The
PATH
of
PRAYER

The

PATH

of

PRAYER

Reflections on Prayer

and True Stories of

How It Affects Our Lives

SOPHY BURNHAM

VIKING COMPASS

VIKING COMPASS

Published by the Penguin Group

Penguin Putnam Inc., 375 Hudson Street, New York, New York 10014, U.S.A.

Penguin Books Ltd., 80 Strand, London WC2R 0RL, England

Penguin Books Australia Ltd, 250 Camberwell Road, Camberwell, Victoria 3124, Australia

Penguin Books Canada Ltd, 10 Alcorn Avenue, Toronto, Ontario, Canada M4V 3B2

Penguin Books India (P) Ltd, 11 Community Centre, Panchsheel Park, New Delhi - 110 017, India

Penguin Books (N.Z.) Ltd, Cnr Rosedale and Airborne Roads, Albany, Auckland, New Zealand

Penguin Books (South Africa) (Pty) Ltd, 24 Sturdee Avenue, Rosebank, Johannesburg 2196, South Africa

Penguin Books Ltd, Registered Offices:
Harmondsworth, Middlesex, England

First published in 2002 by Viking Compass,
a member of Penguin Putnam Inc.

10 9 8 7 6 5 4 3 2 1

Grateful acknowledgment is made for permission to reprint the following copyrighted works:

Excerpt from "Unanswered Prayers" by Larry B. Bastian, Pat Alger and Garth Brooks. © 1989 Major Bob Music Co., Inc., Mid-Summer Music, Inc., Forerunner Music, Inc., and Bait and Beer Music. All rights reserved. Used by permission of Warner Bros. Publications U.S. Inc., Miami, Florida.

Excerpts from *Original Prayer: Teachings and Meditations on the Aramaic Words of Jesus* by Neil Douglas-Klotz, audiotape published by Sounds True, 2002. By permission of Sounds True, Boulder, Colorado.

Selection from *Prayers of the Cosmos: Meditations on the Aramaic Words of Jesus* by Neil Douglas-Klotz. Copyright © 1990 by Neil Douglas-Klotz. Reprinted by permission of HarperCollins Publishers Inc.

Excerpts from *Letters to Malcolm: Chiefly on Prayer* by C. S. Lewis. Copyright © 1964, 1963 by C. S. Lewis PTE Ltd., renewed 1992, 1991 by Arthur Owen Barfield. Reprinted by permission of Harcourt, Inc.

"Gatha" from *Touching Peace: Practicing the Art of Mindful Living* by Thich Nhat Hanh (1992). Reprinted with permission of Parallax Press, Berkeley, California.

Selection by Alfred Romer from *The Choice Is Always Ours,* edited by Dorothy Berkley Phillips, Elizabeth Boyden Howes, and Lucille M. Nixon (R. R. Smith, 1948; revised and enlarged edition, Harper & Row, 1960). Reprinted with permission.

"Seven Steps of Effective Prayer" reprinted by permission of United Research Inc. (www.urlight.org). © United Research Inc.

CIP data available

ISBN 0-670-89464-8

This book is printed on acid-free paper. ∞

Printed in the United States of America
Set in Garamond Three with Phaistos display
Designed by Carla Bolte

This book is dedicated to God,

to anyone who is in pain and suffering,

and to the reader,

you.

The usual notion of prayer is so absurd. How can those who know nothing about it, who pray little or not at all, dare to speak so frivolously of prayer? If it were really what they suppose . . . the dialogue of a madman with his shadow, or even less—a vain and superstitious sort of petition . . . how could innumerable people find . . . such sheer, robust, vigorous, abundant joy in prayer? . . . Could a sane man set himself up as a judge of music because he has sometimes touched a keyboard with the tips of his fingers?

—George Bernanos, *The Diary of a Country Priest*

O Come, let us sing unto the Lord; let us heartily rejoice in the strength of our salvation.

Let us come before his presence with thanksgiving; and show ourselves glad in him with psalms.

—Venite, *Exultemus Domino*

Acknowledgments

This book is written for people of all religious persuasions, but I cannot hide the fact that my upbringing and leanings lead me to Christianity—and this despite my anguish at its failings, blindness, and brutal history.

Nonetheless, I have included prayers from every tradition for it is my belief that if there is to be any reconciliation in this world, it will come from seeing what we hold in common. Many of the prayers may be found in an interfaith book, *All in Good Faith: A Resource Book for Multi-Faith Prayer,* edited by Jean Potter and Marcus Braybrooke, published by the World Congress of Faiths in 1997. Other prayers have been collected over the years in the same way that I collect quotations that speak to my heart. The prayers that have been left out are as lovely as those included, but their collection is left to your personal taste.

You will find this an idiosyncratic book. The Bible quotations are taken from the HarperCollins Study

Bible, New Revised Standard Version, an annotated edition by the Society of Biblical Literature, 1989. But sometimes I have simply paraphrased a text.

It is customary to give acknowledgment to all those who have helped or encouraged a book. In this case so many have contributed to the birth of this small volume—editors, agent, friends, children and adults, strangers and family—that even a partial list would take up all the pages. You must know who you are. In anonymity, please accept my heartfelt gratitude.

Contents

Part III. The Practice of Prayer

CONTENTS

The
PATH
of
PRAYER

Beginnings

I have a friend, Charlie, who was sent on assignment to the island of Bikini. The island is about 2500 miles southwest of Hawaii, and standing there you'd think there is absolutely nothing around it whatsoever, except eternal and unending ocean swells. The island is deserted. Charlie found himself walking on the glistening white sands of an empty and achingly beautiful beach, the sea unfurling itself ceaselessly at his feet. As he walked along, he saw two seashells, each the perfect mirror image of the other, sister shells, lying side by side on the sand. He gave them a nod of passing interest and walked on. A little later he saw two other seashells lying side by side, this pair different from the first but again each one the mirror of the other. He went on and saw a third set of twins, and then a fourth, and by now he was feeling uneasy with this mysterious duplication, and wishing for some signs of untidy civilization when he spotted . . . two Coke bottles lying side by side on the empty, glittering white beach.

Charlie is a spiritual man. He decided that the pairs came as a sign that we are not supposed to live alone. We are supposed to have a partner in our lives. So he got married.

Some years have passed, and now he believes that the

message of the seashells was not about marriage. He thinks it meant . . . that we are not alone. There is something out there watching us, watching over us. We link up with it through prayer.

All over the world people are praying—billions of people praying. They walk down the street praying silently, or they kneel in churches, bow in mosques and temples, bathe themselves in sacred rivers. They make prostrations, walk on pilgrimages, circumambulate their holy sites. They ring bells, light candles, turn prayer wheels, chant songs, sing mantras, fly flags, float prayers down rivers on lotus blossoms or drop their folded written prayers into a God Box or push them into the cracks of a sacred wall. They burn incense sticks that send their prayers up with the smoke (prayers in almost every culture go "up").

If you were born without knowing anything at all about prayer, do you think that you would pray? I say yes. I think it's integral to the human heart; we cannot help ourselves. We think. We pray.

According to one study by the Princeton Religious Research Center, nine out of ten Americans pray.

Ninety-five percent of Americans believe that their prayers are answered, according to a *Life* magazine Gallup Poll.

A 1996 Time/CNN poll of 1,004 Americans found that 82 percent believed in the healing power of prayer and 64 percent thought doctors should pray with those patients who request it—and some do!

"To exclude God from psychiatric consultation," Dr. Arthur Kornhaber of Lake Placid, New York, told *Newsweek,* "is a form of malpractice."

Indeed, so many studies indicate that people deprived

of spiritual meaning live shorter, more unhealthy lives than those who follow some religious path—any path—that you'd think the health insurance companies would ask applicants about their spiritual practices as well as about their histories of smoking, drinking, and disease.

Dozens of hospitals are studying the effects of prayer on epilepsy, leukemia, strokes, cancer, headaches, heart disease, substance abuse, and a host of other ailments. The National Institutes of Health are funding no fewer than ten studies on prayer. Meanwhile, hundreds (perhaps thousands) of studies have been performed regarding the effect of prayer on everything from bacteria and yeast to shrimp, mice, seeds, and red blood cells.

They show that prayer provides statistically significant results.

Nonetheless, we have an ambivalent relationship to prayer.

Both the Senate and House of Representatives, as well as the Supreme Court, open their sessions with prayer. Yet allowing children to engage in prayer in the public schools is controversial (strange inconsistency)—and this despite one British study that demonstrates that schoolchildren who prayed did better on tests and in school overall than those who did not!

You would think it sheer hubris, therefore, for me to tackle the subject of prayer, when there is already so much written on the subject. Even to speak of it as a "path" is both true and, paradoxically, a misnomer, because in a certain sense there is no path! A path implies a well-marked starting point, a journey that passes through various landscapes, with maps and landmarks—this apple tree, that stone wall, this cliff or cleft of rock—and always with the tracks of those who've gone before bending down the grass. A path implies a finish line, the attainment of which brings a thrill of triumphant satisfaction. You have arrived!

But in the case of prayer there is no fixed starting point, no apple tree, no cliff, and not even the same common end point. Each person finds his or her own way. You set off wherever you are, in your own authenticity, and usually (certainly in the beginning) that means with suffering, confusion, tears, fear, doubt. You pray, you stop, you go about your daily life, then remember once again to pray. . . . Sometimes you have one experience while praying, the next time another, and although you may be treading in the footsteps of others, there is no beaten grass to indicate it. Is any activity less understood than prayer?

I pray all the time. Yet still I question it. What is prayer, and why do we do it? Is praying fixed into our DNA? Are prayers answered—and what of those petitions that are not? Are there good and better ways to pray? Or places or rituals or times? And to what are we praying, anyway? Or to whom? What sort of god do we address?

I pray, and yet I find myself, at times and against my will, a skeptic—dismayed and amused that my mind can hold two contradictory beliefs simultaneously and swing easily between the poles of faith and doubt. Then I remember John Donne's saying that "to come to a doubt and to a debatement of any religious duty is a Voice of God in our conscience. Would you know the Truth? Doubt, and then you will inquire."

Or I think of St. Paul in 1 Corinthians: "When I was a child, I spoke like a child, I thought like a child, I reasoned like a child; when I became an adult I put an end to childish ways. . . ."

In recent years I have taken courses at Wesley Theological Seminary. I have studied at the Shalem Institute for Spiritual Formation to become a one-on-one spiritual director or guide. Therefore, I've been exposed to considerable discussion about prayer. I don't remember anyone talking about prayer when I was a child, while almost everyone seems to do so now.

I write this book for several reasons: first for others, because several people have recently asked me to teach them about prayer, and secondly for myself, in order to put down and somehow make sense of what I've learned so far. I write for all those who wonder about prayer, and how and *why* we do it, and whether we are praying to an outside deity or to our own thoughts, and why those rudimentary prayers of petition would be answered anyway, and what is best to pray for. I write for those who, like myself, have wondered what we are doing in our lives, what it's all about. I write for those who are afraid of what happens when we die.

Oh, there are lots of questions! If anyone can learn from these reflections, or take comfort when he is suffering, or be reminded in troubled moments that she is not alone, then this book will be counted a success. I write for those who, like me, feel themselves always a beginner in the practice, always starting over, always learning the same lessons again and again, always struggling to make connection more firmly to the divine.

These stories are offered shyly, recognizing how little we understand of the Great Mystery, but they are offered in love, in joy, in hope that they will give encouragement to others who may have some of the same doubts and questions that have consumed me in my life. I wish the very rhythms of the sentences themselves, the music of the words, will soothe a hurt, caress a soul, and feed an unnamed need. But I think for that I'd have to be someone like the 19th-century Indian poet Hafiz, who wrote some 693 songs of joy to God and who described a poet as "someone who can pour light into a spoon, then raise it to nourish your beautiful, parched, holy mouth."

In the book that follows, at the end of each chapter is a prayer from one of the major traditions. Read these prayers. Let their words sink into your soul, and remember that *au fond* the prayers of each religion are the same. Why would that be? I think it is because all of us humans are the same, no matter our culture or our religious differences. We all have the same needs and wants and longing, all set in us by God.

THE PATH OF PRAYER

The Simple Prayer of St. Nicholas of Flüe[1]

My God and My Lord: Take me away from my own self,
and let me belong completely to you.

My God and My Lord: Take away from me everything
that keeps me apart from you.

My God and my Lord: Grant me everything that draws
me closer to you.

Amen.

Part I

When You Are Hurting
and in Need

Chapter 1

Confessions, Confusions

hen I was a child, I suppose no more than three or four, I knelt beside my bed each night, hands folded sweetly. On one side of me knelt my sister and on the other my mother. She led us through our prayers:

> *There are four corners on my bed,*
> *There are four angels at my head.*
> *Matthew, Mark, Luke, and John,*
> *Bless the bed I sleep on.*

And then:

> *Now I lay me down to sleep,*
> *I pray thee, Lord, my soul to keep.*
> *If I should die before I wake,*
> *I pray thee, Lord, my soul to take.*

In addition, we recited the Lord's Prayer, rattling it off without either thought or understanding, and then we began our litany of "God bless Mummy and Daddy and—"

Now came the fun, as we named everyone and everything we could remember—our aunts and grandparents, the part-time baby-sitter, the ducks (each one by name) and the two horses and the chickens (not by name) and the squirrel or a flight of birds we might have seen that day, and the oak trees and the fallen log we played on in the woods. We went on and on, while our mother prodded us, "Come on."

Finally she would interrupt—"All right, that's enough!"—and toss our giggling little bodies into bed and kiss us on the forehead, turn out the light, and be done with the day!

My sister and I settled into the drowning, stonelike sleep of the pure in heart, knowing we were loved and blessed and never doubting that a magical source of the universe watched over us. How could we doubt? We saw it for ourselves. We lived in the country, and as children we could sense the devas, fairies, elves, and spirits that lived in the shrubs and grasses around us. Each patch of fairy moss was an enchanted tiny landscape, trembling with mystery. The wood-spirits of my childhood were benign, and I think this early sense of goodness, safety, and love pervaded our little brain cells and perhaps has influenced my later vision of life. We talked to trees, to grass, to rocks—a river of prayer, although we never thought of it as that, for prayer as such had rigid definitions.

Mind, I was never taught either in church or at home exactly *how* to pray—not in any sophisticated sense.

"Have you said your prayers?" my mother would ask, in the same tone and with as much interest as "Have you brushed your teeth?" or, if we were settling into the car for a trip, "Did you go to the john?"

Praying was a duty, like wearing clean underclothes. ("Make sure you have on clean underwear in case you're in an accident," she would say; and, while remembering the advise I wonder, Did she say the same thing to my brother, or was this admonition reserved only for the girls?)

Praying was a manner of speech: "You'd better pray that will come out of the carpet."

It was a subject of curiosity: "Did you know the Hopi Indians believe their prayers and dances make the Earth turn?" The idea evoked a certain superior and tolerant amusement at these less enlightened "primitive" people, who hadn't had the good fortune, as we had, to learn the gravitational laws that keep the stars and planets in place.

My mother, of course, had her own ferocious relationship to prayer. When she was a little girl, *her* mother (my grandmother) would turn on the mischievous child. "Down on your knees!" she would thunder. "And pray to God to forgive you for that act!" My mother would have to kneel before her righteous mother, hands folded, and pray for God's forgiveness.

No wonder she could not teach me how to pray. I was lucky with such an upbringing that she didn't pass on to me that unforgiving image of God and prayer!

Whatever prayer was, it was not expected to hold a central place in our lives.

We went to church each Sunday at the lovely, soft, red-brick Episcopal (low-church) structure that had served that community since 1742. We bowed our heads before a deity that no one talked about particularly. The congregation raced through the litany like coursers after a hare, and I had the feeling even as a child that when we reached the triumphant end, and everyone tumbled out of the pews in an explosion of noisy greetings, the grown-ups high above our heads laughing and complimenting one another on new hats or good golf scores the day before, or inviting one another home for a prelunch drink, that we had reached the true purpose of Morning Service: social intercourse.

If praying was what had brought us to church, it was forgotten in the general social din. And maybe that's all right; maybe that's one aim of church—to bind us in unity, with unity, comm-unity. But speaking for myself, church didn't teach me much about prayer. And I was left to grapple with this lack for many years, to find my own way, as I suspect is the norm for most of us.

By our teens my siblings and I were, of course, well read in both the Old and New Testaments—on the theory that anyone aspiring to a true understanding of history and literature required strong grounding in the Bible, the cornerstone of Western culture.

But prayer, our spiritual heart?

That was left for our own explorations.

Sometimes I went to a Roman Catholic church with my friend, Kitty. The mass (as the service was called) was different from my tradition—performed in Latin for one thing, quite incomprehensible. It was a good show, with its incense and gaudy priestly robes. When the congregation filed forward for Communion, Kitty hissed, "Sit down! You're not Catholic."

I wondered vaguely about a God that decided who deserved to be enfolded in His grace and who did not. According to Catholic doctrine of that time, only those saved by Christ—reborn, baptized, and confirmed—could go to heaven. All others—including those people unlucky enough to have lived in the thousands of millennia before the birth of Jesus and those who had made the mistake of being born on foreign continents like Asia or

Africa—were doomed, poor fools, for having come at the wrong place or time.

It didn't seem quite fair.

In my freshman year of college, my brain awash in the heady skepticism of intellectual pursuit, I lost my faith. Did I believe in God? I could find no more reason for there being a God than reason for there being none. (I meant the God of my childhood, the grandfatherly Renaissance portrait—God in the masculine image of man.) I didn't much care for church worship anymore, which I found dry ritual. Nonetheless, still subject to that twinge of guilt that denotes a not-yet-atrophied conscience and concerned by the suddenness of this loss of faith—this enlarging of perspective—I made one last, halfhearted attempt to go back to my innocent old ways. I went to see the Protestant minister at the college church.

I sat in a wing chair, facing him across his paper-laden desk.

"I've lost my faith," I confessed.

He twirled a pencil miserably between his fingers. "You must have faith," he intoned.

I stared at him in contemptuous surprise. "If I hadn't lost my faith," I wanted to retort sarcastically, "I'd still have it." Instead I waited to see if he had anything more to add. He stared down at his desk, not meeting my eyes—and today, years later, I wonder if he was not going through his own crisis of confidence. He must have felt some sense of inadequacy in the face of this determined young woman.

"Yes. Well. Thank you."

I left, and that, tra-la, was the end of my Christian church attendance for many a year. I left God, or anyway I stopped thinking much about a spiritual dimension,

In Peter Barnes's charming 1969 play, The Ruling Class, *Jack, the 14th earl of Gurney, thinks he is the One True God. The family has to prove the earl is sane or else lose its seat in the House of Lords.*

"How do you know you're . . . God?" the earl is asked.

"Because when I pray to Him, I find I'm talking to myself."

and when I met the atheist who was to become my husband, my admiration for his sharp intellect finished off the job. I claimed a wishy-washy agnostic atheism.

On the other hand, I could not stop praying. These were usually petitions, which was at the time my sole definition of "prayer." I'd been doing it since babyhood and found the habit hard to break.

It was humiliating. What was I doing? Talking to myself?

When I was in trouble, I would slip into the dusky, trembling silence of an empty church to kneel in a pew, hands folded. I would pour out my heart to a God I did not believe in—or even *like,* if you consider the historical personage. I would explain my fears and anguish, crying into the void, against my will, "Oh, help."

The odd thing was, I always came away feeling better, except for the tinge of guilt at having *once again* (like a reformed alcoholic *once more* going off the wagon) given in to prayer!

Sometimes I would bargain.

"If you give me this, dear God," I implored a deity I refused to acknowledge, addressing Him, moreover, with unwarranted intimacy, given our lack of relationship, "I promise I'll do XYZ. . . . Please help my husband keep his job. Help us stay in this apartment. Help my little girl get into this school. Help us. . . . Help me. . . ."

Somehow things always worked out. Did I give any credit to my prayers? Of course not! They were merely the expression of my own weakness, and I disliked myself all the more for not even being able, like my husband, to live up to my own convictions of atheistic nihilism.

But that's only part of the story, a half-truth of my experience in those days, for even as an inadequate agnostic, I longed for understanding. I prayed to *understand*. I wished for it on the first evening star. I asked for it, eyes closed, while pulling at chicken wishbones.

Understand what?

All of it! *Understand everything.*

It may have been my consuming prayer for nearly 15 years, until one day with a surge of joy, I grasped (the bolt from the blue, oh, glory!) that the goal could never be reached—and how wonderful! How thrilling that my prayer was not "answered" (except with this understanding, which at the time I did not consider an "answer"); for if I understood everything, I would lose the mystery—and I rejoiced in that realization like a dog rolling in dead seagull guts, undone by that simple fact: How fine life is, how rich, how inexorable, how limitless, how chaotic and orderly, how violent and peaceful, how *right* that we should be utterly at the mercy of the Unknown! In the course of my life I have met many fascinating men and women and studied with enlightened masters or gurus. I have experienced extraordinary visions and mystical moments, some of which I've written about in earlier books. Nonetheless, it seems I am always at the beginning of prayer, as innocent and inept as a child.

Whenever I begin a project, I begin with prayer. For every beginning is born in fear and hope. It seems appropriate, therefore, to begin this one with prayer, however difficult it is to do so publicly. Listen: My prayers are private. I don't like to voice the silent, secret yearnings of my heart, those intimate communications with an energy that is mysterious, intelligent, majestic, and yet so delicately personal, so immediate, so loving (wings bend brooding over us) that we cannot even name it. "God," we say, for want of a better word.

My prayers are unspoken, private, but with what words I have, here is my sense of longing as we begin this exploration:

O God, Delight of my being, O my Beloved: Fill my mouth with Your words, that each person reading them may be relieved of hurt, fear, doubt. . . . Help me to grow so open that I may see with the eyes of God, hear with the ears of God, love with the heart of God, speak with the words of God—You in me and I in You, in the service of all people, everywhere. . . . And may each person find the longings of her heart, if it be for her highest good. . . . I thank You for Your most tender care. . . .

Something like that. Only it would have no words.

Not all of us will express our prayers with such romantic fervor, and that's the first and most important thing to say about prayer itself: that we each find our own way, our own words, our own deity, and anything I have to say about prayer itself . . . you must accommodate and shift and shape to fit your perfect mold.

And now we come to pain.

Why does praying seem so often to begin with pain? With broken minds and hearts? We are vessels of unspoken hurt. Is there anyone alive who has not suffered? Or wondered what to do? Life is full of cares, for no sooner do we love a thing than we find ourselves afraid of losing it, and the more precious it appears to us, the worse is our anguish at the idea of its loss. I think that all of life is formed of change and loss: the loss of our children, the loss of our parents, the loss of homes with their comfortable walls and floors, the loss of dreams and ambitions, of jobs, the loss of status or youth or health, and repeatedly the loss of self-esteem, the loss of those whom we have loved—wives, husbands, mothers, brothers, a good dog or cat, or friend. And always, hanging over us dangles the unnamed loss that will be produced by our own death—the loss of a self we may hardly have gotten to know before it will be extinguished (*not me!*), and with it the subjective loss of this entire thrilling world.

What do we do when we are hurting or in need? We fight our pain and disappointment. We deny it, ignore it, or howl in despair and simple outrage. At some point we try to tackle the problem by willpower and determination. We decide to take control, to change the situation to our advantage and make things come out right, *the way they're supposed to be.* With all our mind and heart we try to make everything turn out the way we want.

We create a new family schedule to brake a teenager's downward spiral. Or we commit to increased hours of weekend work, when we're already over our head with a failing company. We resolve to spend more time on a "relationship," ("we'll *make* it work!") or we volunteer to march for world peace. We struggle to bring order out of the chaos of our lives.

Who was it that said, "When humans make plans, God laughs"? Or there's that other antique saying, known in several languages: "Man proposes, God disposes."

Life is what happens while you're making other plans.

—Anonymous

Do our frantic efforts work? Fat chance.

Some people try to push the painful situation into sub-mission by drive and hard work, while others take to al-cohol or drugs, in an effort either to dull the unwanted sensations or else to vault over them into some exalted, happy state (using spirits to reach the spiritual); and for a short time this course may work. Some people plot vengeance against their enemy. Others stuff down their hurt and anger. They escape into books and films or into hard physical activity and athletics. They drive fast cars to forget their problems, or else they lunge into work or food or chocolate or sex, or even into committing atroci-ties. Still others erupt in fear and bellow in rage and frus-tration at the world or at their mother and father or at the God they don't believe in anyway. At fate. Some-times we lash out in our betrayal, crying for revenge, in-stituting lawsuits, demanding at least justice if we can't have peace of mind. We substitute righteousness for hap-piness, though only mercy can make injustice just.

What else do we do? We talk to a friend, to a coun-selor, or to our private journal. We join a twelve-step program, or perhaps we take our tender, troubled hearts to an astrologer, a medium, a healer or shaman. Just talk-ing helps. We seek respite through massage or Reiki or other forms of loving touch. We dance. We pour our pain into the creative arts. And all these solutions help, but at those times when we cannot take another step, we're forced to pray.

There's the story of a man I know who refused to pray.

He was struggling against an addiction and watching as his life unraveled around him, with an impending bankruptcy, divorce, loss of children and home. People kept saying to him, "Pray, pray." But he was prideful and would not. One day a friend took him aside.

"Do you know what the ox does when it's too heavily laden?"

"No, what?"

"It falls on its knees and refuses to move," he said.

The man thought, "Well, if the ox can fall on its knees, I guess I can." That morning in the shower, where he knew he wouldn't be seen, he very quickly—*tick-tock*—dropped to one knee (help!), and came back up again. Oddly, he felt better, and the next day while in the shower he dropped onto both knees and stayed there a little longer to say his prayer, there, where no one would see him. After that, he found he could pray at night before climbing into bed or in the morning on first opening his eyes. Dropping to his knees even for a moment opened the gate to prayer, to submission to something higher, to the universal energy field, as I call it; that's the only thing we can do when life's breakers boil us in the sand.

A Jain Prayer for Peace[1]

Lead me from death to life, from falsehood to truth.
Lead me from despair to hope, from fear to trust.
Lead me from hate to love, from war to peace.
Let peace fill our heart, our world, our universe.
Peace . . . Peace . . . Peace.

Chapter 2

What Is Prayer?

I wish we had another word for prayer, it sounds so rigid and righteous. In fact it is probably what we are doing most of the time. Walking down the street, we hear our little inner voice calling, "Help, help, help, help help." Or sometimes, "Rage, rage, rage, rage." In their most ordinary form our thoughts are prayers, and we'll see later how our thoughts cup and influence the universe to such a degree that even a good atheist could comfortably pray, if only he realized he could call it "thought."

The word "prayer" comes from the Latin *precare,* meaning "to entreat, ask, beg, request," but it's more than that. It is intention, too, and we'll talk a lot about intention and thought throughout this book.

I think we are praying all the time, only most of us don't know it. Years ago I came across a saying of the Buddha, quoted in the Dhammapada. It stopped me short.

We are what we think.
All that we are arises with our thought.

With our thoughts we make the world.
Speak and act with an impure mind,
And trouble will follow you
As the wheel follows the ox that draws the cart.

We are what we think.
All that we are arises with our thought.
With our thoughts we make the world.
Speak or act with a pure mind,
And happiness will follow you
As your shadow, unshakable.

These words of the Buddha hit me forcibly.

I read and reread the short verses, copied them out in my quotation book, for here lay a clue, the secret tool to happiness: Think and act with a pure mind, and everything will work well. The only question became, What is meant by "pure"? That one stumped me for years, but the implications were clear: With our thoughts we create reality. Do we see the glass as half empty or half full? Do we decide to remain in the problem, worrying our discomfort with terrier teeth, or do we try consciously to guard against our very thoughts?

With our thoughts we create our reality. Think of that. Our emotional balance depends on the projections of our minds. What if we were to monitor our thoughts like spies in the night and clap them in prison when they turn on us? What if our prayers were expressed as love notes to a joyful universe? What if instead of thinking, "Help! I'm scared," we called into the loving spheres, "I see you! Thank you for your help! Here I am, my darling. Take me"? What if we called out as a lover to her beloved, increasingly and wastefully squandering thoughts of love?

It's possible to learn to pray like this, but first come

I cannot believe that the inscrutable universe turns on an axis of suffering; surely the strange beauty of the world must somewhere rest on pure joy.

—Louise Bogan

years of doubt, of seeking and questioning about the correct approach to God; for first we have to know, Is the universe a friendly place? Is it on our side? What if it's not? The earth is splattered with blood. Suffering lies all around. If there is indeed a loving deity, how could it permit such pain? And these, of course, are the questions that underlie this book and that I hope will be a little bit resolved by the time you reach the end.

What is prayer? It is quite simply *a yearning of the heart.* We don't even have to voice it. It arises from the depths of our anguished suffering or from the power of our love. It erupts, flowers, dies down, pours forth again.

It is *thought concentrated* and distilled. "With our thoughts we make the world," said the Buddha. If we take this statement literally, then *worrying* also constitutes a prayer.

"Worry," says the Hopi Indian Grandfather David, "is like praying for your worst fears to happen!"

What else is prayer?

Prayer is the *irresistible urge of our human nature* to contact and communicate with the source of love, with the energy of the universe. In prayer we ask for help at those moments when we feel totally inadequate to deal with a situation.

Prayer is *communication with our highest spiritual part,* with the state of loving and of being loved. It's the effort

25

to commune with supreme wisdom, truth, beauty, passion, safety, strength; with Christ, Mary, the goddess, with nature—whatever word we use for this spiritual realm. And, for some people, prayer may also be a way of placating an undependable, quixotic, demanding, and even bloodthirsty deity. (We'll get to that a little later, too. Keep in mind that both as a people and as individuals, our understanding of the mystery of God has evolved across the centuries, changing and evolving as we have, though cracking the mystery is beyond our pitiful capacities.)

Prayer is *the doorway to the thin places* between the physical and spiritual worlds, the shadowy portal through which we see into the other dimensions and through which we draw down spiritual help.

St. Augustine said that prayer is *love.* "True, whole prayer is nothing but love."

Dr. Alexis Carrel, Nobel Prize recipient for his work in suturing and transplanting blood vessels, said that prayer is *energy,* "a source of luminous, self-generating energy," and he continued that "true prayer is a way of life; the truest life is literally a way of prayer."

There's the story of a peasant who's sitting in the back of the empty church, just sitting there, when the priest walks by.

"What are you doing?" the priest asks.

The peasant looked up at him, radiant. "I am looking at God, and He is looking at me." He could have said that he was wallowing in love. He was subsumed in luminous energy, pulsating with light.

This is true prayer, but it's not the kind of prayer we make when we're first beginning or when we hurt; and I repeat: It's perfectly all right to *ask* with all the anguish of our hearts, pour out our despair, tell the Beloved what is troubling us, and even how we'd solve it, too, if we were in charge; and only then gradually can we let go and move, step by step, into the deeper layers of the prayers of gratitude and adoration—into the simplicity of resting in God. Of looking at God and having Him look at us.

What is prayer?

It is a tool providing strength and energy. You know how singing helps you work. Singing gives energy. Chain gangs once chanted work songs as they wielded their sledgehammers, and slaves working in the cotton fields sang spirituals. Not long ago, when I was sea kayaking with a party of others in a drenching rain, paddling exhausted against a running tide, one or two of the group began to sing. It gave them strength—and us as well. Well, so does constant and repeated prayer.

Years ago I read of a man who fell overboard off one of the Hawaiian Islands. All night he swam on surging waves. At a certain moment he knew he couldn't make it. "God, help me!" he prayed, and then he felt a swell of energy carrying him, swimming for him—angels holding up his body in their arms. The next morning he reached the beach and safety, collapsing on the sand.

You don't have to be in so great a dilemma to pray. Just doing the laundry, exhausted from your chemotherapy, just kayaking against an incoming tide, just meeting a seemingly impossible deadline, or caring for a colicky baby, you'll find work easier when you sing or

But they that wait upon the Lord shall renew their strength;
they shall mount up with wings as eagles; they shall run and
not be weary, and they shall walk, and not faint.

—Isaiah 40:31

WHAT IS PRAYER?

pray. Praying draws into you the energy of the universal life force, the power and strength of God.

So prayer is longing, communication, love, energy. And it's also thought. Let me say what prayer is not.

First, prayer is not lip service, memorized recitation in which your mind is off thinking about something else as you race through meaningless words. Prayer has to have an emotional component. "My words fly up, my thoughts remain below," says King Claudius in *Hamlet,* when vainly attempting to pray. "Words without thoughts never to heaven go." He might have said, not "thoughts" but "heart."

"The head is not a very good place for prayer," writes Anthony de Mello, the famous priest. "If your prayer stays there too long and doesn't move into the heart, it will gradually dry up and prove tiresome and frustrating."[1] It is only when you move in the arena of feeling that prayer brings transformation and deep peace.

Second, prayer is not prideful. It's not a flaunting of your piety. There is a correct attitude toward prayer, one of humility, of vulnerability, and of surrender into the arms of something you do not understand. And that is why so frequently we cannot pray until we hurt.

Surely suffering is important to our lives, for doesn't it nudge us constantly toward prayer, and hence toward happiness? Toward love? In suffering, our shells are broken open. We are accessible, teachable, guidable. If God is love and if love is God, then we pray in order to roll around in love and happiness, like a horse in a pasture, like the dog with its seagull, like a child with chocolate. But for most of us, prayer begins with suffering.

Of course we are afraid. We doubt. We're like blind people feeling our way barefoot in black night down a paved macadam road. We know the road only by the firmness underfoot, and unable to see we sometimes wander onto the shoulder (gravel! briars!). We grope our way blindly along, never knowing if the next step is going to plunge us off a precipice. *Of course we doubt!*

"Truly, it is in darkness," wrote Meister Eckhart, "that we find light, so when we are in sorrow, then this light is nearest of all to us."

There is another reason why we pray: Prayer brings results. Everyone has stories of answered prayers. Scratch a stranger and you will hear a story. Sometimes it is dramatic, like that of the German woman who wrote me recently telling of her bouts with cancer and her miracle of healing prayer. Other times the story is so insignificant, so trivial and inconsequential (except to the person praying) that you'd hardly dare disturb the Force of the Universe with the plea to answer such a call.

I have a friend who is a casting director for films. Not long ago she was looking for a little girl between the ages of three and five, to play a particular part. She interviewed hundreds of children, and none was suitable. They clung to their fathers' legs, or they sat, utterly confused by the lights and cameras and the ambitious grown-ups who demanded they perform. Finally my friend's time was up. She needed a child *the next day!*

That night she fell to her knees. "O God, I can't do this," she implored a force she cannot describe. "I need a child actress now. Please bring me the perfect little girl."

The next morning the child of her heart walked in, the

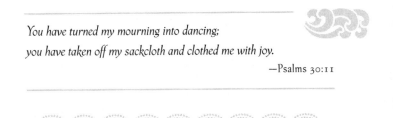

You have turned my mourning into dancing;
you have taken off my sackcloth and clothed me with joy.

—Psalms 30:11

first to be auditioned. "It was because I prayed," she says with absolute conviction. "God brought her to me."

I think we cannot live without prayer. Once, before we were born, we came from somewhere else, and our souls still long for that Xanadu, though we cannot quite remember exactly what it was we may have known. The touch of love. Someday we will return to it, and meantime, during this brief and perilous journey called life, our souls yearn for that state of pure love we knew before. Prayer is our link to that place, that state.

Imagine there's a great pipeway between yourself and the invisible spiritual world and, if unused, it gets clogged up with mud and sludge. No water can move through. By prayer we keep the channel clean. Moreover, this prayer cannot be muttered once a year by dutiful or rebellious rote—not if we want to clean out the muck of distress that accumulates every day, not if we want to remain in serenity, confidence, peace of mind. We are given a spiritual reprieve only one day at a time.

Each day we must begin again. Each day we must make contact with our higher self.

We pray, therefore, in order to come back to this sense of being loved and of knowing that everything will be all right.

While I was first setting down my stumbling thoughts on prayer, I had a dream. Many times our prayers are an-

All will be well,
and all will be well,
*   all manner of thing will be well.*
    —Julian of Norwich

swered in a dream. In my dream I found myself in a strange landscape where everything was a little "off," lopsided or slightly displaced. I was going home, but I was lost, and as I walked along a path beside a river, I saw a house. I stepped in as easily as Goldilocks, walked confidently inside with no more thought of trespass than of bears. The house was empty. It was beautifully furnished. I made myself comfortable, but all the time I knew I was going home, and this house was not it.

I was on the telephone asking the operator for directions—"How do I get home?"—when down the stairs poured a river of little children, flowing around their lovely mother or foster mother. We greeted each other, the mother and I, with open pleasure. She was as serene as the Madonna of Guadalupe, and the children played happy as puppies at our knees. The woman was not the least upset at my having intruded in her house. Smiling, she told me the way home.

In my dream I continued my journey, walking beside a river, and suddenly I met my own mother! Now, my mother has been dead for twenty years, and in my dream I knew it. We were so happy to see one another! We faced one another, looking in each other's eyes, and she said, "I love you," and I said, "I love you," and she said, "I love you." And I said, "I love you."

Then I woke up.

But I knew the dream was about prayer. Praying is how we get to go home, and when we're home, it's our Mother we meet—not necessarily the mother who failed us or had her own problems, but the mother of our hearts, and she is looking in our eyes and saying, "I love you, I love you." She is saying, "I love you," while looking in our eyes.

The Opening Prayer of Islam (Fatihah)

This prayer has been called the Lord's Prayer of Islam. It is the opening sura of the Koran, and is recited for each new beginning:

In the name of God, the Merciful, the Compassionate.
> Praise be to God, the Lord of the Worlds,
> The Merciful, the Compassionate One,
> Master of the Day of Judgment:

Thee alone we serve, to Thee alone we cry for help.
Guide us in the straight path,
> The path of those whom Thou hast blessed.
> Not of those with whom Thou art angry
>> Nor of those who go astray.

Chapter 3

What God Do You Pray To?

When, as a teenager, I abandoned my first images and definitions of God, I didn't know I was really asking how to pray. I thought the Great Question was "Who am I?" Or maybe "What's going on?" Neither did I know that it was utterly appropriate to leave behind my childhood images of God. Today I wonder what would have happened if that clergyman had merely listened to my confusion, my confession, and suggested, smiling, that my loss of faith was a blessing—was appropriate, ideal in fact, something to be applauded, not concerned about. What if he'd said that I had lost faith not in God but in the God of my childish understanding, and that my very concept of God would change many times in my life, enlarge, widen, until finally it would involve no images at all?

Spirit, YHWH, Allah, Goddess (Kali, Mary, Lakshmi), Shiva, Buddha, Christ. How we pray, and when, reveals everything about what we think of God. Which is to say, what we think of the meaning of life. Is our vision optimistic, trusting, or is it dark and full of sin and guilt?

It makes no difference as to the name of the God;
since love is the real God of all the world.

—Apache

The fact is, God cannot be seen. He's like the wind. We see the wind only in the veils of snow blown across a white waste pastureland; we feel the sting against our skin and hear it whistling across the glittering surface of the sea, spinning the frothy spume high into the dancing air. But air and wind are invisible to our weak eyes. It's the same with God, whose presence is glimpsed only in His works and seen only with the eyes of the heart.

Note I used the word "His" although I don't believe in a male deity. It is hard in our Western culture to avoid the influence of the white-bearded grandfatherly pan-creator. In the East we come upon images of the fickle blue-skinned Krishna or of a variety of goddesses, from Kuan Yin the compassionate, to the black-faced Kali, to eight-armed deities dancing on one leg or to others with a thousand eyes. They are symbolic depictions, of course, as is Michelangelo's painting of God on the ceiling of the Sistine Chapel—the old man reaching out to touch and enliven the dormant Adam. It makes you understand why some faiths permit no images of God at all, lest they limit the limitless mystery.

Prayer presupposes a deity, but it need not be the masculine, tender, or suffering Christ nor the guilt-inspiring Great White Judge in the Sky—nor, for that matter, any figure leaning down to listen to our pleas. People who have had an abusive or violent or alcoholic father visibly shudder at Jesus' metaphor of Our Father in Heaven—they'd rather have no God at all!—go atheist to save their sanity rather than submit to this vindictive prosecutor. (We want mercy, forgiveness—not judgment and justice!) I know people who refuse to cringe in guilt before the Holy One, aware only of how far they fail. Their life task is avoidance—to ensure that the beam of His attention falls on someone else!

The God of my understanding, meanwhile, evolved as I matured from being the pure spirit of my childhood to a figurative father or mother, to the mystery of both an impersonal and simultaneously intimately personal one. It is transcendent, immanent, eternal, unknowable. Yet as a human I also require a personal relationship, and I pray, therefore, to my Beloved, which is my husband, my sister, my mother, friend, and Lord. Sometimes I see it mediated through an angel. Sometimes it appears (a gasp of delight!) in a blooming flower. I think of the saint who prayed only, "O Thou my Joy! O Thou my All!" Bathing himself in bliss.

However God is seen, all the mystics and sages agree that this spiritual energy is merciful. For those who have had a near-death experience, the Holy Spirit is *composed* of love, and nothing but burning love surrounds us. Indeed, all the great avatars and boddhisatvas—those who have come down like Christ to enlighten us—all teach that there is only this shining love offered in the face of all our suffering and ignorance.

In cold climates God is seen as light, warmth, fire, and heat: "God of God, Light of Light." In hot climates God is often seen as shade. There is in India a prayer that

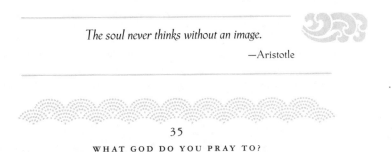

The soul never thinks without an image.

—Aristotle

transliterated sounds like this: "Hey Bhagavan, may abki shar ó n may hgn!" (the last syllable being too strangulated to spell). It means, "O Lord, I have come into your shelter." And I cannot murmur these Sanskrit words without imagining myself slipping under the tent flap into the cool, dark safety of God's tent.

The Greek writer Xenophane noted that "The Ethiopians say that their gods are snub-nosed and black, the Thracians that theirs have light blue eyes and red hair." Our images are formed by what we are. For Buddhists, who have no belief in a creator God, all deities and demons are seen as projections of the human mind, as reflections of ourselves.

St. John of the Cross wrote of finding the lover in darkness. The Hindus describe our longing for God as being like that of maidens mad with love, who wander the dark woods all night, searching the ground for the footprints of Lord Krishna.

What, then, is our image? Are we approaching a tender mother? Attracting the attention of an absent-minded gift giver? Are we like St. Teresa, adoring the Christ, "His Majesty"? Or walking hand in hand with our best friend?

I know a nun who now laughs at her mistrustful Irish upbringing.

"If I wanted it," she explained, "God did not, and if God wanted it, it was going to involve hard sacrifice." If yours is an image of a punishing God, here's some advice: *Divorce it!* Choose one that's on your side. If God is in our

If triangles had a god, it would have three sides.

—Charles de Montesquieu

minds, a projection of our highest being, then select a splendid deity.

I have a lot of trouble with the word "God." I like to use words like "source," "force of the universe," or just "universe." Not only do I wish we had a better word for God but an ungendered one as well: not He, not She. But I am training myself to use the word "God," because it occurred to me recently that I'm the loser in the fight. I only know that there is something Out There and that it is also inside of me. It is both on my side and at my side. It is a part of me—and of you, and of that tree, that cat, the measureless waters of the ocean, the stars in an infinite night sky. The voice of the divine is singing in everything, and everywhere we look, if indeed we see with a loving heart, we see God flaming out. It is within me and simultaneously bigger than me, so that I am a part of this Other as a drop of water contains the essence of a pond, or lake, or ocean. It takes 100,000 forms, visible and invisible, crooning its soft lullabies and forming and reforming itself into all manner of accidents and creations, and the whole time it is laughing, loving us. It is!

It is no accident that YHWH, the vowelless Hebrew word for "the One Whose Name Cannot Even Be Pronounced"—is related to the verb "to be." God is pure essence. Beingness. It is YHWH: "I AM WHAT I AM" (as Moses learned at the Burning Bush). The Buddhists call it "suchness."

Do we dare to pray, therefore, even when we don't know what it is we're praying to?

Not everyone can.

I have a near relative who is a true atheist. I asked him, "Do you pray?"

He said, "Sophy, I don't believe in God. It would be intellectually impure for me to pray. What would I pray to?"

I am, you anxious one.

Don't you sense me, ready to break

Into being at your touch?

My murmurings surround you like shadowy wings.

Can't you see me standing before you
  cloaked in stillness?

Hasn't my longing ripened in you
  from the beginning
  as fruit ripens on a branch?

I am the dream you are dreaming.

When you want to awaken, I am that wanting:

I grow strong in the beauty you behold.

            And with the silence of stars I enfold

Your cities made by time.

—Rainer Maria Rilke, *Book of Hours: Love Poems to God*

I know another man of whom I asked the same question: "Do you pray?"

"I prayed once," he said, "when I was very young and my son was just born." His son was a week old when he needed surgery for a hernia. "At that time I prayed to God. Because I believe in God." He nodded. "I prayed that if my son lived through this operation I would never ask for another thing in my life. And I have never asked for another thing. I've never said another prayer. I made a deal," he said stiffly, "and I stick to my deals."

He gives a curious view of relationship. After fifty years you'd think that any contract might be renegotiated.

He was telling me this as he lay in the hospital recovering from triple-bypass surgery, and I couldn't help but wonder whether in his deep unconscious he had let loose a flicker of a prayer. I know he was happy to accept my prayers for him—*they* did not count. Someone else could pray for him! I went away marveling at this view of an Almighty source of the universe that would grant you one prayer in your lifetime, and only one.

My daughter Sarah held a similar view. She said that for a long time she was really careful what she prayed for. She wanted to pray only for the most important things. Or she would pray for other people—because intercession seemed more worthy than a prayer for her own small, selfish concerns. It was as if there were a quota and she had to be careful not to use up her apportioned lot—until one day it occurred to her that this concept placed limitations on the Creative Element, the benevolent One, however that is understood. She was saying that God would not be able to decide what was important and what was not. With that new insight, she began to pray for both passing desires and passionate needs. Now she says she prays for anything! I tell the story as one small example of how this image at the center of our being, this relationship with the divine, grows and expands with time.

One woman I know feels that God is like somebody driving down a highway while fiddling with the tape deck in the car, who takes His eyes off the road, leans over to try to get the tape in . . . and crashes. That's her view of God: incompetent.

But the Hindus speak of the thousand faces of God, and one explanation for the ways of God uses the image of Lord Krishna as a mischievous little boy. In this story

WHAT GOD DO YOU PRAY TO?

That only which we have within, can we see without.
If we meet no gods, it is because we harbor none.

—Ralph Waldo Emerson

God is playing with his treasures in a sandbox, building castles and roads and cities and armies of toy soldiers—when his mother calls. At the sound of her voice, joyfully he rises, turns, steps on his castle, crushing his cities in the sand, and runs into his mother's arms! It's all done out of love, without malice or concern, for tomorrow he'll make up new games, find new tin soldiers, and play with his toys some more.

I've been talking about our image shifting over long periods of time from one of a fearsome to one of a loving God, but sometimes it happens the other way around. The change can hit you in an instant. You are content with your God. You trust in a spirit of loving kindness and intelligence. Then one morning you wake up, your throat clasped by the fist of fear. Suddenly you are overwhelmed by the power of a God of Impersonal Violence that wipes out a town with a tornado or sends screaming hurricanes over the earth and seas; the God of our ancestors, so to speak, the awesome, terrifying one who demands we sacrifice . . . everything—to death, fear, desolation of heart, hopelessness, despair, and darkness. What can you do with that insight but, like Elijah, cover your head with your cloak and tremble in awe? This is the fierce aspect of God, represented so dramatically in the Buddhist and Hindu traditions. This is the God of grief. The God of the Irish Nun.

Where do such thoughts come from? In our Judeo-

Christian creation tales, God never created destruction, waste, ruin, fear, despair. Were they the "Second Creation," never written of? And how does one pray to the God of despair?

Conversely, after days of desperation, you are walking down the hopeless street when suddenly, as if brushed by an angel's wing, the mantle of fear slips off, and you are washed by joy. Peace floods your heart. You're home. That's how elusive are our images of God.

Awhile ago my nephew visited me for the day with his little daughter, then five years old. We went for a stroll in the park, where she picked up a stick, a broom handle taller than she herself, and she was delighted with her find. When it was time to leave, as we were drifting to the car, she suddenly remembered her stick.

"My *stick!*" she cried. "I lost my *stick!*" She completely broke down. She was desolate!

Her father looked at her in surprise, uncertain what to do. "We can get another one."

But she folded in on herself. "No, I need *that* stick!" Her shoulders crumbled forward, and her face contorted with dismay. Just then our houseguest came striding along, carrying her broom handle.

"You forgot your stick."

Her face lit up. The sun sprang back into the shining sky. "My stick!"

I thought, watching this scene and the father's dismay and confusion, of how much we long to help our children. And of the kind words of Jesus, who asked what father would give his son a stone when he asked for a loaf of bread, or a serpent when he asked for a fish? "If you who are evil know how to give good gifts to your children, how much more shall your Father in heaven give good things to those who ask him?"[1]

I pray all the time. I pray not because I am saintly but because I'm not: I need help so badly. I pray when I'm sure of my Beloved, and I pray especially when I lose touch with Him. There's no bad time to pray.

"I have so much to do," wrote Martin Luther, "that I cannot possibly get by on less than three hours of prayer a day."

The Dalai Lama prays for four hours every morning before his workday begins at 7:00 A.M.

Mother Teresa ordered her nuns to pray for several hours every day—otherwise, she said, they wouldn't have the strength to do their work.

I pray as I'm running errands. "Help!" I whisper. That's much of the time: praying for strength and courage, for understanding or wisdom. I'm hanging on to the subway strap, asking to be quiet enough to listen, patient enough to wait for answers, sharp enough to notice the unexpected little messages or gifts that are scattered at my feet, in answer to my needs.

Sometimes I make prayers of surrender or intercession for others who lie on my heart and mind. Sometimes I'm just asking for direction: "Here I am. What do you want me to do next? How may I serve?"

But sometimes my heart lifts up, rejoicing, and I am overcome by gratitude: "Oh, how beautiful!" my soul cries out. This, too, is a kind of prayer, and now I'll let you in on a little secret about your soul and God. The universe responds to praise! It loves to be noticed, and when you receive its gifts with gratitude, it does cartwheels to send you *more!* You don't have to believe me; put it to the test. Try it out; see if it doesn't work for you. One day, when you are flushed with humility and gratitude, give in.

"It doesn't get any better than this!" you silently cry; at which—as if you've sent a challenge to the Universe—*it does!* It's as if the spiritual dimension is so delighted by our recognition that it outdoes itself, reaching for further applause. "You ain't seen nothing yet!" it boasts.

The strange thing is, you don't even have to be struck by joy to have this happen. I know a man who was driving home after work in a blue, sad mood. He had just received disappointing news concerning the promotion he'd expected. He was irritated with himself—his expectations smashed, ambitions drained. "It's not okay," he thought, and then, remembering a conversation we'd had, he forced himself to lift his eyes and mutter dutifully, "How beautiful the sky is. It doesn't get any better than this!" The next instant he was struck by how clearly he could see the sky, the grass, the other cars, by how startlingly beautiful everything was—and then by the realization that he could quit and learn the business he'd always wanted to go into. "How wonderful! It can't possibly get any better than this!"

Oh, gratitude is a powerful instrument, and so is the power of praise, reminding us all the time by a lucky phone call or a serendipitous event that Spirit is madly in love with us, dropping little love notes all the time.

A Hebrew Prayer[1]

O God, guard my tongue from evil and my lips from speaking guile. Purify my heart that there be in it no malice, but a prayer for the good of all. Lead me in the ways of righteousness, that I may hurt no one; and help me to bring the blessings of love to others. Open my heart to do Your will. Strengthen my desire to obey Your commandments. May my thoughts and my prayers be acceptable to You, O Lord, my Rock and my Redeemer.

Look with favor, O Lord, upon us, and may our service be acceptable to You. Blessed is the Eternal God, whom alone we serve with reverence.

Chapter 4

Looking into the Terror

Once in India I stood on the topmost tower of a palace that reared up from the edge of a cliff. The escarpment dropped hundreds of feet straight down to the level plain below, where a city spread out for miles and miles, and beyond the outskirts of the city we could see the hesitant suburbs give way to the distant green brocade of fields that unrolled right to the hazy blue smudge of mountains at the horizon. As I leaned like Rapunzel out the little casement window of this tower, I could hear the murmur of the city like the hum of bees in a hive: cries, cars, cows, feet, bicycle bells and auto horns, and the voices of all the people down below.

It's what God hears, I thought. *That's what it sounds like to God.* Immediately my heart was wrenched with compassion for all the suffering in this little world—so many longings, so many hurts and fears and desires. Does God choose one (I wondered) and say, "I will answer that one" and "That prayer I won't give"?

In *The Masks of God: Oriental Mythology,* Joseph Campbell tells a creation myth of India preserved from about 900 to 700 B.C.E. in the Brihadaranyaka Upanishad:

> In the beginning the Universe was only Self in the form of a man. It looked around and saw there was nothing but itself, whereupon its first shout was, "It is I!"; whence the concept "I" arose. (And that is why, even now, when addressed, one answers first, "It is I!" Only then giving the other name that one bears.)

In the story, God is both male and female in one clumsy, lumpy body, as large as a man and woman embracing. However, this Self lacks delight (therefore we lack delight when alone, and desire a second). This Self then divides into man and woman, male and female. The male embraces the female, and from that the human race arises. But she reflects, "How can he unite with me, who am produced from himself? I will hide." She turns herself into a cow—but he mates with her as a bull and creates cattle. She turns into a mare—and he a stallion; she turns into a nanny goat, doe, ewe, and so all animals are created—goat, stag, ram—as God pours forth all pairing things, down to the littlest ants.

Then God realized, "I, actually, am creation; for I have poured forth all this."

The story ends with the moral: "Anyone understanding this becomes, truly, himself a creator in this creation."[1]

How different from the Judeo-Christian-Islamic creation tale, in which the source of being creates things out of mud and dirt that seem to stand outside Himself! He creates humankind with free will to deliberately disobey and displease. In this creation the first being to be split in two is man, who is fast asleep in the innocence of a garden, while God fashions his partner and wife. In our

Western tradition we often look outward to God, and only the mystics look inward, to a higher self.

Oh, but the sheer energy of love! In a beautiful poem, "The Creation," James Weldon Johnson's God (as in the Hindu myth)

> *. . . stepped out on space,*
> *And he looked around and said;*
> *I'm lonely—*
> *I'll make me a world.*
>
> *Then God smiled*
> *And the light broke . . .*

Later he walked around and looked at his moon and stars and world with all its living things, but he said, "I'm lonely still. I'll make me a man."

> *Up from the bed of the river*
> *God scooped the clay;*
> *And by the bank of the river*
> *He kneeled him down;*
> *And there the great God Almighty*
> *Who lit the sun and fixed it in the sky,*
> *Who flung the stars to the most far corner of the*
> *   night,*
> *Who rounded the earth in the middle of his hand;*
> *This Great God,*
> *Like a Mammy bending over her baby,*
> *Kneeled down in the dust*
> *Toiling over a lump of clay*
> *Till he shaped it in his own image;*
>
> *Then into it he blew the breath of life,*
> *And man became a living soul.*
> *Amen. Amen*

47

How different this is from the Hindu myth, where God creates man from his own woman-side! However we conceive God to be—that is what shapes our prayer.

For thousands of years, for tens of thousands, the Antagonist God formed a prevailing view. We think of First Woman standing at the brink of a glorious pink and yellow dawn as the sun rises over the vast veldt, bathing the dewy world in glory; her heart must have risen in awe; but everything was unknown, dangerous. Think of the feelings of First Woman and First Man as they tenderly bury First Child. They scrape an oval hole in the dirt and lay the infant, knees to chest, hands curled at the chin, as if in sleep (we find these graves today), and surrounding the babe they place the familiar objects he may need when he faces the invisible spirit world: a bowl, a toy, a totem, some food on which to feed himself in that other place. But everything is scary, uncertain. Death lurks at every corner, inexplicable.

I spoke earlier of losing track sometimes of my loving God and falling into terror of the night. It happened again not long ago. For 25 years I have lived mostly in the light, my soul certain of the goodness of the universe and of my place in that beating heart. One day, while on a spiritual retreat, I went into the dark, and in that quiet and contemplative convent, where all we had to do was listen to slow lectures and make intercessory prayers, suddenly the dangers were roaring in my face like lions, black caverns opening at my feet. I was caught by horror, loneliness, a shattering loss of faith! What if everything I've dared believe is wrong? The image of a God of love places its own limitations on the mystery.

This perception began with my own willfulness. There was something I wanted. Suddenly it occurred to me I would never receive it. I was fighting for my own way, and I could see no way out! Boxed in, I refused to surrender and found my dark perspective enlarging to encompass *everything,* as I fought for what I thought I needed to survive. I could see all the things that were wrong with my life, with the world. For four days I wrestled, angry, defiant, lonely, afraid. And in that time, writhing against the God I hated, I understood the prayer of sacrifice and the courage of our ancestors, millennia ago.

For thousands upon thousands of years (certainly as early as 4500 B.C.E. and right down to the nineteenth century C.E.) it was the custom to offer to the gods whatever was most precious to you. For millennia the fires blazed in the temples; blood poured in rivers from the knives of priests: grains, sheep, goats, doves, even babies sacrificed to the maw of God. Why not? The gods would take it anyway! Why not offer it in hopes of salvaging some small grace in return? Or offer it in hopes that, while feeding, the hungry gods would not notice when you yourself slunk away, as I was slinking along the edges of that retreat, raging in my heart at these selfless idiots around me, who hadn't even the imagination to understand the questions! Raging at God. Which refused to give me what I needed! I was willing to bargain with any sacrifice. If I only knew with what.

Sacrificial practice has been found in India, in Africa, in the early Americas, in prehistoric Mesopotamia, and in corners throughout the world. In India, the black goddess Kali, who is known as "the Inaccessible" (*Durga*), is one aspect of the Divine Mother. She is Shakti, personification of the female creative force. She is the destroyer of all evils. She is depicted as dancing madly with a necklace of skulls hanging from her neck, and over the centuries she has swallowed streams of sacrificial blood. It flows through carved stone channels into her divine

49

mouth, where, still living, it fades into the source. I am told to this day during Kali's nine-day autumn festival, known as the Durgapuja, seven or eight hundred goats are slaughtered in the Kalighat, her principal temple in Calcutta. The heads are piled before the image, and the devotees receive the meat: sheep, pigs, fowl, water buffalo. Before the British stopped the practice in 1835, the black goddess fed on human sacrifice as well.

"In the year 1830," writes Campbell, "a petty monarch of Bastar . . . offered on one occasion twenty-five men at [the goddess's] altar in Danteshvari." But this is nothing in comparison to one 16th-century king of Cooch Behar who immolated 150 victims at one time.[2] Supposedly both victim and priest merged in perfect prayer with the inhabiting principle, casting off a worn-out body and willingly putting on a new and finer one.

The voluntariness of the sacrifice may be romanticized, for surely some victims did not go gently into that good night (as I was certainly not going gently into the dark of my own sacrifice!). Else the kidnapping of victims and the capture of warriors and slaves in war—to be sacrificed to Aztec or Hindu or Mesopotamian gods—would not have been so widespread a practice.

What to me is the multitude of your sacrifices? Says the Lord; I have had enough of burnt offerings of rams and the fat of fed beasts; I do not delight in the blood of bulls or of lambs or of goats . . . your hands are full of blood . . . cease to do evil, learn to do good; seek justice, rescue the oppressed, defend the orphans, plead for the widow.

—Isaiah 1:11–17

The practice was known in early Israel, too. Just south and west of the walls of Jerusalem lies the valley of Gehenna ("the sons of Hinnom"), where lay the pagan Tophet altars, said to be named for the noisy drum that devotees of the god Moloch would beat to drown out the cries of sacrificed infants. Today the ravine begins as a benign valley for chic Israeli gentrification, but follow it deeper into the rocky hills, and the valley, I'm told, becomes a place of briars and snakes, where the raw sewage seeps down a cliff face from the Christian convent above[3] and nothing grows but the memory of the stench of fear. It is a trash dump of constant, slow-burning fires. You smell decaying offal, the congealed stink of garbage.

From 2000 to 1500 B.C.E., it was the site of cultic child sacrifice. The alien non-Semitic practice was prevalent in the eighth century B.C.E., when several Israeli prophets inveighed against it, and sacrifice was still in fashion 200 years later, when Jeremiah and Second Isaiah were still decrying it. It is thought that the practice may have continued secretly right down to the time of Christ.[4]

Judaic sacrifice may have taken strength from a misinterpretation of the Jewish law (Exodus: 22:29–30) that required the symbolic giving of the first fruit to God, and it may have been encouraged by human offerings to the Canaanite god Moloch[5] (the word in Hebrew means "king"). It is thought that the fires burned ceaselessly in this bleak, frightful valley of human slaughter. Apparently there was a wooden scoop or shovel on which the infant was placed (can you hear it screaming, wailing with fear at the heat, the chanting, the loneliness, the bristling sound of flames?). This scoop may itself have formed the outstretched arms of the great wooden figure of Moloch, which at the appropriate moment swiveled or

51

With what shall I come before the Lord . . . ?
Will the Lord be pleased with thousands of rams,
    with ten thousands of rivers of oil?
Shall I give my firstborn for my transgression,
    the fruit of my body for the sin of my soul?
He has told you, O mortal, what is good:
And what does the Lord require of you,
But to do justice, and to love kindness,
And to walk humbly with your God?

                                       —Micah 6:6–8

pivoted and tipped out the contents of its wooden ladle, dropping the baby into the flames below. Hundreds of infants into the flames!

So many mothers' tears! So much heartache.

Was that sacrifice a prayer?

Did a loving God hear it, or was it operating at about the same level as the chain letter that tells you that if you pass the news on to five people within ten minutes of receiving it, you'll get your wish and if you don't, a curse will fall on you? (I make it a point to break the chain. I refuse to pass such ugliness along.)

I've wondered many times about why the darkness came over me during a spiritual retreat in a Maryland convent. Was I picking up the sorrows and fears of thousands of people who have come over the last hundred years to that convent? Did I simply lose my way? Or is there another explanation for the terror? Did I experience the darkness because I was clinging to my own demands about how things should be and what should be mine by right? Now that it's passed, I look back and give thanks for the experience, because I understand in ways I never had before how, yes, I might sacrifice even my most precious child if I thought it would save my people or bless my flocks or rescue this poor, frightened, threatened world. Or let's be honest: save myself. We do it all the time. We send our sons to gallant war, we subject our daughters to abusive situations—men or work—we constrain our sisters and brothers into lives of slavery disguised in various gaudy apparel. . . . We're so afraid.

I was fighting the God of indifference. Yet all during that dark time, I was praying to recover the gentle God of my former understanding. *"I offer myself to You,"* I prayed. *"Do with me as You will."* I put my despair into His hands. I asked for help. None came. Eventually, exhausted, I gave up—resigned to spending the rest of my life with the incomprehensible fierceness of an indifferent deity . . . and then suddenly, like a child released from a prison dungeon, I found myself upstairs in God's lighted public palace, in rooms swirling with gaiety, music, wine, and food. All of it was dear again, and there was my Father's loving glance on me and my lovely Mother's pleasure at finding me again.

"Where have you been?"

"In hell," I could have said.

I still don't know quite how it happened. One day while I was praying, there came a Presence. How can I explain? I lay once more in the lap of healing comfort. I poured out my despair (as I'd been doing for days), but this time I *knew* without the shadow of doubt that my prayer was heard. It was so simple.

No promises were made, no guarantees given that anything would happen in my favor. That's not the point. Everything was right again, and I was God's simple donkey, trotting happily to the stable, where I knew I'd be fed with grain and hay; I couldn't tell you why I had balked and bucked so furiously, and I couldn't tell you what exactly permitted me to stop, let go. So long as we live, we experience pain and hurt. The promise is not that we'll have none. The promise is that we do not suffer it alone. In the midst of anguish we are comforted.

I was glad to be back home. I had seen into terrors unimagined before, and I knew that I would never be the same.

In C. S. Lewis's *The Screwtape Letters,* the devil writes to his young demon-nephew about how our relationship with God works as a kind of undulation of peaks and troughs, and it is in the troughs that the devils can do their best work—insidiously introducing doubt into our minds.

On returning home, almost the first book I opened contained the following passage, written by Alfred Romer, an American professor of physics. The paragraphs came so serendipitously to hand that I felt as if the universe wanted to explain itself, show me the meaning of my terror on the retreat:

There has come to me an insight into the meaning of Darkness. The reason one must face his darkness, and enter into that darkness is not that he may return purified to face God. One must go into the darkness because that is where God is. The darkness is not sin, not evil. Those are by-ways, side paths by which one can escape. The darkness is pure terror, and the last terror of all is to know as one turns downward that there is no God. Then the darkness is upon you, and there is God Himself, *for God is the greatest destroyer of Gods* [italics mine].

It seems as though we must each make himself a god of his own, one not too big to carry. For some, the Good will be God, or Nature, or the Creative Idea, or the Indulgent Father. One must stay with him and in His universe, or go down into the darkness alone. It is as though one had to take a hammer and smash his god to bits, only to find that here on the instant stood God, God Himself, filling the universe and personally near.

The meaning of the Crucifixion must be like this. One can imagine the disciples talking among themselves: "How could God have let him be killed? He was so good, so kind. He was surely doing God's work if ever a man did. What kind of a God lets His own followers, His best follower, die so?" Until at last they had to deny their God, the God who would waste a good man's life—and in that instant they found the God who sent them all

The kingdom of God is within you.

—Luke 17:21

over the world, the God about whom no more can be said than that He Is.

God is. That is so real that to talk of His love, or of serving Him is saying less, not more. He is, and He is with us, and there is no need of promises.[6]

Throughout this book I will keep repeating the importance of monitoring, watching, guarding your thoughts. It is especially important after a horrific experience to heal, pull quickly back into tranquillity, hope, trust, and love.

If you ever find yourself in the terror, here is a special chant taken from Isaiah 43:1–4. It was arranged by Tracey Marx of Lancaster, Pennsylvania. She calls it a Scripture echo. There are several ways to use it, depending on whether you are alone or have the support of a group.

1. If you are alone, read it aloud several times. Listen to the words. Let them sink slowly into your heart.
2. If you have the privilege of praying with others, select two or even three people who will speak the words aloud, sometimes whispering, sometimes strongly. The voices should alternate, each person reading one line. The others listen. Let the words wash over you, redeeming hope and love.

A Chant for Fear

The Lord, the one who created you, the one who formed you, says

"Do not be afraid, for I have redeemed you. I have called you by name and you are mine."

Do not be afraid, for I have redeemed you.

I have called you by name and you are mine.
Do not be afraid.
Do not be afraid.
Do not be afraid, for I have called you by name.
By name.
I have called you by name and you are mine.
Do not be afraid.
Do not be afraid.

When you pass through waters, I will be with you,
and through rivers, they will not overwhelm you.
I will be with you, when you pass through waters.
I will be with you.
I will be with you.
I will.
And through the rivers, they will not overwhelm you.
They will not overwhelm you.
They will not
Overwhelm you.
When you pass through the waters, I will be with you.
I will be with you.
I will be with you.
I will be with you. Do not be afraid.

When you walk through fire, you shall not be burned,
And the flame shall not consume you.
When you walk through the fire,
You shall not be burned.
You shall not be burned.
You shall not.
The flame shall not consume you.
The flame shall not consume you.
The flame
Shall not consume you,
When you walk through fire,

When you walk through,
Through fire,
Do not be afraid.
Do not be afraid.
Do not
Do not
Do not be afraid.
The Lord, the one who created you, the one who formed
you, says, Do not be afraid, for I have redeemed you. I
have called you by name and you are mine.

You are mine.
You are mine.
You are mine.
You are mine.
You are mine.
The Lord says, Do not be afraid for you are mine.
I am the Lord your God . . . and you are precious in my
sight, and honored, and I love you.

I love you.
I love you.
I love you.

A Hindu Prayer[1]

O Supreme Spirit! Lead us from untruth to truth.

Lead us from darkness to light. Lead us from death to immortality.

O Lord, in Thee may all be happy.

May all be free from misery, may all realize goodness, and may no one suffer pain.

Chapter 5

When Thought Can Touch

I fretted the other night at the hotel at the stranger who broke into my chamber after midnight, claiming to share it. But after his lamp had smoked the chamber full and I had turned round to the wall in despair, the man blew out his lamp, knelt down at his bedside, and made in low whisper a long earnest prayer. Then was the relation entirely changed between us. I fretted no more, but respected and liked him.

—Ralph Waldo Emerson, *Journal* (1835)

We can name the prayer of contemplation, the prayer of sacrifice, the prayer of action, the prayer of touch. But one thing they all have in common is *intention,* thought. So far we've been talking how you are influenced by your own thoughts—by what you think. But here's another fact: Your thought affects the world.

They say that anything you think about for 17 seconds you attract into your life. They say that praying from lack increases lack (certainly it reinforces the impression of lack and thus increases fear). They say that if you expect the best, the best comes pouring onto you, and that this is why you should train yourself to pray with thanks and praise, all wants fulfilled! Your cup running over. Or else, in anguish, to pray to have your ugly thought removed.

A friend, Isabelle, once told me how as a child a friend of hers was sitting under a tree, overwhelmed by misery. She was just a little girl at the time, forlorn in the speckled sunlight, when suddenly—out of nowhere—she began to pray fiercely the famous Jesus prayer: "Lord Jesus Christ have mercy on me." But being little, she gave it a childish twist: "Lord Jesus Christ," she prayed, "have mercy on *me-ee!*"

Instantly her dark thoughts vanished, and her unhappiness. She went away impressed. This girl, now an adult, told her discovery to my friend, who not long ago passed it on to me.

"Try it," said Isabelle. "But the important thing is you have to say it exactly like that. You have to put the accent on *me-ee!*"

Since then I, too, have used it many times and always found immediate help. Now whenever I notice myself judgmental, pessimistic, resentful, worrying, whenever I find myself less generous than I'd like, or caught in nets of fear, confusion, doubt, whenever I see myself concentrating on what I think I lack, I silently cry, "Lord Jesus Christ have mercy on *me-ee!*" Moments later I will realize always with a surge of surprise that my thoughts have shifted to tranquil paths. It's impossible to hold a negative thought if you pray like that!

Then Isabelle told another story. She said that she had started saying the Jesus Prayer over and over, in a kind of constant mantra, and that after a few months she noticed that judgement, resentment, doubt, and pessimism seemed to have diminished, or perhaps even vanished, leaving only worry, "those pesky moments of uneasiness."

Commit your cause to the Lord; let him deliver—
let him rescue the one in whom he delights.

—Psalms 22:8

"Whenever I'm rushing away from tranquillity," she told me, "I say, 'Lord Jesus Christ have mercy on *me-ee!*' And it helps. But there's more. You know, the one thing I can't stand is having the chain of a necklace all knotted up," she continued, fingering the delicate gold chain at her neck. "One day I was trying to get it unknotted. I was in a hurry, standing at the front door, unable to untangle the necklace to put it on. I stopped myself, held the chain in my hand. 'Lord Jesus Christ have mercy on *me-ee,*' I repeated, and then—can you believe it?—the chain unknotted itself in my hands!"

I laughed. I could well believe it. But the resolution of a problem is of less importance than the transformation that comes to the person praying—to the soul. We can't transform ourselves by ourselves. But in prayer we can offer ourselves to be transformed.

"And we can always tell when it has happened," added Isabelle, leaning forward with her penetrating, luminous eyes. "We tell by the fruits of the Spirit. And the fruits are love, joy, peace, patience, kindness, generosity, faithfulness, gentleness, and self-control.

"Whenever I'm upset or anxious, I say to myself, 'Love, joy, peace, patience, kindness, generosity, faithfulness, gentleness, and self-control.' It's from St. Paul's letter to the Galatians," she added, laughing. "By saying it again and again, I'm dwelling in those moments. Love, peace, patience . . . and then they come to me."

It's a living example of how to guard your thoughts,

62

THE PATH OF PRAYER

assuming that whatever you think about for 17 seconds will be attracted into your path.

Simone Weil likened prayer to school, the purpose of which (school) is not only to instill information into young heads but also to develop concentration. Praying brings the mind to attention. You think. You concentrate with singleness of heart.

But the heart is as important as the mind. The desires of the mind must align with those of the heart, and if they do for even a fraction of a second, not only do you receive relief, *you influence the world!*

Some people may doubt such an exaggerated statement, but experiments at the Princeton Engineering Anomalies Research lab (PEAR) in Princeton University's School of Engineering are demonstrating the power of intention. The studies began at PEAR in 1979, when a student persuaded the dean of the school, Dr. Robert Jahn, an aerospace engineer and physicist, to let her study the effect of human consciousness on machines. Since then the results of several *million* experiments have been published. (For more detailed information, you could get hold of Dr. Jahn's book *Margins of Reality* or of any of the scientific papers available on PEAR's Web site—www.princeton.edu/~PEAR.)

The important thing is this: The experiments work only when using machines exquisitely calibrated to generate random results. One clue to a success in these experiments on the power of thought is *randomness.* One machine is a breadbox-shaped Random Event Generator (REG), spewing out random numerals. Another is a gravity-operated "pinball" machine, where 9,000 small balls bounce off a series of pegs cascading with a terrible racket into one of 19 bins. A third device operates as a water jet, rising or falling, and a fourth as a little robot that swivels randomly around on a circular table. Each device has sophisticated photoelectric or electronic counters to record its results over the course of a "run." A volunteer sits before one of the machines and tries *by thinking* to influence its action. The volunteers have no special psychic powers; they are ordinary men and women of all ages.

The scientists found that intention or thought influences the machines at statistically significant levels. We are talking here, of course, about minuscule levels or degrees of change over the course of many such runs, but the overall results leave little doubt about the effectiveness of the power of the touch of thought. (At PEAR they speak of "intention," rather than "thought," since "thought" implies a cognitive activity rather than the deeper emotional level of engagement that is believed to be at play.)

With this established, Dr. Jahn and his team began to wonder about *distance.* They found that a volunteer in Australia or California can send an intention to one of the machines in Princeton, New Jersey . . . and the intention will register in the same way as if the person were sitting in front of the device. "Go high . . . go low . . . bounce

All things are possible to the one who believes.

—Mark 9:23

left . . . move right. . . ." Somehow the machine discerns the idea and adjusts. (Physicists studying subatomic particles have found the same sensitivity and interaction between the photons and observers, the particles behaving so playfully that they almost seem aware of the observer's thoughts.)

The next question concerned *time.* PEAR asked the volunteers to send their intention hours or *even days before* the machine had run its program, and found again that it mattered not a jot! The future bends before the power of intention.

Finally, the PEAR team asked another question: Could thought affect the past? What if a message was sent *after* the fact, after the machine had already made its run? Several studies in this field had been done years earlier both in France and by Dr. Helmut Schmidt, a theoretical physicist then at the Mind-Body Foundation in San Antonio, Texas. Schmidt had worked with tapes and radioactive decay, and he had found that the sender's intention, even arriving days after the "run," could influence a random-operating machine *if the data had not yet been observed.* But if the data were examined and recorded before the volunteer finished sending the intention, then no influence was found. Don't look over the shoulder of the machine!

Now PEAR, duplicating his work with volunteers and the random-operating machines, found (as he had) that . . . *The Past Is Malleable to Thought.*

I don't pretend to understand the nuances of these experiments, though I've now read a considerable amount and visited the cluttered, crowded, happy laboratory at Princeton. What they discovered is that, yes, the sender's intention could influence the machine, but in the PEAR experiments it isn't so much "observing" the results that

65

seems to matter as knowing the operator's intentions beforehand or, in other words, making observations within a specific context of belief. The record of observations must be made without prior knowledge of the sender's intention.

As a scientific institution, PEAR is cautious in formulating conclusions. Its researchers will not state unconditionally that thought can change the past, because there's another possibility: that somehow it was the machine that was influencing the volunteer, the telepathy running backward, as it were. But no longer can anyone dispute that our intellect, desires, longings, and intentions affect even inorganic matter—move mountains, as Christ said!

But what exactly is influencing the machines? Apparently it is thought combined with caring love. Two people working in pairs produce stronger results than a single individual, and on average two people of the opposite sex *have about twice the effect of two people of the same sex.* Moreover, the thoughts of two people who are in love *have nearly seven times the influence* of a single individual. It is not thought alone, then, but *love* that makes the machines respond.

One man was having no success in influencing the Random Event Generator. Finally he stalked into the office to ask Brenda Dunne, the office manager, how to get the thing to work!

"It seems it works by love," she answered. "You have to love it." He stalked back out to his machine, and a few minutes later she heard him shouting at his machine, "Love! Love!"

Competition has no effect, and neither does anger or hate. It is not strong emotion that moves the machines but heart. Should this surprise us? I heard recently of one experiment in France in which a cage of baby chicks was placed at the edge of the table on which roamed a random-operating robotized machine. Chicks imprint "mother" on the first thing they see, whether it is their hen, a stick, a dog, a pair of human legs. In this case it was the robot that the chicks imprinted on, cheeping to the machine as to their mother hen, and the robot (I was told) was found to hover more closely to the cage of chicks than elsewhere on the table, drawn by their cries of love or need.

Many other studies are being undertaken now. All point to one irrefutable idea: that so powerful is the human mind and consciousness—intention, thought—so subtle, so unchained by time or space that we will probably never understand exactly what it is or how it can affect the physical world. The mind is nonlocal (as the scientists say). It picks up information by telepathy, precognition, or by some mysterious ability to view things happening far away. It influences the future and can change the past, and so our every prayer, hope, longing, every thought and intention sends out ripples to a universe predicated (apparently) on two simple, loving words: *Why not?*

If prayer is concentrated thought, distilled and sent out on beams of love out into the stratosphere, if prayer is a passionate longing of the heart, then the task is to pay attention to your thoughts. Are they creative or destructive? Are they worried or tranquil? And if you are by nature pessimistic, then how do you change the thought habits of a lifetime and send out positive, believing prayers? For this, affirmations play a part. You lay claim to your desire! Prayer and affirmations are sometimes confused. It's important to take a look at them.

An affirmation is a statement of what you want to have

WHEN THOUGHT CAN TOUCH

happen! An affirmation is an act of courage, demanding the future you want to have appear. An affirmation is an intention written out in simple language. You read over and over; you write it ten or twenty times a day, and slowly the intention seeps into your unconscious and changes your thinking. Then your thinking attracts to you what you want to have.

"I am worthy of good friends, for the highest good of all."

"I complete my college education with ease."

Posting loving affirmations around your rooms—on a bathroom mirror or on the refrigerator door—gives courage, optimism, strength. Some people tack up Scriptural references:

This God . . . has made my way safe.
He made my feet like hinds' feet,
and set me secure on the heights.

—2 Samuel 22:33–34

Others use affirmations of courage: "I have the ability to feel good in all circumstances."

I am an artist!" still others claim, or "I am brilliant, talented, prolific, successful."

"I work with discipline and delight every day."

"I have the perfect job that fulfills me creatively and financially."

"I have my perfect mate."

Our belief at the beginning of a doubtful undertaking is the one thing that insures the successful outcome of your venture.

—William James

Some people say that prayer and affirmations are the same, that the same principles of positive thinking apply, and it is true that you pray most powerfully when you express the prayer as if you've already achieved your heart's desire. The Unity School of Christianity, for example, speaks of "affirmative prayer."

In fact, some prayers are affirmations, but not all affirmations are prayers.

Years ago I came across a wondrous little work by John Lester that talked about "Consciously Creating Circumstances," or CCC. I had not heard about this business of controlling your destiny by claiming it. This book promised that if I wrote out my desires ten or twenty times each morning and again ten or twenty times each evening, always expressing my desire *as if I already had it* . . . it would come to me!

Wow, that's great! thought I. Did I need money? (The book was mostly attuned to money.) I had only to affirm that I had money to spend, to lend, to spare, to save—I had so many thousands or millions of dollars—and abundance would pour upon me. Did I need love? A job? I should merely affirm, "I have the perfect partner" or "I have the perfect job." The adjective "perfect" gives power to the affirmation. Years later I would read with admiration Norman Vincent Peale's book *The Power of Postive Thinking* and be struck by the *rightness* of what he said as well: that we must always expect the best and train our minds to believe in the power of the Holy One, which is helping us. The *belief itself* draws our destiny to us. Negative thoughts attract destructive events, and positive thoughts attract positive ones. In that book Dr. Peale gives one example after another of men and women overcoming insurmountable obstacles by the power of

> "Whatever you bind on earth will be bound in heaven," pro-
> claimed Jesus, "and whatever you loose on earth will be loosed in heaven."
>
> —Matthew 16:19

their positive thinking. (It is one of the books I keep by my bedside, so important is this idea.) But my first introduction to positive concentration came with that publication by John Lester on Consciously Creating Circumstances.

Who does not like that idea of directing fate? We're taught to admire self-reliance, to control our circumstances. I experimented with CCC for some time, and I have to report that all the affirmations I wrote out in those long-gone days have since come true, though some took years to manifest themselves. Are you feeling insecure, inadequate? Then you consciously retrain your unconscious mind, reprogramming the ancient voices of inadequacy with new adjectives: "I am strong and capable," you write. "I am beautiful, brave, generous. . . ."

"I have the perfect conditions to create the work that is in me. . . ."

"I let God's creativity work through me. . . ."

Are you imprisoned by an addiction? "I am free of alcohol and drugs," you affirm. "I easily stop smoking."

Are you troubled by your weight? "I weigh 130 pounds. I easily and effortlessly keep my perfect, healthy weight."

You write out your longings, you sing them in the shower, you whisper them to the skies and clouds. Indeed, the rules for making an affirmation are much like those for prayer.

1. Keep it clear, one simple phrase at a time.
2. Keep it concise. Don't rattle on, with clauses and subclauses.
3. Use the present tense, as if the thing has already happened.
4. Avoid negative words, like "not" or "hate."
5. Use positive words, like "perfect," "balanced," or "harmonious" in each affirmation.
6. Finish with "for the highest good of all concerned" or else "this or something better is coming to me now."

Do you want more friends? Affirm, "I am worthy of good friends, for the highest good."

I didn't know all these rules at first, but I found this idea of Consciously Creating Circumstances intriguing. At the time I suffered from terrible skin rashes that would erupt in red, raw, itching, flaming areas over my arms, neck, face, and chest. One evening I was in London packing to leave next morning for the United States, when my nervous rash broke out once more. Aha! I knew what to do! That night as I lay down to sleep, I silently repeated over and over, "My rash is getting better. My rash is getting better."

The next morning my rash was so much better that it had spread over my whole body! I was covered with open, oozing sores. No time to go to a doctor —I had to catch a plane. But as I settled in my seat and buckled the seat belt, I realized I had made the affirmation wrong. I then decided that the rash would be gone by the time the plane reached Washington, D.C., and, closing my eyes, I began to repeat, "My skin is clear, my skin is perfect. My skin is healthy and perfectly clear." By the time we landed, seven hours later, the rash had completely disappeared! I have never suffered from eczema since.

WHEN THOUGHT CAN TOUCH

Doing our own will is usually what harms us.

—Teresa of Ávila

But was that a prayer?

I think not. I'll tell you why.

It was concerned solely with the self. *My will be done!* I cried without regard to a higher end. I certainly never thought to ask "for the highest good" or mutter "this or something better." (I hadn't learned that yet.) Still, the power of thought produced the desired effect.

Let me be clear: I like affirmations. Affirmations can bolster self-esteem, boost courage, or change a bad habit or attitude. Before an opera, when the other singers backstage were warming up their voices with rising and descending scales, the great tenor Caruso would sing, "I am the greatest singer in the world! My voice is mag-ni-fi-cent!" Things like that.

A friend used to swim laps for exercise. So boring did she find the undertaking that she began to use alphabetical affirmations, each stroke a positive attribute or virtue, each lap a different letter, moving from adorable, athletic, attractive, through beautiful, brave, brilliant . . . on to fit, funny, generous, glamorous, past lean, lithe, loving, muscular, patient, persistent, through x-traspecial, youthful, and yummy. By the time she reached zesty (for the highest good), she was in nirvana! She felt powerful, graceful, tactful, creative, and ready to face any challenge.

So affirmations have a real place in our lives. But they are not necessarily prayer.

Nonetheless, they may be used as prayer.

"My strength cometh from the Lord . . ." runs Psalm 118. "The Lord is my strength and my might; he has become my salvation." Are these songs very different from an affirmation? "Rejoice in the Lord who gives aid to the poor."

Affirm your truth; lay claim to the positive in life.

If you are in need, go among others. Rejoice with them. Sing praises. Lift your thoughts to joy and love and help, and you will find cares leaving you, so powerful are intention and thought.

Many people consider our relationship with God to be one of "co-creating." According to this principle, we affirm what we want and God gives it to us! It's a little simplistic, for who are we to know what's best? But it's true that when you pray, affirming, and when you *visualize* what you want, what you are working to achieve, your thoughts can bring it to you. When you surround an ailing person with healing prayer and light, you are creatively visualizing the (future) healing that has taken place. And when you make intercessory prayers for your friend to heal or find the perfect job, or the perfect house, or the perfect school for her son, aren't you sending out an affirmation—creating together with the universe the longing of your heart?

Sometimes, however, the affirmation lacks one essential component of true prayer: It lacks humility. Unless done carefully, affirmations skim close to the terrain of the magicians, of shamans and wizards, of the conjurer woman who throws spells and mixes love potions, will-

---

"Again truly I tell you, if two of you agree on earth about anything you ask, it will be done for you by my Father in heaven."

—Matthew 18:19

---

fully trying to manipulate the universe. Curses fall into this space, too—as negative affirmations, negative prayer. They work, but, oh, be careful what you do!

There's the difference in a nutshell. Affirmations don't seek grace. The fact is, we rarely hear of someone asking, with an affirmation, "What do you wish me to pray for, God?"

Moreover, no matter how long you repeat it or with what single-minded faith, an affirmation will never lead to mystical experiences and insights, to raptures and favors, to the sacred encounters with the Mysterious One that change a life forever.

Finally, some affirmations (or prayers, for that matter) are impossible to achieve. "If wishes were horses, beggars would ride," runs the old adage. We can affirm till the cows come home that the shell of our body will live 200 years, and, lo, it will not.

The key distinction between prayer and affirmation, then, lies in the degree to which you are willing to trust, to open yourself to the marvels of the universe. Because the fact is, we simply don't know what is best for us and others. Which is why, in true prayer, we try to align ourselves with the will of God.

This phrase "the will of God" is often tossed about. When something bad happens, people say, "It was the will of God"—a phrase, I might add, that brings cold comfort. What does it mean, "the will of God"?

You have made us for yourself, O Lord,
And our hearts are restless until they rest in you.

—Augustine of Hippo

It's instructive that the word "will" in Greek and Hebrew is related to "yearning." It means "God's yearning"—a yearning to love and be loved—which includes the wild, extravagant freedom implied. We like to think that our calling will come with screaming sirens, a motorcade, a drumbeat tattoo to signal the Will of God. We'll know when it comes by its searchlights and thunder and the trumpets of angels. Unfortunately, the will of God often comes with so subtle a call that it's easily ignored.

Once I asked my spiritual director the troubling question "How do I know the will of God? How do I know if this longing is really what the universe wants of me?"

She looked at me in her thoughtful, quiet, prayerful way. "Did it ever occur to you," she asked, "that God puts desires in your heart, in order that you will execute them?"

It had not. Yet it seems an appropriate response. Each of us has some mission or purpose here on earth. The purpose may change as we grow older, so that the purpose in our twenties may not be at all the one we have in our seventies. But if we listen deeply, we will know what is the highest good for ourselves and others. We will know the will of God concerning that moment. We will come to trust the universe and our own intuitions.

Here is what I know about the will of God, which presents itself, I find, in a thousand little ways, through accidents, or other people, or by a recurring nagging thought that just won't leave you alone.

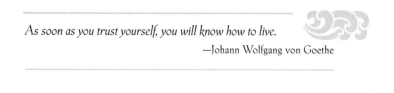

As soon as you trust yourself, you will know how to live.
—Johann Wolfgang von Goethe

1. The will of God is inexorable. It will happen. There is nothing I can do to speed or stop it, and when it comes, its solutions are always elegant.
2. God's will is steady, constant. It doesn't drift.

Skeptics may take me to task for this second statement. "So when I long for something constantly," you argue, "does that mean it's the will of God?" The answer is yes and no. I think we are like a two-year-old—so easily distracted! One moment he's poking a hairpin into an electric socket, and the next he's playing with the pot lids in the kitchen or skipping down a road, delighted by the flowers to either side. Beside him walks the mother, moving with stately calm. As he dashes from one enticing curiosity to the next, the mother watches, allowing her baby the freedom to explore, yet ready to prevent real harm. That's how it is with God. Certain. Steady. Just watching us and waiting for our response.

There are two other tests for the will of God.

3. The will of God brings *joy.* The heart leaps up with *yes!*
4. Last (but not always), there is a physical response— an electric charge running off your fingertips, the hair rising on your arm, or sudden tears. The will of God feels different from your ordinary whim.

But we were talking of the difference between prayer and affirmation.

Some years ago I had a great friend, Dorothy, who lived on my street. She was 86 when I met her and 97 when she died. At 93 she told me with enormous excitement, "Oh, Sophy, I've learned so much since I was 90! I've learned more since I was ninety than in all my life before!"

How could that be? She lived alone in one small room. She was deaf, though her eyes were good enough to read or watch TV. Every morning she got up and dressed herself carefully in underclothing, corset, garters, stockings, shoes, and dress. She put on makeup and a pearl choker at her neck. Hanging on to the chairs and wall for support, she tottered the few steps to the kitchen and ate a fruit yogurt for breakfast, then staggered back to her sitting room and sank into a chair. She spent the whole day in one chair. Some days no visitors came to see her. She might speak to no one for days at a time! She lived like a hermit in a Himalayan cave, eating only a little yogurt, but in this period she relived (sometimes with the most passionate remorse) her wild, adventurous, often wicked life. She read. She thought. She prayed.

One morning she was consumed with anxiety and the urgency to *do something!* I don't know her prayer exactly, but suddenly she was receiving an inner knowing so strong that she snatched up a pen and wrote down the words that flowed into her mind:

"Don't fret," came the silent voice. "You have nothing to worry about! Just relax and let things come along in their proper time. Let Quiet, Peace, and Harmony rule and avoid stressing situations. Let them be born, live, and straighten out pleasantly, not with fretting or urgency but by simply accepting the fact—*it will work out* if you let yourself be *led* instead of trying to force matters. All is well and will remain well!

"Please Heed!"

And then the final direction: "Remember always that Divine Love is a Force. It is Everywhere, *governing, guarding, guiding,* and *protecting* us. It works wonders."

In excitement, she put down her pen and telephoned me. Later she gave me the card on which she'd written this hopeful and extraordinary message. I tacked it on the bulletin board above my desk, where it stands to this day, her beautiful handwriting reminding me of her.

There's a sequel to the story. Years passed, and Dorothy died. I was in New Mexico, and one day I found myself lying on a couch overcome once again by fear and helplessness at a writing deadline. "Oh, God, oh, God," I prayed in the wordless, aching fashion that marks my poorest prayers. No magical affirmations here.

My hermitage in New Mexico is small, and only an hour earlier I had swept and vacuumed it. Now, as I lay miserably on the couch, my eye spotted a scrap of paper on the bare wood floor. How did it get there? In irritation I rose to throw it away—and saw Dorothy's card with that message written in her own lovely hand!

"You have nothing to worry about! Just relax and let

As children bring their broken toys
With tears for us to mend,
I brought my broken dreams to God.
But then instead of leaving him,
Because he was my friend,
In peace to work alone,
I hung around and tried to help
With ways that were my own.
At last I snatched them back and cried,
"How can you be so slow?"
"My child," he said, "What could I do?
You never did let go."

—Anonymous

things come along in their proper time . . . simply accepting the fact—*it will work out* if you let yourself be *led* instead of trying to force matters. All is well and will remain well!"

I held the card in astonishment. How had it gotten there? It was supposed to be on my bulletin board back home, 2000 miles away! Moreover, I had only just finished cleaning. Moments before, there'd been nothing on the floor.

Perhaps that explains the difference between our pitiful attempts to consciously create circumstances and the state of absolute abandon to a spiritual dimension that constitutes true prayer—the touch of thought.

A Buddhist Prayer[1]

May there abound in all directions
Gardens of wish-fulfilling trees
Filled with the sweet sound of Wisdom
Proclaimed by the Holy Beings.

And may the earth everywhere be pure,
Smooth and devoid of rough terrains,
Level like the palm of a hand,
And of the nature of lapis lazuli.

For as long as space endures,
And for as long as living beings remain,
May I too abide to dispel the misery of the world.

Chapter 6

The Four Stair-Steps of Prayer

I think that some part of human nature delights in making lists, in organizing, cataloging, bringing order out of chaos, and true to this imperative are the scores of different kinds of prayer listed by different authorities. Lama Surya Das, in *Awakening to the Sacred,*[1] lists fourteen. Richard Foster, in *Prayer: Finding the Heart's True Home,*[2] lists twenty-one types (good gracious!) of prayer. These include simple prayer, the prayer of self-examination, the prayer of relinquishment, the prayer of tears, covenant prayer, petitionary prayer, intercessional prayer, healing prayer, the prayer of suffering, the prayer of adoration. . . .

But I reduce the list to only four, each type opening a doorway to the next:

1. Petition or supplication—asking for something
2. Gratitude or thanksgiving
3. Praise and adoration
4. The prayer of union

Actually, I don't see any of them as really separate or distinct, for the first hesitant step of petition soon feeds into the prayer of thanksgiving, which when continued turns, to our surprise, into a paean of praise, which with repetition becomes sheer adoration, and this prayer merges so indistinctly into the prayer of union (which St. Teresa called "orison") that it's hard to see the boundaries where one begins and another ends. They are sequential, but the seeker can leap into the middle, ignoring petition altogether in favor of a higher stage. Or she can begin with petition and dash into adoration almost without knowing she's bypassed thanks. I think of them as steps on a staircase, or perhaps rather as a ramp, like the moving roadway in an airport terminal. Each footstep leads to the next until, arriving, you are flooded with joy, with love. And then you send love out to others, either with your heart or with the gentlest touch. Except for the initial supplication, they are each one just stair-steps of love. For that matter, even our frightened, begging prayers arise out of love for our own selves! Or for the person or situation we're praying for; so that all prayers could be said to arise from love.

The first three types of prayer need little explanation. We've already talked about them earlier. Is there anyone alive who does not know how to make a plea for help? How to ask for forgiveness, how to give forgiveness, how to be open to God's love? As for prayers of thanks and gratitude—why, every time you bow your head, overwhelmed by the sight of your children or loved one, every time you fall silent before a majestic landscape or give a cry of joy at the first tulip in the garden, you have made a prayer. You can, of course, kneel at an altar and list those things for which you give thanks to God. You can swim in the simplicity of gratitude. I will add this:

The prayer of help expressed as gratitude for having it already—this is a powerful way to pray.

Even more powerful is the prayer of praise. I spoke earlier of how the universe responds to praise, how it squirms with pleasure at your offering of praise, and how you can even toss out a challenge to the spiritual world: "Things can't get any better than this!" you say, and then they do. Praise is a suitable response to thanks. Praise opens doorways of your heart, so that when consumed in praising, you are lifted into levels of happiness unknown to you before. With praise you teeter on the lip of union. *Hallelujah!*

There are so many ways to practice these types of prayer that it would take days to discuss them all. There is the praise expressed in song or in the Psalms. *Hallelujah!* The praise of bodily movement and dance. There is chanting. There is silence. There is the practice of resting in the palm of God's hand, just listening. Your heart is pulsing with praise.

Here is an exercise:

When you pray, ask yourself which kind of prayer you're making. Is this a prayer of petition, thanksgiving, or adoration? (The prayer of union is not ours to choose.) It's interesting to see which type of prayer you mostly choose to make. It's also interesting to see what happens if you try a different one.

Select one kind and pray it for a time.

What happened? How do you feel? What was different from the way you usually pray? Did you receive a response?

As for the prayer of union, it is not in our human power to achieve. This is the prayer of the contemplative, and it is attained by silence, fasting, meditation, and deep introspection. But no one can reach the prayer of union by herself. Rather, it drops upon us by grace. We don't know when union will come or why it happens at one moment while at another time it remains as distant as the moon. It is the last of my four distinctive types, and yet it, too, can be divided into subtypes if we care to split atoms or hairs: In union we dissolve into a light-struck silence so deep and thrilling that we lose all power to think or speak; we are ravished by love. Sometimes union is accompanied by raptures or ecstasies, mystical visions tossed out at us and accompanied by knowledge beyond the human scope. Other times we feel our souls lifted on the wings of angels to the twisted treetops; and at still other moments we see the face and form of the deity, or perhaps we fall into such a state of formless compassion that when we return to our senses we are forever changed, though we couldn't say precisely what had happened. Perhaps this union is such that, though united with God in love, we remain separate, paradoxical as that may sound, and this occurs especially when visions are involved. But one thing is sure: A single instant of union and, like the suckling child, we find that our faculties of *thinking* and observation have stopped, have been absorbed into the milk of love. Yet when we recover, we recognize that we were separate in union, we on the lap, the universe just loving us. Sometimes, by merely being still, just breathing and resting trustfully in a prayerful state, we can hear the still, small voice of God, receive an answer to our prayers. Sometimes this is close enough to heaven, too.

I call these mystical states a prayer of union because we are in a prayerful state, although unable for that drunken, time-stopped period to speak or move or think.

But true union is not a prayer that we can undertake by thought or will; it's given as a gift, and in my experience it seems to come by humble practice of the lower (if I may use that term) three forms of prayer.

I heard of a man, an ordained minister, who was asked what he thought heaven would be like. He quoted the wonderful images of God's love for us from the book of Zephaniah.

> *The Lord will take great delight in you,*
> *He will quiet you with his love,*
> *He will rejoice over you with singing.*
>
> —Zephaniah 3:17

"When I go to heaven," he said, "I want to hear God sing. I want God to take a look at me coming, and stand up and burst into song."

And I guess that's the point of prayer.

Of all the people who write of prayer, St. Teresa of Ávila has written most brilliantly. Teresa went into a Carmelite convent at the age of eighteen, and because she was wild, beautiful, witty, intelligent, and because she adored men and vivacious company, she found the experience hard. For twenty years she tried to pray. One day, at the age of 38, passing a crucifix in the hallway, she was suddenly smitten to the heart. She fell to her knees in tears, the first of many "favors" of the Lord that she experienced. In her forties, at the urging of her spiritual adviser and always under the eye of the Inquisition, she wrote her books about mystical encounters, prayer, and her spiritual life. In her autobiography she names three categories of prayer—verbal, mental, and silent—in the last of which the soul *cannot* speak without the greatest difficulty.

Mental prayer in my opinion is nothing less than an intimate sharing between friends; it means taking time frequently to be alone with Him who we know loves us.

—St. Teresa of Ávila, *Life*

Verbal prayers are the formal ones recited out loud in church or murmured on a rosary. Mental prayers are unspoken, made-up ones. Silent prayer for her meant orison or union.

In her *Life* she also provides the beautiful metaphor of prayer as watering a garden. Here she names four "degrees" of prayer, moving from hard to easiest.

"The beginner," she wrote, "must realize that in order to give delight to the Lord she is starting to cultivate a garden on very barren soil, full of abominable weeds. . . . It seems to me the garden can be watered in four ways. . . ."

Imagine the arid landscape of 16th-century Spain, when so much work is done on the backs of donkeys or laborers. In the beginning, she says, praying is hard. It's like trying to water a garden by drawing water from a well, hand over hand, and carrying the buckets to the gasping plants. But as you continue—and mind, she knew what she was talking about, for it took her twenty years, from the ages of 18 to 38, before a prayer life came easily to her—as you continue, you reach the second degree of prayer, when it becomes like taking up water from a windlass. You crank it up by a wheel and axle built over the well. Or perhaps it comes on a waterwheel, an invention in which a series of buckets are hung over a stream or riverbed, and as the current fills the buckets, one by one, it lifts them like the seats of a Ferris wheel up to the peak and empties them into an aqueduct.

Now the water of prayer is higher, and you reach what she calls the Prayer of Quiet, embodied in a still heart. Everything brings consolation with little effort, and you may find yourself weeping with joy at the early supernatural and mystical experiences that are given to you now. Neither verbal nor mental prayer must be completely given up, but the soul at this stage wants only to rest in silence in the presence of God.

St. Teresa is careful in all these descriptions to add that only the first effort is ours, while the *results* of the prayer come from His Majesty, who, seeing and loving our effort, sends grace to help us on our way. What the soul does at this second degree of prayer is simply to go softly, making little noise and having no concern that now prayer is done without words; in this second degree the soul will come close to God and retreat, then move closer again, always learning more about itself.

But there is a third degree, when prayer becomes even easier, for now the garden of the soul is watered from a running spring or river that cuts into the thirsty fields. It is marked by a great rejoicing and praise and love of God; all desires for the world pass away at this point into one sublime longing for union, for at this stage, she says, the soul is caught by the fire of love and wants only *that.*

If you have been blessed with union, you are in bliss. But when this state passes away and you return to your body, then memory, will, and imagination create great turmoil in their efforts to recapture and understand what happened, and this is so fatiguing, she says, that the seeker must "take no more notice of the will than it would of a madman."

> *At the same time, . . . no soul on this road is such a giant that it does not often need to become a child at the breast again. . . . For there is no state of prayer, however sublime, in which it is not necessary often to go back to the beginning.*
>
> —St. Teresa of Ávila, *Life*

Finally she names a fourth degree of prayer, in which God Himself, His Majesty, is praying for you. She likens this fourth stage to rain, when all you do is lift your face and taste the water running from the skies. Watering the garden for you. Praying with you, effortlessly. In this stage you receive mystical ecstasies, which change you so completely that you are made into fine gold.

Nonetheless, the soul, she says, is always brought back each time to earth, back to the beginning, so that the cycle always begins anew.

Anything can be a prayer. Singing can be a prayer, lifting your voice in a song or chant. Sitting in the silent *samadhi* of absorbed meditation is a prayer. Or moving your body. Dancing is a prayer—dancing to the full moon, or leaping like David, who danced naked in the streets as the royal procession brought the sacred ark into Jerusalem. Washing the dishes can be a prayer, or tenderly holding your dying father's hand (the silent prayer of touch). Any creative art can be engaged in as a form of prayer—painting, acting in the theater, writing poetry. Anything can be a prayer.

The question is, what is the *intention*?

Intention is what makes a prayer alive.

Are you awake, alert? Are you present to the moment? Are you loving or hating, hurt or afraid—and are you *aware* of the emotion or the need? Are you trusting, daring, thanking?

It seems to me that there is no distinction between morning or evening prayers, prayers of reconciliation, angry prayers or silent prayers or prayers of self-examination. They are all just different ways of talking to God! Or perhaps it would be better to say that they concern different things you're talking about. A prayer of anger, for example, is still, at least, about petition: We want what we want—now! The anger comes at not having it, and we're telling God what should be done! We are demanding, not pleading, but still we're in relationship; we're still talking. The same is true of grief, and comfort comes mysteriously. Perfectly. Elegantly.

Once my friend Donna was praying the rosary. She was very angry, and, remembering the injunction of St. Ignatius to visualize and relive on each bead one aspect of the suffering of Christ, she decided rebelliously she didn't want Christ's suffering! She'd pray the life of Mary instead.

She was praying, therefore, and imagining the Annunciation by the angel Gabriel, then the visitation with Elizabeth, and finally the naked birth—and each episode was colored by her anger.

"Now everyone knows I'm pregnant! The gossip is all over the place."

Or "Here I am on this cold winter night, about to drop a baby, and there's no place but a stable, and I'm not being taken care of. Oh, *fine!*"

Suddenly, as Donna prayed, the story of this birth seemed mysteriously beautiful. She couldn't say how or at which moment her thoughts shifted. She couldn't say what step had been taken. But at a certain moment her anger disappeared. This was not at all what she had

89

expected—not even what she'd wanted, necessarily.
Against her will she was caught by love and lifted into an
awareness of a presence at that birth . . . and the ripples
broke against her own situation, dissolving all her fear
and rage.

Praying is always hard in the beginning. Moreover,
even the spiritual giants sometimes find it hard to pray.
Some days we cannot force a prayer. Other days it springs
unbidden to our lips, our hearts. Sometimes we skip
pleading and move directly into praise and gratitude,
and other days we are brought back to the petitionary beginning, forced to our knees by fear or loss or hurt.

I'd like to boast that I pray only with thanksgiving or
adoration. It would be a lie. Whenever I'm in the grip of
fear, it's impossible to force myself to pray with praise.
I train myself to do it—whistling in the dark, as it were.
I have learned to rush to this portal of safety. But even
there, if I'm honest, I'm still in the prayer of petition.
The fact is, prayer often begins with pain, hurt, fear.

Once I was sitting at my typewriter (this was before
computers). I was paralyzed with fear. I could not write. I
could not move. I held my head in my hands, elbows
resting on my typewriter, stomach churning. My anxiety

arose from my desire to produce. An article was due. I huddled against the sandstorm swirling inside me. No words. No concentration. Every bone in my body shuddered in the winds. By then it was no longer a matter of wanting to write or finish the article. I wanted freedom from fear. I wanted to be happy. I prayed that wordless, heartfelt plea: "Oh, God!" Suddenly it came to me with a flash of insight that the alternative to my fear was not happiness. The alternative was to be dead! So long as I am alive, I get to experience all the emotions, the dark as well as the light. Fear is simply part of being alive.

Instantly I accepted it. "All right!" I said in a manner of speaking. "I choose life."

Instantly the fear was gone.

I lifted my head, ready to go back to work. But what had happened? I had said a prayer and had it answered, not as I'd expected, with removal of the paralysis, but instead with a sudden absolute acceptance of the pain— which in turn demolished it. Then I remembered the words of Goethe, written on a plaque and hung in the kitchen of one dear friend. I used to whisper the words to myself, treasuring them:

> *The Gods, the eternal ones, give all things to their darlings,*
> *All joys, all sorrows, to their darlings, everything.*

A Baha'i Prayer

I bear witness, O my God, that Thou hast created me to
know Thee and to worship Thee.

I testify, at this moment, to my powerlessness and to
Thy might, to my poverty and to Thy wealth.

There is no other God but Thee, the Help in Peril, the
Self-subsisting.

(Baha'u'llahl)

Part II

When Prayers Are Answered

Chapter 7

Pleading and Petitioning

My sister once observed that when we covet our neighbor's house or wife or car or job, it's not the *thing* we want, necessarily, it's the happiness we imagine that it will bring. Think of that when beginning to make a prayer. What is it that we want? Just happiness, love, safety, life—for ourselves and those we love. But usually we're asking for something else, and when we don't get it, we think our prayer's been lost. Or else we think it was refused. Sometimes we don't see that it was answered anyway.

There is an old story about a clergyman who is caught in a flood. The water is rising, and he shouts out, "God will save me!"

A car comes along, and the driver says, "Get in the car."

"No, no. God will save me!"

But the waters are ever rising. Soon the man finds himself on the roof of the house, when a party in a boat comes along. "Get in the boat, we'll take you off to dry land."

"No, no," calls the minister happily. "God will save me!"

The boat goes on. Pretty soon a helicopter comes thundering overhead, and the same thing happens. The man of God refuses the ride. The flood continues, the house is swept away, and so he drowns.

Now he goes to heaven.

"God," he accuses, "what were You doing? I prayed for You to save me. You didn't listen."

"What do you mean?" says God. "I sent a car, a boat, and a helicopter. You wouldn't take them."

Are prayers answered?

Always. But never the way we expect.

Of course, the question "Are prayers answered?" applies only to prayers of petition. No one asks it about prayers of thanks, or prayers of praise, or surrender, or adoration, for when you are lifted into this sublime joy, you're fully satisfied. You have no needs. Either you have reached the kingdom of God within—unutterable peace—or else you have surrendered your life to the care of the Holy One who bestows on you blessings beyond description. Blessings you never thought to ask for. But that comes with a higher stage of consciousness, you might say, and it takes a while to reach that mountain peak.

Meanwhile, there remain our ordinary wants and needs. Our petitions are the most rudimentary prayers,

First of all, then, I urge that supplications, prayers, intercessions, and thanksgivings be made for everyone . . . so that we may lead a quiet and peaceable life in all godliness and dignity.

—St. Paul, 1 Timothy 2:1

Put me to the test, says the Lord of Hosts, if I will not open the windows of heaven for you and pour down for you an over-flowing blessing.

—Malachi 3:10

and probably most frequently expressed. These prayers are not wrong. It's appropriate to ask, beg, plead for help when you're in need. Christ himself enjoined us to pray for our daily food, and if it didn't come, he said, then ask again and again, imploring like the importuning widow with the busy judge.

"Ask and you shall receive," he promised in John 14:14. "Whatever you ask in my name I will give you."

When I was younger, I used to worry the question: I thought a lot of my prayers were *not* answered, even if I tacked on the name of Jesus Christ, as I'd been told. But here is this promise repeated time and again, and not only in the Christian faith but in all religions—Jewish, Islamic, Hindu, Baha'i, Sikh: Fall to your knees in supplication and your prayers will be answered! they say.

For years I had a Hindu teacher in Jaipur, India, a guru. He used to tell me, smiling gently at my ignorance, that I should only absolutely trust. It was Almighty God who fed me, blessed me with pleasures or lessons, and I was not to suppose that money or food sustained me: no, but only God! All things came of God. He didn't use Jesus' story about the lilies of the field, but

Do not fear—only believe.

—Mark 5:36

he indicated the same thing: that we must only believe that Spirit will care for us, trusting in the same way that we trust our lungs to breathe and our hearts to beat. Listening to him, I slowly allowed the thought to seep into my pores. What he was saying was simply that if I threw myself with total abandon upon the breast of the universe, all my needs would be met. My prayers would be answered. All I had to do was to surrender, trust!

The idea is so simple that I found it hard to wrap my brain around. Could Jesus really have meant what he said literally? Did my guru actually *believe* that all things begin and end with God? I'd like to say that my understanding moved from ignorance to enlightenment in one clap-of-thunder moment, or even in a steady motion, step by step, marching along like successive chapters in a book. It didn't work that way. I don't know when I learned which lesson. I don't know at what point I came to believe that what he told me was literally true. It took a lot of experimenting on my part, a constant testing of the spiritual world. But I'll set down some of the rules I've come to understand, knowing that I'm still only at the earliest stages of prayer, and there are many people who know far more than I.

But first some stories. I love the stories. I need the stories. They make firm my faith, restore my hope, strengthen my resolve whenever it gets weak. Some of the stories are magnificent, but you might think others are trivial or even pointless, I suppose, except to the person praying. Each insignificant prayer answered, however, serves as a handhold in our climb to trust, so that we have the courage when the frightening moments come.

Looking back, I see that all my prayers have been answered. Not on my timetable, and never in the way I'd necessarily choose, but with such elegant timing that I'm always surprised, and enchanted as well by the light-hearted delight that accompanies the gift, as if the universe were rocking with laughter all the time, just playing with me. So strong is this sense that today I often sit back and watch with curiosity to see what happens when I send out another prayer, and with what hilarity the answer will arrive.

I used to weigh myself every morning. One morning I thought, *What a bore, I wish I didn't have to watch my weight every morning.* It was not even a prayer, really, just a complaint. The next morning I stepped on the scale and found—it had broken! That took care of that! The odd thing was that tossing it out had never occurred to me before.

Another time, driving for hours through the hot, red Arizona desert, I longed for water. I began to daydream about fish and flowing streams. I wished I could see a fish, and, driving along, I began to sing a song about water. I glanced out the window, looked up. There in a deep blue, rock-hard, dazzling summer sky swam a single cloud in the shape of an enormous fish!

But sometimes prayers are serious.

Some years ago, Mother Teresa came to war-torn Lebanon to carry trapped schoolchildren out of an area that was being daily shelled. "On Tuesday," she told the military, "we will be taking buses into this war zone to remove the children. You should be prepared."

The officers were taken aback. "You can't do that—there's a war on! We can't guarantee your safety."

Mother Teresa had come from India specifically for this purpose. "Don't worry," she said. "We're praying about this. Just be ready. The children will be carried out on Tuesday."

*In my experience the universe falls in with worthy plans
and most especially with festive and expressive ones.*

—Julia Cameron, *The Artist's Way*

On Tuesday the shelling, for some incomprehensible reason, stopped. For the first time in weeks, silence blanketed the empty, devastated streets, and in that unusual quiet the school buses roared into the war zone, picked up the children, and drove them out to safety. Then the shelling began again. Mother Teresa ascribed it to prayer. To God. To the angels watching over us.

I have written about angels in the past. Like many people, I have seen angels and talked with them and recognize that they come in many forms. One day I was walking along the canal in Washington, D.C., and I was in a funk. (In spite of my basic optimism, as you can see, these dark, brooding moods fall over me.) On this day as I walked, I prayed:

"Dear God, I need a sign, and I need it now, and I'm in no mood to interpret something subtle. You're going to have to hit me over the head with it. I just want to know You're there. I need to know that everything is all right." I was pouring out my fear and anguish in this way, when suddenly out of the canal rose a flock of pigeons, wheeling into the sky. Pigeons don't roost in the canal (seagulls maybe, but not pigeons), and I stopped in wonder at the beauty—the flashing, light-struck wings! They circled in the sky, and as they flew over me, one let loose right on the top of my head. *Plop!* Impeccable aim.

What could I do but laugh? Hadn't I just asked for a sign to hit me on the head?

One of the irritating things is the complete *literalness*

Don't take life so seriously, son. . . .
It aint nohow permanent.

—Porky Porcupine

of the universe. You have to tell it *everything!* (Or nothing!) Once I prayed for a young woman to find a husband, the mate of her heart. It was time for her to meet somebody and get married. What happened? A week later she fell in love with a married man. Someone else's husband! Really! If that's how it works, you have to be so careful you hardly dare voice the prayer!

"Be careful what you pray for," runs the ancient adage, "because you'll get it."

There is an Arab saying, too: "'Take what you want,' said God, 'and pay for it.'"

The axiom is illustrated in a joke.

A couple had been married for 40 years, and that same year the husband was celebrating his 60th birthday. They threw a party in their honor. During the celebration a fairy godmother appeared and said that because they had been such a loving couple all those years, she would give each of them one wish.

The wife wanted to travel the world. The fairy waved her magic wand, and *boom!* she had plane tickets in her hand.

Next it was the husband's turn. He paused for a moment, then said shyly, "I wish I had a woman 30 years younger than me." The fairy picked up her wand, and *boom!* he was 90 years old.

The mystic Emanuel Swedenborg, who lived in the 1700s, was the son of a bishop, director of mines in Sweden, an intellectual and brilliant man. He spent the last

PLEADING AND PETITIONING

When the gods wish to punish us, they answer our prayers.
—Oscar Wilde

20 years of his life communing with angels, who stayed with him always, whispering and guiding him, and in one of these interior instructions he learned that, unlike humans, who give way to doubt when things don't go their way and then blame God, angels look on *all events* as proceeding from God. His angels repeated again and again that we poor humans should not worry about the future but only trust in Providence; for Providence will bring all things that we desire, not necessarily while we desire them, "but yet if it be for their good," he wrote, "they obtain them afterwards when not thinking of them."

In other words, you get your prayers when you don't care anymore!

Now, why would that rule hold?

I think it is because when we're suffering, hurting, truly in need, when we're aching for help and held captive by our grief and sense of loss . . . then our thoughts are so concentrated on the thing we fear that the very cells of our body contort. You could say we've drawn "lack" to us, and we're living in a hell of loss and pain.

It's as if the strength of our desire, like the bow wave of a moving motorboat, pushes away the goal; and just as we cannot rid ourselves of any vice or bad habit until we've completely accepted, owned, and honored it (and then let go of hating it), I think that likewise we cannot *acquire* a virtue or longing until we no longer hunger for it emotionally. It's so queer. I've always thought that if there is, in fact, an Ultimate Truth, it lies in paradox.

Not long ago I started a file of answered prayers, but it soon became so long I simply dropped the enterprise. Pages of needs were met with no apparent effort on my part; everything seems given all the time—and not only to me, to everyone! To you! To all of us. You're lonely, and a friend suddenly telephones. You need a parking space in rush-hour downtown, and one appears in front of your destination. So many unnoticed accidents and co-incidences: little things. A scarf is lost—and found. A set of keys. You need a necklace clipped behind your neck: "Can you clasp this for me?" you ask the Invisible, and *snip!* It's done! What happened? You may have struggled with the clasp for five minutes before remembering to *ask.* A ring or wallet is returned, an address is found ("Where did I put it? Please help me find it"), or you find yourself speaking exactly the *right* words at the appropriate moment—words that astonish you. How did you know those things? Little movements occur, events converge to bring an unexpected joy, and the accumulation all adds up to one clear thought: *We're not alone!*

Love letters from the Beloved fall into our hands. A friend once checked into a splendid hotel penthouse suite (business: paid for by her company). She was wandering through the unfamiliar rooms, somewhat disoriented in a strange hotel in a strange city, when her eye fell on a scrap of paper on a spotless, high-waxed pier table in the hall. On it this was typed: *The highest pinnacle of the spiritual life is not about joy and happiness, but is absolute and undoubting trust in the love of God.* How did that note get there, to ease her forlorn loneliness? She wasn't even praying, only scared.

And all we have to do is trust, believe that, despite everything, the universe is working out for good.

Everyone has miracles. My 95-year-old aunt has a caregiver named Ilsa. She has three children, and one day when I was visiting my aunt, Ilsa told me that a few months earlier she had been diagnosed with stomach cancer. The cancer was biopsied. It required surgery. She went home and prayed, pouring out her heart to God. *But she did not pray that her cancer be removed.* What she prayed for was her children. What would happen to them if she died?

She needed one more test before the surgery, but when she went back to the hospital, no trace of cancer could be found.

As far as Ilsa is concerned, her prayer was answered; hers was an unselfish and uncontrolling prayer: "Please help."

Dr. Larry Dossey, who has written beautifully on prayer and medicine, reports that in 1975, Dr. Yujiro Ikemi at Kyushu University School of Medicine in Fukuoka, Japan, studied five cases of spontaneous remission of cancer. Spontaneous remission is so common that doctors use the abbreviation SRC to denote it . . . yet they don't know what it is or why it happens. Inexplicably, some cancers go away. Sometimes.

Dr. Ikemi found that his five cases seemed to contradict the prevailing idea that SRC is accidental, random, and beyond the effects of people's thoughts. One of his

THE PATH OF PRAYER

cases happened to a Shinto teacher, who at the age of 64 developed a tumor on his vocal cords. A biopsy confirmed the malignancy; the doctors recommended surgery, which would leave him with no voice.

"I have no complaint," he responded fatalistically. "This is God's will. What will happen will happen." He did not fall into a depression, as many people might, or demonstrate any fear—and this easy attitude seems to be typical of many who recover spontaneously from disease. *He did not even pray for his own cure.* He merely renewed his commitment to God in gratitude for the life he'd been given.

His church president came to him. "Remember that you are a valuable asset to our church," he said. The cancer disappeared. The teacher died at the age of 78 of an unrelated cause, having lived 14 years with no treatment for his malignant tumor.[1]

Dr. Ikemi suggests that SRC may be affected by one's spirituality, by a profound attitude of prayerfulness, and finally by knowing that you are important to both yourself and others. He means not only having a healthy sense of self-esteem but also feeling that you are *needed.*

I have a friend who had a bean-size cancer of the breast, and she, too, prayed, and it was gone. But keep in mind that the ways of universal intelligence are always mysterious. The mystery of unanswered prayer returns us always to humility. I remember, for example, still another friend, a film producer, who died of breast cancer in less than a year, while firmly believing that her disease could be cured with herbal remedies and prayer alone.

Some 182,000 American women are diagnosed annually with breast cancer, and 46,000 of them die each year—26.4 deaths per 100,000 of the total population. Every one of them must have prayed! If prayer were always "answered," surely more sons than daughters would be born in China or India or certain Muslim countries, where parents, disdaining girls, are pleading, begging, prostrating themselves praying for the birth of boys! Yet the birthrate of boys to girls is roughly the same there as in every other country of the world.

It's all a mystery. I think that there are times when what happens is less important than how you respond to it. There are times when you don't know why you're being asked to perform your martyred tasks. You know only that you must rise courageously to the challenges of life, and somehow the task involves the puzzle of love. I think of my present spiritual director, Liz Ward, who one day was talking and praying with me.

"I have come to believe," she said, "that there is a presence, God, the universe, a Holy Spirit—whatever you call it—that cares deeply for us. I think 'it' cares much more about our souls than about the external facts of our lives: God cares tremendously about our souls. God may be more interested in how the events of a life affect someone than in the events themselves. A person may be sick and yet overflow with serenity and faith and joy, while someone else under the same circumstances will lose heart. As a spiritual director, companion, and guide, those I worry about are those whose hearts are hardened to compassion and hardened to justice.

"'What's happening in your heart, in your mind?' I ask. 'Are you becoming more loving (whatever that means), more truthful (whatever that means)?' It's the soul's response that matters."

Sometimes you don't know for years that your prayer was answered. When I was twelve, a happy tomboy, it suddenly dawned on me that I was growing up. There wasn't a minute to lose! If I didn't do something, I'd end up a *woman,* trapped in housework, subject to male whims (this was before the women's movement). Then I knelt down and nightly prayed with all my heart to become a boy.

Six months later, nature made it evident that my prayer had been refused. Well, what can you do? Later still, I discovered the enormous power that girls wield over boys, a fact that went far toward consolation. I used to laugh, however, that here at any rate was one prayer Providence had ignored! Today I realize that the prayer was answered all along.

It wasn't that I'd really wanted to turn physically into a boy, complete with external body parts. What I'd wanted was the independence and freedom that were open to boys and closed to girls (I thought)—the ability to work, travel, explore, have adventures, to live a full, rich, independent life. And I've been given them! My prayer was answered: I simply hadn't known what I'd been praying for!

Sometimes your prayers are answered in such jolting, unexpected ways that it takes your breath away. I'm reminded of the bitter words of the Roman poet Juvenal about those extraordinary prayers "that the gods in vengeance grant." Some years ago a film came out. (I can't find either the title or director's name—was it Spanish?) It was about a young boy who is blind in one eye. The other children tease him, push him away, throw rocks at him. His life is so miserable that his grandmother decides to take him on a holy pilgrimage, where the Virgin Mary will restore his sight and relieve his torment. They hear mass, take the Eucharist, pray on their knees at each Station of the Cross, and in every way invite a healing miracle. Yet none occurs. Sadly, they join a group to travel home. One night while they're sitting around the campfire, someone in their party throws a firecracker into the flames. It explodes in a spray of sparks. One hits the boy's good eye. He returns home blind in both eyes.

Now his grandmother is satisfied. He will no longer be tormented. Her prayer was answered.

Do we even dare to pray? It's the kind of horror story that gives us pause: "What if my prayer is answered and its scorpion tail curls around to stab me in the neck?" How do I ask for what I want? How do I even *know* what I want? Would Jews for centuries have prayed for the return to Zion had they known it would come at the cost of six million in the Holocaust? Such questions lead us to a shuddering understanding of why we are told to end our heartfelt pleas with heartfelt submission: "Thy will be done," we finish humbly. "I belong to You. . . . I place it in Your Hands."

Everyone wants to be happy. Everyone wants to love and be loved. The constant task is to open our hands. Live lightly. Think positive and optimistic, happy thoughts. Do our work and love as much as little hearts can love. Surrender . . . everything. When you do, when you find that you want unselfishly only to serve the ineffable for the glory of God and for the welfare of others, then something happens. God starts working for you, bringing bounty, happiness.

Not long ago a friend, Eliana Rivera, phoned me out

of the blue. Five years earlier she'd had a horrible year. In one short period of time, her mother, brother, and sister had died, one after another. A cancer had recurred for the second time. Then her best friend drowned while scuba diving; loss piled on loss. She shook her fist at God in angry hatred: "How can you do this to me?"

She knew about courage, willpower. When several years earlier she had first been diagnosed with breast cancer, she'd made herself a promise: "I'm going to kick this disease, cure this myself!" She took control.

"I was really butting heads with God. I thought being healthy," she told me, "meant controlling my life, especially my emotional life." Now, faced with so many losses, she found herself tortured as well by migraines and back pain. Finally she could not take another step.

"God, this is yours, not mine," she said. "I'm turning my life over." She had made that promise before, but she had always pulled back from full commitment.

"Others commit suicide," she said as she laughed to me over the phone. "I turned my life over . . . and suddenly everything changed. I quit my job and immediately found a better one I love. Now I've found a man, my soul mate. It's amazing. All I did was surrender! If you'd told me five years ago that I'd be so happy, that my life would be so good, I wouldn't have believed you. Anything can happen, and now I have this new understanding that my life path is to help others to heal." She gives free massages to the ill and dying, especially to women with breast cancer and people suffering from AIDS.

We talked more, she and I, about the purpose of pain, for she found treasures hidden in the caves of pain.

"I experience higher consciousness in times of great joy," she said, "but I experience it more in times of great pain. Here's a fact: Once you surrender to God, you cannot do evil anymore, you cannot even think it! Once you surrender, you can think only good, and then good pours through you. You become a vessel of universal energy, and you feel yourself moved here or there, where you can be of service."

Oddly, the blessings also bring you happiness.

Where then does free will come into play? You have free will to come to God and wisdom—or not to. You can always refuse to surrender; you can always refuse to accept your suffering or to see in your pain an invitation from God. You can always forge doggedly ahead, jaw set, self-reliant, determined to have your own way. You may get it, too, for aren't prayers always answered? But will it bring you happiness? I promise you that if your plan is selfish and purely self-serving, your pain will only get worse, no matter how much you pray.

We are back to my sister's wise words: that what you covet is the happiness you imagine that object will bring. We are back to the words of Emanuel Swedenborg: that everything you need will be given, *if it be for your good,* but you'll only get it "afterwards, when not thinking about it."

A Hebrew Prayer

Blessed art Thou, O Lord our God, King of the Universe, Who has made the world lacking in naught, but has produced therein goodly trees wherewith to give delight to the children of men. Blessed art Thou, Who has given wisdom of Thy hands to flesh and blood, that beautiful cities might rise to Thy glory. Blessed art Thou who has created joy and gladness, mirth and exultation, pleasure and delight, love, brotherhood, peace and fellowship, O Lord our God, King of the Universe.

Chapter 8

Three Ways to Ask in Prayer

We will talk at length later in this book about the principles of prayer, but at this point we must stop to consider three ways to express a supplication: directed, undirected, and in surrender.

Directed prayer asks for a specific thing, a particular outcome: "Bring me food." "Please, heal my daughter's leukemia." "Dear God, help with my grandson's operation." "Ease my back pain; hear my prayer."

Or else we ask for things that we don't want: "O God, don't let my son die!" "Don't let me lose my job."

As we discussed earlier, with directed prayer, you may also visualize the desired outcome. This increases the power of your thought. You see yourself happily in your job; you see your daughter alive and healthy, practicing ballet, taking exams; or you visualize prosperity, understanding for your friend. As when making an affirmation, you end your prayer by giving thanks and by the admonition for "the highest good."

Undirected prayer, on the other hand, operates as a

kind of wordless glowing at the heart. In this petition you draw up the image of the person or situation you are praying for, but instead of visualizing anything concrete, you simply surround her (or it) in a globe of light, a passionate balloon of love. By praying, you raise your own vibration, and then, glowing with life force, you send out the concentrated power of your thought in a wave of love and energy. With undirected prayer you have no need for words (you may need none with directed prayer as well), but if you were to speak, your mental intention might be stated thus: "Into your hands, O God . . . the highest good."

Hold this globe of light around the person or thing, resting in love for as long as possible, and when the force of your intention fades (we do get tired), you say simply "Thank you" and move on about your busy day, for studies have shown that *undirected prayer is two to four times more effective than directed prayer.*[1]

Scientists arrived at this startling conclusion by studying healers who prayed over seeds or molds. They found that those seeds that were prayed over by asking only for whatever is best for the organism grew stronger and that molds multiplied faster than with directed prayer.

In purely practical everyday life, of course, we use both directed and undirected prayer alternately. Consider the frightened woman who is lost in a foreign city and makes first a directed prayer ("Dear God, bring my husband to find me"). She holds the prayer in mind but then con-

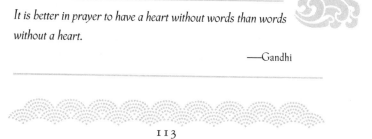

It is better in prayer to have a heart without words than words without a heart.

—Gandhi

cludes by leaving the solution to God ("Please help"). In a flash her directed prayer has been converted into undirected prayer.

The third type of petition is surrender, another musical slide. You could say that surrender is the final coda of directed prayer. It is a melody hidden in the fugues of undirected prayer. But it also plays out its own motet. It is the great chorus of prayer. Possibly it's the most important one of all, yet so subtle you'd hardly think of it as petition.

With the petition of surrender, you make no demands at all, not even open-ended ones. You merely present yourself: "I am yours, O Lord. Do with me as You will." You address the mystery full face, asking nothing, unless it be to serve.

I remember my guru once telling me that when you surrender everything to God, you are taken care of utterly.

Surrender is not the same as giving up. Surrender is an active exercise, repeated over and over, minute by minute, in a continual dance of letting go and taking back control, then letting go again. With surrender, you empower yourself by a joyful acceptance of *what is.* Making this prayer takes discipline. It takes trust. You work for your dream, yet relieve yourself of the burden of any special outcome. Surrender is not passive. Surrender is not the same as indolence.

"Pray as if it all depends on God," they say, "and act as if it all depends on you."

And, "If you pray for potatoes, grab a hoe."

I find that my prayers these days are answered almost without my expressing them anymore. Is that because I've spent so many hours in the practice of surrendering? Not long ago I was eating up the food in the house, pursuant to leaving for a month. Two days before my departure I saw that nothing was left in the refrigerator but peanut butter—not even a cracker to put it on. "I wonder what I'll do for dinner tonight?" I thought idly, for a spoonful of peanut butter is not very appetizing. "Well, I'll think about it later."

You can't really say it was a prayer, an observation rather. The whole subject was of so little interest it didn't warrant prayer. But less than two hours later a friend dropped by, bringing me a meal—and guess what? It was enough to cover my last two days. "Just thinking of you," she said, and I laughed with pleasure, thanking the universe for putting the blessed idea in her head. God feeding us. Lilies of the field.

But no sooner did I thank the angels of God for feeding me as the ravens fed Elijah than I began to doubt. Was I crazy? Here I was engaged in writing a book on prayer; did I really dare to assert that God takes care of everyone? What of those who die each day of starvation and disease? Now I began to pace the house, metaphorically wringing my hands with distress.

How can you say (argued Logic) that you are always fed? Maybe it was just accident, like the hundreds of coincidences that occur every day in our city, or maybe these apparent blessings (continued acid Analysis) are no more than the reflection of your own need for order and symmetry in a chaotic world. Perhaps the only thing you've demonstrated, Sophy (Doubt finished with a daunting, triumphant smirk), is how much you want control! It was a devastating argument. Yet poor Intuition, while having no logical argument to throw up in defense, would not be run off the battlefield. The Beloved provides, it kept repeating helplessly.

How to resolve the dilemma? I prayed for insight. A

few hours later I picked up a book that I haven't looked at in years—*The Autobiography of a Yogi,* by Paramahansa Yogananda. It almost fell off the bookcase at my feet, the pages opening to a story of the young boy Mukunda.

"Swamiji, I am puzzled about following your instruction," says Mukunda, who one day would become the renowned Yogananda. "Suppose I never ask for food, and nobody gives me any. I should starve to death."

"Die, then!" This alarming counsel split the air. "Die if you must, Mukunda! Never believe that you live by the power of food and not by the power of God! He who has created every form of nourishment, He who has bestowed appetite, will inevitably see that His devotee is maintained. Do not imagine that rice sustains you nor that money or men support you. Could they aid if the Lord withdraws your life breath? They are His instruments merely. . . . Cut through the chains of agency and perceive the Single Cause!"[2]

In the story Mukunda decides to surrender everything to God, including all concerns for food or making a living ("God first and money second"). There is a law of demand and supply, he insists, in which when we have a need, the universe supplies it from unlimited stores of goods. His older brother ("Money first, God second") challenges him.

"All right," cries his brother. "You say God will do everything for you. Words are cheap. Life has shielded you." Then he sends his little brother and Jitendra, a fellow disciple, to another city for one full day.

"I'll buy you the train ticket to Brindaban," he says. "You must not take a single rupee, beg for food or money, or reveal your predicament. You must eat all meals, see all the sights, buy train tickets home and be back before midnight without having asked for a thing. We'll see whether God provides."

The two youths set off, and once in Brindaban they are provided with royal meals by a self-appointed escort, a stranger, who guides them by horse carriage around the holy city of Lord Krishna and in the evening presents them with sweets and bonbons and two free train tickets home. When they arrive that night, Yogananda's astonished brother, submitting finally to "the subtle laws of demand and supply," asks his younger brother to initiate him into the path to the divine.

I closed the book in awe: Was this my answer from the universe? But surely it only raises further questions, doesn't it? Don't we also have to work for our living? What of those who live in poverty? I have no easy answers. I only know that for myself I've come to trust.

I've almost stopped using directed prayer, it has such limitations. I've had to learn this lesson the hard way. Once I fell in love (only once?). The relationship was very painful. I didn't know what to pray for. I thought and thought about how to phrase my desires. Finally, triumphantly, I prayed to have the pain removed from the relationship. There! That was a safe prayer!

Within a week the man was gone.

Oops.

That wasn't what I'd wanted at all.

I'm not saying we cannot make a directed prayer. We do it all the time, and directed prayer delivered from the pure, right heart and enhanced by laser-sharp, one-pointed, focused thought is a powerful tool. But always you must surrender, afterward, for how do you know what's best for yourself or someone else?

Let's tell more stories. I like the tales of miracles, the ones that demonstrate that a loving Spirit is an active participant in our lives, diving down to intervene.

"Have you ever seen an angel?" I asked the bellhop at a hotel as he showed me to my room. I could have asked, "Have you ever had the experience of God?"

"Oh, yes, I was a paratrooper in the army," he answered without hesitation. "We had a night training maneuver, in which we jumped from a very low height, and as I dropped from the plane, my 'chute caught. It opens automatically from a clip as you leave the plane, but mine spun out in a long, tangled web. I was falling. If I pulled the reserve, both 'chutes would have twisted up together. I didn't know what to do.

"Just then I heard a voice above me. 'I've got you,' he said. 'Don't pull the reserve.' I looked up and saw in the darkness that the man who had jumped after me had gathered my parachute in his arms. He was carrying me down to earth.

"We landed. He laughed and called out, 'It's been a long time since I jumped!'

"I was busy unhooking my harness and gathering up my billowing parachute, and when I turned to thank him, the man was gone. He'd vanished. I couldn't find him anywhere. Later I got hold of the roster of all the men on the plane for that jump, and I went to every single one of them, but the man who had saved me—he wasn't one of them. He wasn't there that night. He was my guardian angel."

Surely this man had not prayed, or if he did, it was no more than a cry of terror and surprise. No prayer as we define the word, no thoughtful requests on bended knee, no sending out of the prayerful energy of love. No thirty-minute period of prayerful intensity, or rejoicing, praise and thanks. Yet the answer came, slammed down in the shape of a living man who drifted above him in the night.

My friend Molly is a theater director, tough, pragmatic, funny—a doer. She is strong and sturdy, with black hair and forceful black eyebrows. Her partner, Suzanne, told me how some years ago Molly was diagnosed with breast cancer. She was in the hospital for chemotherapy as several nurses and doctors hovered around, trying to insert a needle into a vein that constantly rolled away. After ten minutes of futile trying, the doctor caught her vein. The chemo had begun its drip, when suddenly the needle popped out. If chemotherapy goes anywhere but into the blood, the patient could die. Suzanne sat in a corner, praying.

"Oh, God, oh, God."

The surrender of an undirected prayer.

She opened her eyes, she says, and saw two enormous winged angels standing behind the doctor. She says they were seven feet tall and thin as a Giacometti statue. Silently she called out to them, "Oh, help!" One of the angels turned its gentle head, looked down at Molly, and—

"We've got it!" said the doctor, as the needle slipped back into the vein. Slowly the two angels dissolved into the walls.

Another time Molly lay in her hospital bed, so sick that every visitor had to wear a mask and gloves, to avoid infecting her. Six or seven friends, dressed in their masks and gloves, were praying at her bedside. The window was open a few inches. As she prayed, Suzanne glanced up and saw a host of tiny yellow moths sweeping through the window screen. They swarmed around the bed. She thought they were flower petals. Then she saw that they were tiny, tiny angels, no bigger than beads of light. They fluttered out the window and were gone. No one else saw them, but Suzanne felt God's love surrounding and enfolding her dear friend.

After that, Molly recovered.

How mysterious is this whole question of prayer! We know that it is related more to a state of mind than to words falling from our lips. We know that it must arise from the absolute, undiluted truth of our hearts, fearless and unscathing. We have to trust—believe that our prayers are being answered, although the person being prayed for *doesn't even need to know a prayer is being said!* In prayer we enter a space of lucid quiet, and this state is deeply connected to love. It carries power.

Yet despite all our efforts, bad things happen. Not even the spiritual masters get off scot-free. Indeed, so sensitive are saints that often they seem more frail and sickly than tough-skinned sinners do. St. Teresa of Ávila suffered from illness most of her life. The Buddha died of food poisoning. Sri Ramana Maharishi died of cancer of the stomach. Christian Scientists get sick and die. Death will be the end of us all—no prayers will stave off death. Being spiritually pure, then, and praying well does not relieve us of loss or pain or physical obliteration. It only brings us comfort in distress.

"There is a great deal of pain in life," said R. D. Laing, the psychologist-mystic, "and perhaps the only pain that

Unhappiness is the ultimate form of self-indulgence.
—Tom Robbins, *Jitterbug Perfume*

can be avoided is the pain that comes from trying to avoid pain."

In prayer you learn to bend to the Tao, like a tree in the wind. "Don't close your fist on a thorn," runs a Buddhist saying, referring to the way that by clinging to our desires we increase our pain. In prayer you learn to let matters work out as they will, and still you pray for them to change.

I remarked earlier how truth is found in paradox. We know that nothing is certain concerning prayer, and yet it seems some general rules apply. If you try them, you'll find that, strangely, the universe seems to tilt in your favor, bringing happiness. Experiment and see. Tithe, for example, and you will find that somehow money flows back to you. The roots of all the laws of Providence lie in the soil of generosity and trust. "To them that have shall be given," said Jesus in one of the most horrible laws we can imagine, the most unfair; "and to them that have not shall be taken away, even what they have."

The rules of happiness below refer to anything— money, love, gifts, energy, compliments—or, conversely, to complaints and self-pitying whines.

FIVE RULES OF LIFE

If you're holding on too hard, you've already lost it.
The more you give away, the more you have. (Even money seems attracted by your generosity).
You feel poor when saving, rich when spending.
The more you practice letting go, with open-hearted in-nocence, the more you find that all your needs are met.
When you expect the best, the best will come.

The rules of prayer are equally bizarre. Keep in mind that what you're really praying for is always peace, prosperity, and happiness.

THE PARADOXICAL RULES OF PRAYER

You receive what you want when you aren't thinking about it anymore.

You receive your prayer when you surrender utterly to the Absolute, accepting whatever comes.

You receive your prayer if it is unselfish, for the highest good of everyone concerned (fear not: this includes yourself).

You receive your desire if the prayer encourages harmony, love, joy, laughter, and well-being.

The more you notice when you have received, and give thanks—be glad—the more will come to you.

Don't take my word for it. Experiment. See if what I'm saying is untrue. Years go by, and one day you look up in astonishment and say, "Good gracious, I remember having prayed for that! And here it is. I never noticed." Your very soul will tilt in awe and wonder at the elegant way in which the creative principle has worked things out.

There is one other curious law: The more optimistic, the happier and more grateful you are, the more will good things flow out to you. Such is the power of the principle of thought.

Native American Prayer

In beauty may I walk
All day long may I walk.
Through the returning seasons may I walk.
Beautifully will I possess again.
Beautifully birds . . .
Beautifully joyful birds . . .
On the trail marked with pollen may I walk.
With grasshoppers about my feet may I walk.
With dew about my feet may I walk.
With beauty before me may I walk.
With beauty behind me may I walk.
With beauty all around me may I walk.
In old age wandering on a trail of beauty, lively,
may I walk.
In old age wandering on a trail of beauty, living again,
may I walk.
It is finished in beauty.
It is finished in beauty.

—Navaho, "Night Way"

Chapter 9

Loosing in Heaven, Binding on Earth

There is an ancient saying that whatever is loosed in heaven shall be bound on earth: "On earth as it is in heaven" or "As above, so below." It's worded differently in various cultures, this idea of the inexorability of fate, but this particular saying about loosing and binding implies that we play a part in what is loosed, in fate; and our part is played by prayer.

In this little book many of the stories about the miracles of answered prayer concern health, life, death. Perhaps this is because anything else seems trivial by comparison. It's in times like these that we forget all rules, howl out a cry of the heart so anguished that it touches the very heavens above and looses a response. That which Spirit commands takes form on earth.

An Hispanic man told me of his terrible battle with alcohol. It is a violent, ugly tale, experienced by thousands all the time, a story of watching in horror as his hand moved up to his mouth with the bottle. He was drinking several quarts of alcohol a day, helpless to stop.

He lost his job, his girlfriend, his money, his house, his memory. Lonely, despairing, isolated, he was reduced eventually to a car and one quart of alcohol, nothing else. At this point he fell to his knees and uttered that most helpless cry to a deity he did not even believe in: "Help!" Hardly had the word passed his lips than he noticed across the four-lane highway a church, beckoning to him. Somehow he managed to cross the highway without being killed. The church door was open (another cause for surprise). Alone inside, he knelt in hopeless prayer.

But as he prayed, he felt flooded with an extraordinary sense that everything would be all right. Many people will recognize this pure sensation. The experience lasted only a few seconds, but for the rest of the day he hovered in its echo, and that day he did not take a drink. The next morning he once more fell to his knees and prayed, and that day, too, he did not drink. Within a week a friend found him: "Would you like to go to a meeting of Alcoholics Anonymous?"

That was sixteen years ago, the man told me. He hasn't taken another drink of alcohol since, and every morning he prays to be relieved of the compulsion, and every evening he gives thanks for the day of freedom that was given him. As a result of his sobriety, he has become a useful member of society. He knows that he is loved.

An Alaskan woman of my acquaintance, a Native American, tells how she went to a bar on her birthday.

Tonight I'll find out if I'm an alcoholic! she said to herself. She got completely smashed. She came out of a blackout to find herself sitting in a strange car in front of her house. Two other Indian women were with her—strangers. She remembers them helping her into her house, after which she blacked out again. The next morning she awoke to find her house destroyed, the sofa cushions slashed with a knife. She was furious!

Who were those women? she thought.

Then she found a note: "I hope never to see you again in my life."

She was horrified. Had she trashed her own house? Had she turned on the women with the knife? She fell to her knees, weeping. She knew she was going to die.

Are tears a form of prayer?

That evening two other women came to the door, again both strangers. How had they found her?

"Do you want to stop drinking?" one asked.

"Yes."

"Here are your directions. Get on your knees and pray. Can you do that? Can you pray on your knees?"

"Yes," she said.

"Your prayer is simple: 'God, keep me from drinking today.' Can you ask that?"

It is a straight, directed prayer they gave her, but that day she did not take a drink. In the evening one of her saviors called.

"Did you drink today?"

"No," she answered.

"Then get on your knees now, while we're on the phone, and say, 'Thank You, God, and please keep me from drinking tomorrow.'"

"Is that all?"

"That's all. Do it now." The woman on the telephone waited until the prayer was said, then continued, "You must make this one prayer every day of your life, because you are given a reprieve only one day at a time. You can't manage by yourself, alone."

My friend has followed these directions now for more than ten years and never taken another drink. Note that she is saying a directed, specific prayer, and it works fine.

Perhaps no story is so impressive as that of Charles and Myrtle Fillmore, who healed themselves of tuberculosis, malaria, partial deafness, and a shriveled leg. Myrtle was born in Pagetown, Ohio, in 1845. She was frail and sickly from early childhood. She was so sick that she moved to Texas, in hopes the climate would be better for her.

Charles, born in Minnesota in 1854, was not in much better shape. He was deaf in one ear. At the age of ten he had dislocated his hip, and between the rheumatism that set in and damage done by the doctors who treated him, his hip socket was totally destroyed. He lived in chronic pain. His left leg, encased in a heavy leather and metal brace, was four inches shorter than the right. He hobbled on crutches, his left shoe lifted on a four-inch platform sole.

Charles met Myrtle in Texas, where he worked with the railroad. They fell in love, married in 1881, had three sons, and around 1884 moved to Kansas City, Missouri, in an effort to restore Myrtle's failing health. But Myrtle grew sicker still. Finally the doctors gave her three weeks to live.

In Kansas City, however, the Fillmores had come into contact with Ralph Waldo Emerson's philosophic New Thought, with Buddhism, Theosophy, Rosicrucian studies, and the ideas of Dr. Emma Curtis Hopkins's Theological Seminary in Chicago. The Fillmores completed a course of study with Dr. Hopkins.

From early childhood, Myrtle had been told that consumption (tuberculosis) was the "family" illness. Having contracted the disease in 1885, compounding existing problems with malaria and intestinal weakness, she believed that she had inherited the family trait. When she was given only a few weeks to live, friends suggested to

LOOSING IN HEAVEN, BINDING ON EARTH

the Fillmores that they attend a lecture on healing given in a local meeting hall. Desperately wanting to find help for Myrtle's condition, they decided to go.

The lecturer was Dr. E. B. Weeks, a teacher sent to Kansas City by Dr. Hopkins. During the lecture, Myrtle heard the words *You are a child of God; therefore you do not inherit sickness.* For the first time she questioned her long-held belief that, because of her family history, her illness was unavoidable. Night and day she began to pray, using that phrase to affirm life and health: *I am a child of God, and therefore I do not inherit sickness.* Soon she rose from her deathbed. In 1888, two years later, the TB had disappeared. She was completely healed.

Myrtle died in 1931 at the age of 86, having lived from the time of her realization an active, passionate, energetic life.

Notice that she had asked for nothing. Her prayer may seem more a statement than a supplication, thus showing how closely linked are affirmation and deep prayer. But she did more:

> . . . it flashed upon me that I might talk to the life in every part of my body and have it do just what I wanted. . . . I went to [the various parts] and spoke words of . . . strength and power. I asked their forgiveness for the foolish, ignorant course that I had pursued in the past, when I had called them weak, inefficient and diseased. I did not become discouraged at their being slow to wake up. . . . Then I asked the Father to forgive me for taking His life into my organism and there using it so meanly. I promised Him that I would never, never again retard the free flow of that life through my mind and body by any false word or thought: that I would bless it and encourage it. . . .

Your desire is your prayer. Picture the fulfillment of your desire now and FEEL its reality and you will experience the joy of the answered prayer.

—Dr. Joseph Murphy

I did not let any worried or anxious thoughts into my mind and I stopped speaking gossipy, frivolous, petulant, angry words. I let a little prayer go up every hour that Jesus Christ would be with me and help me to think and speak only kind, loving, true words. I am sure that He is with me because I am so peaceful and happy now. . . .

I want everybody to know about this beautiful, true law, and to use it. It is not a new discovery, but when you use it and get the fruits of health and harmony, it will seem new to you, and you will feel that it is your own discovery.[1]

Her husband was impressed. Charles was a real estate salesman, a practical-minded businessman with a rational, intellectual, and scientific frame of mind, but he, too, began to pray. At first he found this hard, for he did not quite "believe." But each morning he went off by himself, to sit alone in a chair and listen—merely listen; and as the years passed, he discovered to his surprise that dreams provided his pathway to "a wider intelligence." He began to have prophetic dreams, then that he also was slowly getting well.

His shriveled leg began to grow. His hearing improved.

When I began applying the spiritual treatment, there was for a long time slight response in the leg, but I felt better, and I found that I began to hear with my right ear. Then gradually I noticed that I had more feeling in the leg. Then as the years went by, the ossified joint began to get limber, and the shrunken flesh filled out until the right leg was almost equal to the other. Then I discarded the cork-and-steel extension and wore an ordinary shoe with a double heel about an inch in height. Now the leg is almost as large as the other. . . . I am giving minute details of my healing, because it would be considered a medical impossibility and a miracle from a religious standpoint. However . . . I know it is under divine law. So I am satisfied that here is proof of a law that the mind builds the body and can restore it.[2]

Charles died in 1948 at the age of 94. Charles and Myrtle had spent their lives in constant prayer. In 1890 they founded the Society of Silent Help, now Silent Unity, the prayer ministry of Unity School of Christianity. In 1907 it consisted of five workers. It is now a huge organization. It works out of several calm, lovely Italian Renaissance-style buildings on the serene grounds of Unity Village, Missouri, just outside Kansas City. Its mission is to pray, and it invites anyone to phone twenty-four hours a day, seven days a week—or write—or send an e-mail to ask for prayers. Those who have no means of paying for the call may use a toll-free 800 number.[3]

A prayer associate, man or woman, answers the phone: "How may we pray with you?" The tenderness of that voice, heard when you're in need, is enough to bring tears to your eyes. Many times I have called, and, hearing that soft, sure voice praying with me on the other end of the phone, I felt flooded with peace. Sometimes I am enveloped by light. Or I feel a little *click*—and know the prayer was heard.

Silent Unity then holds you in prayer for 30 days. The vigil is kept 24 hours a day, 7 days a week. I do not know how they pray, for no one is allowed in the Silent Unity prayer room. Do they read through banks of names one by one? Do they hold a book of requests in their hands and send it to the grace of God? But I know this: Miracles occur. Pick up any issue of their monthly magazine, *Daily Word,* and read the testimonials.

A baby girl with pneumonia has a high fever for five days. The parents call Silent Unity, and the fever breaks. A man is diagnosed with cancer and told the doctors can give him no hope, until, after phoning Silent Unity for prayers, the doctors discover the tumors diminishing in size. A mother wants prayers to help her son find the perfect job and writes that soon afterward he fell into conversation with a stranger on a train, and the relationship develops into a fine job.

There may be a reason the prayers of Silent Unity are so powerful. Walter Weston, author of several books on healing prayer and touch, claims that the power of prayer is strengthened not by the number of the people praying but by the *square* of that number![4] If five people are praying for you, for example, the prayer has not five times but 25 *times* the value of a single person's prayer. If a Jewish *minyan* of ten people are praying, their prayer, multiplied again by ten, is *100 times greater than that of a single individual.*

Did not Christ himself declare this of the power of the human mind? "Whatever you bind on earth will be bound in heaven, and whatever you loose on earth will be loosed in heaven. Truly I tell you, if two of you agree on earth about anything you ask, it will be done for you by my Father in heaven. For where two or three are gathered in my name, I am there, among them." (Matthew 18:19)

Sometimes, in praying, it is not the situation that changes. It is you. Then the problem no longer holds us in its grasp.

A Hindu Prayer

O God, the Giver of Life, Remover of pains and sorrows,
Bestower of happiness, and Creator of the Universe.
Thou art most luminous, pure and adorable.
We meditate on Thee.
Inspire and guide our intellect in the right direction.

Chapter 10

The Mystery of Unanswered Prayer

Sometimes I thank God for unanswered prayers
Just remember when you're talking
To the man upstairs
That just because he doesn't answer
Doesn't mean he don't care
Some of God's greatest gifts
Are unanswered prayers.
—Garth Brooks

This brings us, reluctantly, to unanswered prayer. It is foolish, even heartless, to ignore the reality. When I hear myself say, "God takes care of me in all sorts of ways, clips necklaces, finds lost keys," it doesn't mean I'm insensitive to the enormous suffering around me. All of us hurt or grieve, everyone on earth. We feel remorse. We weep. There is great cruelty in this world.

"Even in our sleep," wrote the Greek playwright Aeschylus, "pain we cannot forget falls drop by drop upon the heart. . . ."

We watch the genocide and migrations of peoples, read of terrorism, torture, atrocities (or, God forbid, experience them), see our children shot in schoolyards, have our lives and those of our loved ones hurt or killed by famine, fire, storm, and war; and we want to scream aloud, like the man in the Edvard Munch painting, with horrified hands to our ears and our mouths an open sore: "No! No!"

Weren't those people praying, too?

"Every war," wrote C. S. Lewis, the English author, "every famine or plague, almost every death-bed is a monument to a petition that was not granted. At this very moment thousands of people in this one [land] are facing as a *fait accompli* the very thing against which they have prayed night and day, pouring out their whole souls in prayer, and as they thought with faith. They have sought and not found, knocked and it has not been opened."[1]

This questioning of God—"Why? Why?"—is as old as humanity. An ancient Mesopotamian story tells of the virtuous King Tabi-utul-Enlil, who lived around 1750 B.C.E., and who is known as the Babylonian Job. Like Job, he was a pious man. Prayer was his royal delight. "I taught my country to guard the name of the god . . ." he says. "I thought such things were pleasing to a god." Nonetheless, he is stricken first blind, then deaf, then twisted and bowed in leprous misery, pain, and disease. "I cried to God, but he did not show his countenance; I prayed to my goddess, she did not raise her head."

Already, thousands of years ago, people were struggling to understand and were baffled by the great metaphysical mysteries. The king recites:

What, however, seems good to oneself, is to a god
  displeasing,
What is spurned by oneself finds favor with a god.
Who is there that can grasp the will of the gods in
  heaven?

*The plan of a god, full of mystery—who can
   understand it?
How can mortals learn the way of a god?[2]*

Like Job, who followed this king years later, the old man sees his faith rewarded. He is carried to the sacred waters of a holy place, where miraculously he is healed. All things are possible with a loving and attentive God, says the Mesopotamian author.

*He wiped away the blemish, making the entire body
   radiant.
The crippled frame regained its splendor
On the banks of the stream . . .
The brand of slavery was erased and the fetters
   removed.[3]*

But the questions refuse to die away. We rant at God. We defy him in our suffering. We question our unanswered prayers. Twelve hundred years later, around 500 B.C.E., the Jewish exiles in Babylon raised the same question: How could Jerusalem have fallen? What had they done wrong? The answer came back with almost the same words as those of Tabi-utul-Enlil: *"For as the heavens are higher than the earth,"* says the Lord, in Isaiah 55, *"so are my ways higher than your ways, and my thoughts than your thoughts."*

Viewed from the smallest and most selfish view, without the telescope of time, prayers go unanswered all the time. And it's not through any fault of how we prayed!

Misfortunes will happen to the wisest and best of men.

—Pawnee proverb

Let's be clear about that. Throughout this book I talk about the various rules of prayer and ways to pray, but mark this well: When your prayers go unheeded, it's not necessarily because you did them wrong.

We have only to look at Jesus in the garden of Gethsemane—the ultimate example of unanswered prayer. He may have been the son of God, but he was also a frightened human being. He always called himself a mortal, "the son of man." He knows what is about to happen to him. He has seen crucifixions. They were a common Roman punishment, fields of crosses with their hanging, living flesh. This image is not some fairy tale to him, based on pictures in churches or museums. He has heard the screams of convicts lashed for days on a cross.

It is the middle of the night. He has had his seder dinner. He knows that Judas has gone off to betray him. He almost ordered it. He asks three of his friends—Peter and the two brothers, James and John—to come aside with him into the garden on the Mount of Olives, to stay awake with him and watch. The small, square garden is there today. You can visit it, with its black-barked, gnarled, and twisted olive trees—trees from the very stock that sheltered Jesus on that night. He tells his friends to pray, then goes off alone, for his heart is sorrowful, and he prays out loud. "Let this cup pass from my lips," he begs in desperation. We know he is praying out loud because his words are reported in three of the Gospels (Mark 14, Luke 22, and Matthew 26). Later he goes to find his friends, and they're asleep. They've had a big day. They can't keep their eyes open. He wakes them up.

"Couldn't you stay awake one hour with me?" he asks plaintively. "Pray that you may not enter into temptation [of sleep]." He goes off a second time and again prays in the same passionate way.

"Abba, Papa, Daddy, all things are possible to you; remove this cup from me; yet not what I will, but what you will." Overhead, the gold stars swing across an indifferent black night. Can you imagine his loneliness, his sense of hurt betrayal? According to Matthew, he returns to his sleeping disciples still a third time (the symbolic number three). Then it is too late. The soldiers with their lanterns march in, arrest and cuff him. He goes quietly, without a fight—even healing the slave whose ear was cut off by one of his disciples.

Apparently, 2000 years ago people prayed out loud. They did everything out loud. Three hundred years later St. Augustine (not yet a saint) came upon his mentor, St. Ambrose, bishop of Milan (also not yet a saint), reading under a tree. Augustine was astonished, for, standing right next to Ambrose, he says, "you cannot see his lips moving and you don't hear a word!"[4]

For centuries people read to themselves out loud, and they prayed out loud, and they palavered loudly in the hall or the marketplace, coming to political, economic, and philosophic consensus by loud discussions. So when Christ instructed his followers to pray quietly in their room, speaking to God in secret, and not shouting in public like the hypocrites who want to be seen and praised for their piety, he did not necessarily mean to pray as we do today in the silence of our hearts, but only modestly, lips moving in intimate, mumbling conversation, while remembering that the Holy One knows what's in our hearts before we cry aloud.

The prayer of Jesus in the garden was a straight, directed prayer of petition. There is nothing wrong in ask-

THE MYSTERY OF UNANSWERED PRAYER

ing for what we want. But he followed it with complete abandon: "Thy will be done." That's one of the lessons of this story. The other is simply that not all prayers are answered as we want.

Sometimes there's a larger picture that we cannot see.

———

The fact is, we do not know why some people are healed of dread diseases and others are not. We do not know why sometimes a need is answered in ways so beautiful it leaves us breathless with joy and gratitude, sometimes in ways so awful that we think the very angels must weep.

Concerning this second possibility, we often find that if we wait another year, the situation we thought so terrible has blossomed into flowering delight. "Wait three years," goes a Buddhist saying, "and every disaster turns into a blessing."

And this is why, as the years pass, we begin to understand with deep humility that we cannot even distinguish anymore what's good, what's bad. What we thought a blessing often has such thorns we can hardly hold it in our hands, while what we thought was terrible turns out to wear a crown.

To a degree, pain is built into us. If we did not have tender skin, as Alan Watts observed, thorns would not prick or sharp rocks hurt. Hard, soft, bright, dim, smelly or fragrant, ugly or lovely—it all depends on our human senses. Good and bad, fortune and disaster, even justice and fairness are human judgments.

"Some people," wrote the medieval mystic and professor of theology Meister Eckhart (1260–1327), "want to recognize God only in some pleasant enlightenment, and then they get pleasure in enlightenment, but not God."

Some six hundred years later Alan Watts expressed the same idea. "Human consciousness must involve both pleasure and pain. To strive for pleasure at the exclusion of pain is in effect to strive for loss of consciousness."

Suffering simply is. Yet curiously, in its spiritual sense it does not exist at all.

Today something like eight million people are said to have had a near-death experience (NDE)—to have died, in other words, so completely that the doctors can find no brain or heart activity. Mysteriously, they return to life. In one case a man was brain-dead for 40 minutes. His sheet-covered body had been laid on a gurney pushed to the corridor and marked to be sent to the morgue, when a nurse's aide noticed the sheet quivering as he breathed.

It is an extraordinary fact that on returning to life almost every person who's experienced an NDE reports having had a spiritual encounter with a great light or with beautiful beings of light, and this light is also seen as intelligence. Sometimes they have been met on the "other side" not only by angels and great sages but by dead relatives gesturing and welcoming them, and in some cases they have met relatives they didn't even know existed. (I'm thinking of one child who after his near-death experience told his father he had met a little brother—at which his father burst into tears and confirmed that an older baby had died before the child was born.) These blessed people, returning like messengers to tell us of the spiritual dimension, also uniformly report *knowing* that everything in the universe operates perfectly, by a perfect plan—even suffering, famine, torture, child abuse. Including our unanswered prayers. On their return they are transformed by the near-death experience and often can no longer tolerate the material world, with all its illusions, anger, fakery, and small-minded judgments of what is good, what's bad. Nothing

The way I see it, if you want the rainbow, you gotta put up with the rain.

—Dolly Parton

appears to them as it was before. Not even suffering and unanswered prayer.

"Pain we cannot forget," wrote Aeschylus, "falls drop by drop upon the heart, until at last, in our own despair, against our will, wisdom comes through the awful grace of God."

Once I was undergoing a particularly trying time. Every bone in my body hurt. I wept uncontrollably, praying wordlessly, "Oh, God, oh, God," not even knowing what to pray for. I don't remember how long this period lasted, but one day, like a bolt from the blue, I *understood.*

I was standing in the bathroom, of all unlikely places. I will not forget how I had turned unhappily toward the door, and in the moment between lifting one foot and setting it down, knowledge brought my head up like a startled deer's. I was shot by the sure and instantaneous realization that through adversity we are tempered by the fire of God's love. We are forged like a fine Toledo blade into true steel, flexible as a willow wand and strong as the girder of a bridge. A flood of joy swept over me. As metal is plunged first into the hottest flames and instantly in cold water to temper steel, as gold must pass through fire to make fine jewelry, as carbon is chipped out of rock and cut before the light can flash off its diamond facets, so are we tempered by the hand of God.

Do we dare to be fashioned into gold?

"Even in our sleep," wrote Aeschylus, "pain . . . falls

drop by drop upon the heart, until at last, in our own despair, against our will, wisdom comes through the awful grace of God."

Legend has it that all the buddhas of the cosmos got together one day and compared notes. In their different times and worlds they taught by diverse means: some through music or poetry, some through aromas, still others through dance and movement. They marveled at the dedication of the Gautama Buddha working in our earthly realm. "How do you do it?" they exclaimed. "Those beings are so dense and ignorant that they cannot be reached except through suffering."

No teacher addressed the question of suffering (and by implication unanswered prayer) more thoroughly than the Buddha. He never mentions prayer as a way to ease it. He explains, instead, the Four Noble Truths:

1. That life is full of suffering.
2. That suffering is caused by attachments to those things you want.
3. That the way out of suffering is through living lightly—nonattachment.
4. That nonattachment is achieved through daily practice of meditation and careful self-examination, watching and guarding our minds, our speech, our actions.

Accept the truth, taught the Buddha, and suffering departs. It's not a question of unanswered prayer, because when you are balanced in peace and wisdom, you no longer can perform those acts that cause yourself or others to suffer; you try to speak and act in ways that do no harm, in ways that help. If the outcome is different from your intent, at least you acted from integrity and purity

I slept and dreamed that life was joy.
I woke and found that life was service.
I served and learned that service was joy.

—Rabindranath Tagore

of heart. You acted from a spiritual motivation, out of love.

It is important to note that suffering is caused not by the desires and the longings of your heart but by your *attachment* to gaining these desires; and the way out of your pain, this abstract nonattachment, is not to be confused with not caring, not loving. Nonattachment is another word for surrender, I think, for bending with the Tao, for acceptance. Living lightly. Indeed, in struggling for this wisdom, you grow more compassionate. You long to help others and to serve. Through service you find joy, and then you no longer hurt.

"In my own limited experience," says the Dalai Lama, "I have found that the greatest degree of inner tranquillity comes from the development of love and compassion. The more we care for the happiness of others, the greater is our own sense of well-being."[5]

Buddhist practice is all about cultivating a loving heart, which is the source of happiness, and in a way ends all questions about unanswered prayer. Loving, or being in a state of love, takes the attention off yourself. Loving

The sign of a fully merciful heart is when it burns for all creation.

—Isaac of Syria

gives you strength to overcome the obstacles in your path. Which is just what prayer does, too.

How curious that the traditional Buddhist does not believe in a creator God! Yet Buddhists pray. They turn prayer wheels, fly flags, make countless prostrations, and lift voices in chorus and in chant. Nonetheless, pure Buddhism extols the philosophy of karma, or the law of cause and effect, above the practice of prayer. Karma dictates that everything we do or say changes our surroundings. Every thought sends ripples around the world. When we pray, our thoughts create a shift and an effect. Intention arouses energy, energy flows forth.

But now we're off the subject of unanswered prayer, except to say, concerning suffering and unmet needs, that according to Eastern religions some people by their generosity and karma, take on heroic tasks, agreeing to be reborn cycle after cycle, as the homeless, the poor, the war-torn, the diseased, or those subject to torture and atrocities. These holy ones (whose prayers remain unanswered) offer more privileged people the opportunity to offer compassion, alms, service, help. I don't know if it is true.

It hardly matters.

The point is, we see appalling suffering in the world. We could all become like angels if we only understood.

"What karma really means," says Pema Chödrön, an American-born Tibetan Buddhist nun, "is that we continually receive the lessons we need in order to open our hearts."

I used to think that my prayers were left unanswered because I had prayed wrong. It's a common misconception that derives from trying to retain control. If I'm the one at fault (we unconsciously reason), then I can change whatever I am doing wrong: I'm still in charge. I'll *make* the universe bend to my demands by working harder, doing better, *praying properly.*

I remember an Episcopal priest once saying, "The hardest thing to learn is that I'm not God."

Fundamentalist Christianity affirms that your prayers went unanswered because you sinned. You don't deserve to have your prayers responded to. Fundamentalist Islam echoes the idea. Your prayers were not answered because you read the Koran but did not act on it; or you believed in God but did not live your life as if there were such a holy text; or you prayed five times a day to Mecca, but without a clean, pure heart. The fault is yours.

You know what? It's all a mystery. Even our predilection for guilt and unhappiness is strange.

I used to play in the garden of rejection. How I learned it, I don't know. It must have dated back to childhood, when, finding my desires thwarted, I would go away alone and dream about how sorry my parents would be when I died! *Then* they'd regret the actions that had made me sad! I took delicious comfort in my self-pity, little knowing that a habit was developing that would carry me as an adult into immediate despair.

In my adulthood it became a game. One day I'd notice the garden gate beckoning me toward rejection, with all the pretty flowers of abandonment, and I'd think how

Thoughts are like arrows: once released, they strike their mark.

Guard them well or one day you may be your own victim.

—Navaho saying

much fun it would be to feel bad for a time. Like a child, I'd push open the innocent white wicket gate to go feel sorry for myself (eat worms, as my mother called it). I'd step inside to sniff one enticing flower of victimization, take one step, still holding on to the gate—and as if by magic the exit would vanish! I was lost inside rejection. I might spend days in that despairing state—depression, abandonment, fear, self-loathing—until one day by accident I'd stumble out the hidden gate and find myself panting breathless on the other side, swearing never to go back.

Wow, I'd tell myself. *I won't do* that *again!* My promises were soon forgotten. Before long I'd be tempted once more just to peek into that pleasurable self-rejection. . . .

It's not hard to lose your way, be tortured by the accusing inner prosecutor. It's not hard to take on the role of victim. Everything in commercial Western society, after all, is committed to making you feel bad about yourself. "You're not good enough, smart enough, thin enough, curvy enough, old enough, young enough, pretty enough, rich enough. . . . You are not loved—*as you would be,* sing the Sirens from their far-off rock, *if you bought the product being advertised!*

No wonder some people believe that God would punish us by deliberately not answering our prayers.

But listen. The universal energy, the primal principle, God, creative intelligence, is composed of love, and it can no more stop loving than the sun can stop shining. It pours out love indifferently, and so generous is the Holy Spirit, so attentive to our longings, that it will give us everything. If we want to live imprisoned in our own resentments and sullen anger, eat bitter shame and grinding guilt, or burn with jealousy (the "not enough"), then Providence is happy to oblige. Another answered prayer!

Does my argument sound like the hollow comfort of the friends of Job—who, rather than sympathize or offer help, berated him for his wickedness? The friends brought up the righteous party line: that God comes like a merchant in the bazaar selling material and spiritual wealth, rewarding the just and punishing the sinful. God is just, they said, and rewards the righteous. Therefore, suffering must come as punishment. *Repent!* they said. *Since you've been punished, you are wicked, too.* This same theory of retributive justice was expressed 500 years later, when the disciples asked Jesus what sin had made the blind man blind, and he answered with the radical instruction "He has done nothing wrong, and neither did his parents or any of his ancestors before him. No past-life karma. Nothing to work out. *It just happened!*"

The concept is still in vogue today. "If I think right

Life is God's novel. Let Him write it.

—Isaac Bashevis Singer

thoughts and perform right actions," runs the wishful argument, "I will receive health, wealth, and happiness." Yet love rains on the just and unjust equally, often arousing such hurt howls of betrayal, such ethical questionings of what is fair and just, that we are forced to reexamine our belief in God and the deal we think we've cut.

There is no deal.

Christ did not promise material wealth and power when he spoke of the kingdom of heaven. Neither did the Buddha offer his *bikkhus* fortune, safety, fame. They promised only love, peace, joy, comfort, happiness, even in the midst of pain. To be taken care of.

We don't have to do a thing to earn it. Love is given as a grace.

Prayer of St. Francis

Lord, make me an instrument of Your peace.
Where there is hatred, let me sow love.
Where there is injury, pardon,
Where there is doubt, faith,
Where there is despair, hope,
Where there is darkness, light,
Where there is sadness, joy.

O Divine Master, grant that I may not so much seek
To be consoled as to console,
To be understood as to understand,
To be loved as to love.
For it is in giving that we receive,
It is in pardoning that we are pardoned,
It is in dying that we are born to eternal life.

Chapter 11

The Prayer of Touch

So far we've been talking about prayer principally as intention, thought, surrender, but there is another form of prayer so subtle that we hardly ever think of it as prayer at all: the healing power of touch. The largest organ of the body is *skin!* It is so sensitive that by touch alone you sense the other person's mood, his vibrational frequency or energy field. (Indeed, you don't even need to touch; you can pick up another's mood merely by his entering the room.)

The simple act of placing two fingers in sympathy on a grieving woman's wrist is a wordless prayer. It heals.

This prayer of touch is related to telepathy, but the touch itself carries energy, and this has been proven by scientists today. David Benor, an American psychologist researching spiritual healing, reviewed 131 controlled

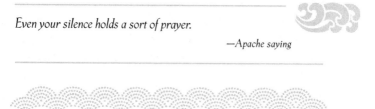

Even your silence holds a sort of prayer.

—*Apache saying*

experiments on prayer and the laying-on of hands and found that 56 of the studies showed statistically significant results. The odds of that happening by chance alone were less than 1 in 100. For decades researchers have studied the effects of healing touch on seeds, mice, chickens, shrimp, plants, on red blood corpuscles, on cancer cells. They respond to the energy of the healer's hands. In one study seedlings held by a healer grew at twice the rate of other seedlings. In a second test the healer held a flask of water, and the seedlings watered with this energized and prayed-over water grew significantly faster than those watered normally. Conversely, cancer cells diminish when prayed over with a healer's hands. Each organism seems to strain toward health.

I talked earlier of the invisible touch of thought—how intention transcends space and time. Well, so, too, does the prayer of touch. The distant healer holds between his flaring hands the *idea* of the seeds or the shrimp or the wounded mouse—intention combined with healing touch—and the seeds or mice get well. Dr. William Braud, while at the Mind Science Foundation in San Antonio, Texas,[1] reviewed 149 long-distance experiments of healing "touch" practiced on fish, animals, and humans, and found that half showed statistically significant results.[2] This is interesting, for clearly belief or faith on the part of the plant or fish has nothing to do with the results of prayer.

There are many schools of healing touch: Therapeutic Touch, the Rosen method, Barbara Brennan's Hands of Light, Reiki, Mari-El, Bioenergetic therapy. Not to mention massage, acupuncture, polarity, cranial-sacral work, Feldenkreis. . . . And then there is the simple touch of a mother reaching out to kiss away the hurt of her son's scraped knee. Our hands heal naturally. Everyone can do it. It's only prayer made physical! It's only love. We give it through our hands in numerous ways—with blessings, hugs, with handshakes that tender our word of honor, our hospitality, our friendship and our peace. "Peace be with you," we say, offering our hand, offering this prayer of touch. It is so natural for us to touch that I heard of one instance in which paramedics could hardly reach the victims of an auto accident for the press of the crowd of strangers, all straining to touch and hold those who were lying hurt beside the road.

Let's return for a moment to the formal schools of healing touch. I suggest that the interested reader explore all kinds of schools to find the one that suits her personality. The one I know best is Reiki, and that's what I'll describe, but not because it is the only one. Much work is taking place with the human energy field, as much as on human consciousness. Slowly we begin to understand its place in prayer.

It is almost 20 years ago that I first heard of Reiki. I was at dinner with a friend when she turned to me suddenly. "There's a class I want you to take. An exceptional teacher, Ethel Lombardi, is coming to town the end of May. Sign up."

"What is it?"

"It's called Reiki"—she pronounced it RAY-key—"and I won't tell you any more about it than that. Just take the class."

"You know I'd do anything for you," I answered, "but

I look at God, I look at you, and I keep on looking at God.

—Julian of Norwich

THE PRAYER OF TOUCH

I'm flying to England then. I've already paid for my ticket."

"Don't be silly. These opportunities don't come every day. Change your ticket. If you're supposed to go to the class, it will work out."

I argued about the cost, about my time, I raised other difficulties; but in the end my friend simply cocked her head, giving me that *look* that closed discussion, and then she carried in the dessert.

I signed up for the class and found, to my surprise, an even cheaper, more convenient flight. It was one of my first experiences in synchronicity. Was it possible, I wondered, that some force wanted me to take the class?

The class met in the basement rumpus room of a suburban Virginia house. I glared suspiciously at the 20 to 25 men and women in the room, some waiting quietly, others—to my disdain—chatting about their sun signs or the colors of their auras! When I discovered that the class was in spiritual healing, I was dismayed. *What had I gotten into?* Looking around the room, I decided I wouldn't let any person there lay a finger on me, much less try to *heal me!*

I believed in spiritual healing. I had met the renowned healer Olga Worrell, who died in 1985 and whose energy had once washed over me in waves of light so perceptible that it almost made me faint. What left me skeptical was the idea this gift could be *taught.* To just anyone! To me!

This was my first experience with the subtle energies

Lay your hands on the sick, and they shall be healed.

—Mark 16:18

that scientists are still unable to measure but which seem to underlie all life. Later I would discover that there are schools for learning healing touch, and I would find out how touch dovetails with other forms of alternative medicine, not to mention prayer. But in those days I knew none of that. In those days none of this was considered "reputable." It was embarrassing.

We sat in the dim basement (it was painted pink), while one by one each participant was called upstairs to be "tuned in" or initiated. We were told to remove our wristwatches, lest they break under the powerful energies being given us! Each person went upstairs nervous and unsmiling, and each came back with a startled look.

"What happened? What did she do?"

A shrug. An uncertain smile. "Wait and see."

When my turn came, I went to the living room upstairs. Ethel, this motherly, practical, red-haired woman, directed me to a straight-backed chair.

"Close your eyes," she said.

She stood behind me. I don't know what happened that first night. I could feel her hands fiddling at the crown of my head . . . and I fainted. I came to with her clapping her hands, saying, "Come back. Come back."

She was not pleased.

"You just slipped out of your body. You do that all the time, don't you?"

"I fainted," I defended myself. She took no notice.

"Don't you know you were given your body in which to live on this plane? Now, you stay in it! I don't want to see you *ever* leave your body again like that. You can't do any decent work if you're going to leave your body all the time."

I returned to the group abashed.

The second evening I felt as if the top of my head had been opened up and a column of pure white light poured into me, down as far as my waist.

The third night I felt the light descend, but darkly, like a heavy weight, through the trunk of my body to my buttocks on the chair.

The fourth night I felt nothing.

Now, years later, I am myself a Reiki "master," with the ability to pass this extraordinary touch to others, and I am more familiar with the power of this energy. Yet in truth I understand little of the mystery.

"What are you doing in an attunement?" I asked Ethel. She pursed her lips, thinking how to express the matter.

"It's like tuning an engine to make it work better, or tuning a radio to a particular frequency. In the process, energy blocks and emotional traumas are released. You get clearer. You can't do any healing work without it."

I think it also lifts your vibration. The same thing happens when you pray and meditate, for the clearer your soul, the higher the frequency of your vibration. Imagine that the soul is like a beautiful ruby covered in hardened mud and dirt. The mud comes from anger, war, unmet expectations—all the disappointments, abuses, and betrayals of life—but only you can clean the jewel of your own soul and lift your vibration. Prayer and meditation are your tools. Through prayer you chip away the mud bit by bit, until you are left a light-struck jewel.

Reiki, this energy of touch, also cleanses you. It releases the mental, emotional, and physical blocks that hold you back. It makes you more wholly yourself, and free, which means you emanate great, palpable beams of love. This sounds ridiculous perhaps, absurd, abject, to

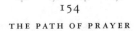

someone who has never experienced this special touch, and yet it's sacred, too.

I asked my classmates what they had felt during their initiations. One saw colored lights before his eyes; another sensed a tingling through her body; another felt the hair rising on his scalp—until he remembered he was bald.

The word "Reiki" comes from the Japanese, meaning "universal life force." The Japanese *ki* is the equivalent of the Chinese *chi* or *qi*—as in *t'ai chi* and *qi gong*. It may be what physicists call tachyon energy. According to quantum physics, tachyon energy is an invisible, faster-than-light universe existing independently from our visible universe, where the speed of light marks the limits of possibility. Tachyon energy lies beyond electromagnetic energy. It is the theoretical source of subatomic particles. Tachyon energy exists everywhere simultaneously. This energy needs no time to travel, recognizes no limits of space.

But what are they saying, the physicists? It's just a scientific word for God!

Over the weekend Ethel made us practice giving healing touch (it is done with the client fully clothed), learning how and where to place our hands and allow this *stuff*, this energy to pour through us into the other person. You feel it surging off the palms of your hands, prickling and urging you on. It is delicious to receive and just as enjoyable to give. Your hands know where to go, when to move and when to rest in one place on your client for minutes at a time. You come to utterly trust the intelligence of this independent energy field, this Reiki.

I wish I could tell you—tell everyone, shout to the

world—how to use the prayer of touch. I dream sometimes that one day everyone in the world will have healing capacity, will learn it in childhood perhaps, and then we will pass this energy like honey back and forth among ourselves, and no one will be allowed to hurt for long.

Reiki is so powerful that it can heal cancers, heart problems, emotional disturbances, allergies, asthma, depression, addictions. Is anything impervious to the prayer of touch? So powerful is Reiki, and now so acceptable a practice, that some hospitals have set up special Reiki units for the treatment of heart or cancer patients, in addition to regular medical practices and their regular studies in the effects of prayer. George Washington University has recently completed a complementary alternative medicine study—including Reiki—for the treatment of multiple sclerosis. Memorial Sloan-Kettering Cancer Center uses Reiki in conjunction with standard medicine to combat cancer.

Reiki is pure energy. When receiving, you feel it as a *substance* remarkable for light and heat. You are surrounded by a sense of safety, comfort. You feel the healer's hands as hot as waffle irons! As for the healer, she is receiving, too, even while giving it. The healer almost merges with the patient, just as, when praying, you *become* the prayer. She blends her consciousness with that of the one receiving, sinking into a prayerful state and listening to the other's body and spirit, sending it pure

It is a very remarkable thing that the unconscious mind of one human being can react upon that of another without passing through the conscious. This fact is incontestable.

—Sigmund Freud

THE PATH OF PRAYER

love. This is prayer physicalized. Moreover, it is not her personal energy she is giving away (to do so would tire her), but the universal life force.

This energy is so strong that you can see it.

Once I attended a lecture by the gifted healer Olga Worrell. For many years she and her even more exceptional husband, Ambrose, were renowned for their abilities. Ambrose was an aeronautical engineer, and he had met Olga, his future wife, when they were both still children. His book *The Gift of Healing* remains a classic. During their lifetimes both Ambrose and Olga were studied furiously, and their healing touch was recorded by Kirlian photography, a form of photography developed in 1936 by Semyon Kirlian to capture visually the electromagnetic energy field that haloes every living thing. All beings vibrate with electromagnetic energy. Kirlian photographed the energy field of thousands of organisms, including a newborn baby's hand and the healthy aura of a flourishing leaf compared with the torn, weak energy of a diseased one. When Olga's hands were photographed in an ordinary, resting state, the photos showed only a subtle light around her fingers, as would be true of anyone, but when she entered the healing state, this light streamed forth in long daggers of color: blue and yellow and green and red.

Olga was an old woman when I heard her lecture, but sitting in her presence I could feel the waves of warmth and light that pulsated from her, like ocean breakers. It was the same force that I felt with my guru, Maharaj, and that I would later feel when in the presence of the Dalai Lama. The closer you sit, the more powerful is the sensation of these waves of light breaking over you. If your intuition is very clear, you can see the light flaring off the skin of an enlightened spiritual teacher. It's nothing strange. Don't we comment on it daily? Saints are depicted with a halo at their head. And ordinary people are known to shine with light. "She must be in love; she's radiant," we say. "His face lit up when he saw her."

The more loving the person, the higher the vibration. The higher the vibration, the stronger the healer.

Remember the story of the woman who, having suffered for twelve years from constant bleeding, squirmed through a crowd to reach the side of Jesus? She wanted to be healed, but at the last minute, aware of her own uncleanliness (for menstrual blood was unclean to the Jews), she bent to the ground (she *bowed*) to finger the hem of his garment. In doing so, she brushed his aura.

"Who touched me?" Jesus asked. His disciples laughed.

"Master," they said. "You're being jostled by a thousand people, and you ask who *touched* you?"

But he had felt the surge that passed—do we say, "out of" him? It slammed into the woman, the prayer of touch, and instantly her hemorrhage was healed. It is the touch of love.

David McClelland, a Harvard Medical School Ph.D., once demonstrated the tangible effect of love by showing a group of students a documentary of Mother Teresa lovingly addressing and caring for the dying. Both before and after the film McClelland tested levels of immunoglobulin-A in the saliva of the students. This is the substance that makes you immune to disease. He found that merely watching a film of Mother Teresa's love, even if the students considered her a fraud, raised their immune levels.

This energy has the capacity, directed by thought, to pass through time and over distances. The touch or intention can be "sent" across vast oceans. Quick as thought. Your friend will *feel* the healing light a thousand miles away. Jesus did it when he told the centurion to go home, that his servant was already healed. You (the healer) can send healing touch to an ill friend, to a puzzling situation, to world peace, and the same healing benefits are received as in a hands-on session. You can "tag" the energy to be received at some future date when convenient to the client. ("I am now ready to receive my Reiki treatment from [name]," says the client when sure she will not be interrupted.) In addition, the healer can send a positive intention, an affirmation that will take root in the other person's mind and slowly begin to change a habit or bad attitude. (Need I add that this is done only with the other person's consent? Both healer and client agree ahead of time on the wording of the prayer.)

Even more extraordinary, Reiki can be sent *after* it was already received! All rules of time and space collapse before a proper prayer. We saw this demonstrated by the experiments at PEAR, but I discovered it by accident one day when working with a friend, who is herself a Reiki master. We had agreed that one evening she would send me a long-distance healing between 6:00 and 6:10. At 6:00 P.M., as I was puttering around my house, the Reiki caught me by surprise, for I'd forgotten to watch the clock, and when it unexpectedly hit, it left me reeling. I staggered to the couch to lie down, to relax into the luscious force that I felt pouring over me. It felt wonderful. The session lasted ten or fifteen minutes, then abruptly stopped.

The next day I commented on the treatment to my friend. She looked a little sheepish and then confessed that unexpectedly she had had to meet with a client at 6:00 P.M. and had been unable to send to me as planned.

Instead she had sent the treatment *an hour or so later,* tagging it to have been already received.

Even the past is malleable to your intention.

I cannot emphasize this enough. Nothing is impossible to God. Thought, intention, prayer, surrender, love—they are all one thing. Just as the healer merges his consciousness with that of the patient, carrying them both into a higher plane, a spaciousness of healing love, so thought merges in prayer with the consciousness of the universe—with God, with love—and healing comes or answers to our need.

A Buddhist Prayer[1]

May I become a medicine for the sick, and their physician, their support until sickness come no more.
May I become an unfailing store for the wretched, and be first to supply them with their needs.

My own self and my pleasures, my righteousness, past, present and future, may I sacrifice without regard, in order to achieve the welfare of all beings.

Part III

The Practice of Prayer

Chapter 12

A Hundred Ways to Pray

The Hindus speak of the thousand names of God, and surely there are a hundred ways to pray. A Zen master once addressed the matter with a story. A man and a woman, he said, were dressing for a party. The man washed his face and shaved it clean. The woman applied creams and makeup to hers. They were both going to the same party, but can we say one is right and the other wrong? We are all going to the same place, all seeking God.

Sometimes we can hardly move, we go numb, unable to find our voice. I don't know if this is prayer. I write this at such a moment, on the day after the plane bombings of the World Trade Center and the Pentagon, with thousands killed and wounded, and all of us shocked, the country shaken to its roots. Today I take a taxi, and the driver, a handsome young Cameroonian, is so highly agitated that he twists around in his seat to look at me as he talks, almost squirming from the pressure of unspoken thoughts, the pent-up feelings, until, approaching my destination, he bursts out, "I have to go to church. I need to pray now. This is a time to pray."

All over the country, all over the world, people turn to God. Prayers are being spoken in cathedrals, in parish churches, in synagogues, temples, mosques. Yesterday, the day of horror, I found I could not pray. I mean with *formal* prayer. I watched the TV, glued to the disaster, watching the same scenes shown over and over again, unable to disentangle myself from the visual horror long enough to go away alone, to commune with my Lord. In the face of immediate disaster, the mind goes blank and then is swamped by a confusion of emotions—hurt, anger, anguish, sorrow, disbelief, despair. How to reach out for hope? Formal prayer came later to me, although others were already on their knees in their places of worship, already turning to the Comforter.

"Yea, though I walk through the Valley of the Shadow of Death, I shall fear no evil."

Perhaps, however, I was praying all the time, as I held my new niece to my heart, a tiny sleeping baby, only three weeks old, with her perfect fairy fingernails and toes as small as pearls. I held her sleeping form and watched the towers collapse again and again, and I hoped that just holding, loving her, would count as prayer—I mean, as more than the swift and horrible "Oh, help! Please, God, oh, help!"

The first thing you need for long, extended prayer is space and quiet. You turn inward then, away from the

Be still, and know that I am God.

—Psalms 46:10

roaring of the television and the violent frantic panic in the announcers' voices. You turn toward love.

In crisis, however, our first instinct is often to run around, to be *doing*. You rush to donate blood, to phone a friend, or else you watch the disaster, hugging yourself in anguish and choking out half-formed and silent prayers. Later, when the adrenaline calms, you can remember what's important and, like the taxi driver, search out a quiet, sacred place of God and kneel or stand or bow in prayer. For what? For all those hurt and suffering, for yourself and for the loss of those you loved, for the terror, your powerlessness, and fear of the unknown that is lurching toward you. For centering. And then, beginning all over again at another level, perhaps you may continue praying—but shifting now to thanks and gratitude for all God's blessings, for comfort in distress, for love. For angels riding to our aid. And then, moving still further on the ramp of prayer, you may find yourself slipping into praise and adoration, but now you are far removed from the disaster itself, and I think your prayers are very strong. At this point you may leap wildly to your feet again, back into the scramble of *doing*! Then you must begin it once more, with discipline forcing yourself to breathe, to pray, to surrender over and over, until you know that God, too, is reaching out for us.

The practice of prayer is a lifelong enterprise, sometimes easy, sometimes hard. Everyone has her own favorite way of prayer, and the curious thing is that every way works. Yet so weird are we humans that we will go to war (imagine!) in disapproval of how another offers prayers. Are we crazy? We kill another because we don't like the way he prays or to what name for God?

There are a hundred different ways to pray, and we must each one of us find a path.

I have a friend in Baltimore, Janice Darrell, who signed up when Johns Hopkins University Hospital Department of Oncology approached members of her church about praying for terminally ill patients. Interestingly, the cancer unit, now called the Sidney Kimmel Comprehensive Cancer Center, devised the project not as a research study but as a valuable adjunct to cancer care, knowing that more than just medical attention is needed in a lot of cases. Janet received a list with the names and case histories of some 30 patients, and each morning for nine months she took her folder out on the sunporch to sit in meditation, praying for them, one by one. (At present her church is not involved, while other churches have been enlisted for periods of three months at a time of serious prayer.)

Janet never met the people on her list, but she felt so close to them by virtue of her prayers that when one man died, she burst into tears! She felt she knew them. They became dear to her. The rewards, she says, came to her. It is she who benefited from prayer.

John Ryan is a handsome gentle, gray-bearded man who, a Jesuit for nine years early in his life, teaches theology and philosophy at a local university. I asked him how he prays. Every morning he sits with a cup of coffee for 20 to 30 minutes "just staring into space," as his partner in life put it, playfully. He says he is "connecting."

"I go to my center," he said simply, as if my question were as common as asking what he wanted for dinner, "and see what comes up. I don't do any Eastern stuff, but I do pay attention to my breathing. I become aware of my absolute dependence on God. This is the fundamental essence of piety, the expression of our relationship with God: ultimate dependence."

We talked a little more. *"Introibo ad altare dei,"* he

quoted. " 'I will go unto the altar of God.' I see it as my life," he continued with sweet gravity. "My life is an altar of God. Sitting there, I am going into my life, which means surrendering to God. You know that in Islam one of the names of God is 'Merciful.' Islam means 'surrender,' and you surrender to the mercy of God, into the life of God. I'm going into the juice and vitality of God."

Sometimes you pray by action. A New Mexican woman, Snowflake Flower, paints a sacred eagle feather on her pottery and thinks of the daughter, Patricia White Bull, who has come out of a coma after sixteen years. "When I paint the pottery," she is quoted as saying, "I paint [the feather] first, and I say, 'This is a prayer for you, Pat.' I feel better."[1]

Jeanie, a Reiki master, says she does not pray. Instead, she forms a kind of intention, a carefully thought-out statement describing a situation, then sends Reiki, or universal life force, to that situation, in whatever way will serve the highest good, assisting herself or any people involved to become open to change. She does not call it prayer.

I like the words of the Anglican monk Dom Chapman: "Pray as you can, not as you can't."

All languages are understood by God, Yahweh, Allah, Krishna, even our inarticulate moans, and we can take comfort that even when we do not know how to pray—

Likewise the Spirit helps us in our weakness. For we do not know how to pray as we ought, but the Spirit himself intercedes for us with sighs too deep for words. . . .

—Paul, Epistle to the Romans 8:26–27

A HUNDRED WAYS TO PRAY

or indeed that we are praying at all, as we hold the baby to our heart—the Spirit is praying in us.

In prayer you begin wherever you are—in anger or disgust, in jealousy, hurt, hate. In prejudice and intolerance, frustration, self-pity, or anxiety. I think they are all various expressions of fear; they arise from fear; they could be written out mathematically as divisor and dividend: jealousy/fear . . . hate/fear . . . bigotry/fear . . . frustration/fear. But dividing is not quite accurate either, for each emotion is undivided, pure, complete in itself, and real. The important thing in prayer is to speak with absolute honesty in your own voice, spontaneously whatever is in your heart. As you pray, the anger will drift away, replaced by other forms of grief. And each person will find her own voice by which to pray, in her own personal way.

A woman prayed that her agnostic husband learn to pray. One day he called her into the living room. "Listen to this music."

Okay, she was listening to the music.

"No, *listen!*" he said urgently, and suddenly she realized with a wash of humility that music was for him a form of prayer. He heard more in music than she did; it carried him to interior spaces where she could not follow.

Thich Nhat Hahn, the Buddhist priest and teacher, thinks of mindfulness as his prayer life. "How do I take in my food?" he asks, savoring with eyes, scent, taste. Each moment he is practicing awareness. "Present moment," he murmurs, "beautiful moment." The point is to be alive to every moment, as if coming on it fresh, alert, as innocent as the first time ever seen. (Or "Lonely moment, frightened moment.")

Margaret Poloma, a sociology professor at the Univer-

Breathing in, I know I am breathing in.
Breathing out, I know I am breathing out.
In/Out.
Breathing in, I see myself as a flower.
Breathing out, I see myself as fresh.
Flower/Fresh.
Breathing in, I see myself as a mountain.
Breathing out, I feel solid.
Mountain/Solid.
Breathing in, I see myself as still water.
Breathing out, I reflect things as they are.
Water/Reflecting.
Breathing in, I see myself as space.
Breathing out, I feel free.
Space/Free.[2]

sity of Akron, names four ways of praying: *colloquial,* or talking to God; *petitionary,* asking for things; *ritualistic;* and finally *meditative* or silent prayer, which is sometimes called contemplative or centering prayer. But I keep reverting to my earlier list of the four stair-steps of prayer:

1. Petition or supplication
2. Thankgiving
3. Praise or adoration
4. Union with God

We are always doing one or another of these prayers, even without knowing it, and therefore we shouldn't feel intimidated by the thought of beginning to pray or not knowing how to pray—and certainly not guilty that we keep returning to petition. We are always beginners in prayer.

Since we cannot achieve union by willpower (for it comes only by the grace of God), the prayers of praise and adoration are the most powerful ones that we can make, those that glorify God. Every religion underscores this fact. We think of the Jewish *Baruch atah, Adonai, Eloheinu, melech ha'olam*—"Blessed are thou, O Lord our God, King of the Universe." Or *Kadesh, kadesh, kadesh, Adonai tzvaot*—"Holy, holy, holy is the Lord God of hosts."

The same prayer appears in English, spoken or sung, in various Christian services. I think that every religion is glorifying God. The Muslims are singing, *"There is no God but God, adored is the Lord God, great is God, great is Al-lah."* They sing, *La Ilaha Ilalahu.*

But sometimes you cannot pray with praise and adoration. Sometimes so great is your distress that you cannot lift yourself to such a space. Then try to pray with thanks. I'll talk further about this principle below, and the importance of pulling yourself up into a state of gratitude. If you are upset, lost, if you are in pain yourself or grieving at the suffering of a friend, then *force yourself* to make a gratitude list, naming all those things for which you are grateful that day. "Count your blessings," my mother used to say with an impatient toss of her head, in scorn for our whining and complaints. She was of that disciplined generation that gave no weight to misery. Deliberately finding things you are thankful for moves you out of self-centered concerns, offers peace to the troubled soul. Is this a selfish thing to do, insensitive in the face of destruction or other people's hurt? I think not. For now your serenity flows outward onto others, blessing them.

I know a man who was walking one day on one of the soft dirt paths that wind through the beautiful heather of Nantucket. He felt blue. Nothing was wrong, but nothing was interesting either, or particularly good. He could think of no reason to be happy. He had heard of counting your blessings, however, and walking along, disgusted and disgruntled, he began to try. At first he could think of nothing to be grateful for. He looked at his hand.

All right, I'm grateful for my right hand, he thought resentfully, bringing it reluctantly to eye level. *I'm thankful for my muscles and thumb and for fingers that move and grip. . . .* He wasn't grateful. They were only words, but the more he looked at his hand, the more astonishing it appeared; and then there was his wrist, with the tendons that pulled his hand backward or forward, not to mention the brilliant way his forearm rotated on an elbow joint. Soon he was marveling at the intricacy of his hand, his wrist, his arm, his strong legs, his feet—with toes that permitted him to tramp along this golden path between the blooming pink rosebushes, and suddenly he *could see* the brilliant little flowers skylarking under a brazen blue dome. He almost fell to his knees in humility . . . and yet, he assured me, he was not certain there even was a God. Nonetheless, his prayer (for it was a prayer) shifted his attitude from bleakness into utter happiness and awe. It also brought him further questioning, for to whom was he grateful, or to what?

Make a gratitude list before you fall asleep. Lying in bed, going over the day just past, start to list the things you're grateful for (it's not even a prayer yet, just a list), and you will find that gratitude has blended into praise, and praise is gathering such delight that you hardly have time to notice it, before you fall into the pool of sleep. With gratitude for blessings poured on you and blessings

God, fill this night with radiance.
Let me sleep in peace and wake with joy to the light of the
new day.

you have garnered and given others, your sleep is quiet, deep, and sweet.

Often I think we make too much of this word, "prayer." It comes weighted with rituals and formalities, a heavy duty dragging at us, as something we're supposed to do right! When in fact, if you have an open and pure heart, there's no wrong way to pray! Recently I met a man, whom I'll call Joe. He had just returned from the Betty Ford Center in Palm Springs, California. He told his counselor that he didn't know how to pray.

"Just talk to God," said his counselor, with a shrug. "Nothing fancy." Margaret Poloma's "colloquial" prayer.

That evening Joe took two chairs out onto the lawn down by a lake. There was no one else around. He settled in one chair; the other was for God. He began to talk.

After a time another Betty Ford participant came along.

"What are you doing?" he asked Joe, starting to sit down.

"I am talking, but you can't sit there! *Don't sit in that chair! Do you know what you're doing!?*"

The other guy was confused. "No, what?"

"You're sitting on God! Get up! That's God's chair!"

"You oughta be in the loony bin," said the other man, and he stalked away.

The next night Joe went out to the lake again, carrying his two folding chairs. He was setting out his chairs when whom should he see coming across the lawn but the skeptic of the night before, lugging his own two chairs. By the time Joe left the Betty Ford Center, he says, the lawn at dusk was dotted with clients talking to their empty chairs, whispering to God.

At the other end of the spectrum is the prayer that I call simply "being." It takes no words.

I spoke earlier of my friend Isabelle. One Easter morning, she and her little granddaughter, then about three and a half, were sitting in the attic window seat of her house. She wanted to say something about this special Easter day, the day of the Resurrection of Christ.

"Charlotte," she said, peering deeply into the little girl's eyes with her intense, intelligent, probing gaze, "Charlotte, look at the sun shining in the blue sky. Look at the soft green leaves budding on the trees, and the golden daffodils. Look at this beautiful world God made!"

The little girl was looking at all this out the window, nodding with her grandmother and admiring, and then she turned, "Grandmom, what is God doing now?"

Isabelle was taken aback. "O Lord," she prayed in panic, "put your words in my mouth!"

When she looked down at her granddaughter, she answered, "God is loving you and me. He is loving this."

———

And still we hurt, we need.

"Pain has taught me much," says Orestes in *The Eumenides,* "and it has taught me the wisdom of ritual."[3]

In suffering we turn to the comfort of ritual, and especially to the customs of our tradition. If there are many ways to pray, there are many rituals as well, each with its cultural roots.

In hot, Eastern cultures people sit cross-legged on the floor. In Northern ones the custom is to sit on chairs, for who wants to sit or kneel on the cold stone floor of a Norman cathedral? In the Russian Orthodox tradition, which took root 1000 years ago in a climate even colder than that of medieval Europe, the congregation stands throughout the four- or five-hour services. Standing is a sign of respect and reverence.

"When the servant comes in from the field," wrote Brother Pimen, a Russian Orthodox monk in a letter to me on the subject, "he does not sit down to be served, but stands to serve his Master, and then he is served. In Church we are in the presence of the King of all. Shouldn't we stand?"

Western dress also encourages sitting or kneeling on furniture, just as central heating permits many people today to take up the Eastern habit of settling on cushions on the floor. But whatever the ritual, the purpose is to focus and concentrate the mind.

In the high Himalayas, where monks live at altitudes of 18,000 to 20,000 feet, and where maintaining a healthy body temperature is important, hard physical activity stimulates blood circulation. There the monks practice full-body prostrations. It's hard exercise! With folded hands, the devotee touches heart, throat, brow, then drops to his knees and with both arms extended thrusts his body forward until he is lying full length on the floor. Afterward he rises to his feet, hands folded and dropping from his forehead to his heart, to his sides. Each prostration is a prayer. (The word "prostration" comes from the Greek *proskinisis,* meaning "being a dog before" the One who is Adored.)

They say that in the preliminary practice you must make 100,000 prostrations in which body, mind, and speech are all three engaged, as you gesture from heart to throat to brow and then stretch out in full prostration.

As a devotee, you make 100,000 mandala offerings and repeat 100,000 syllables of a mantra—and *only then* are you ready for the real stuff!

Muslim prostration is somewhat different. Islam has rigorous rules on how to pray five times a day (or twelve!) and exactly what to say at each hour. In the Muslim tradition, the knees touch the ground first, and then forehead, nose, hands, and the soles of the curled toes. A good Muslim does not stretch out his hands "like a dog" but keeps them close to his sides, fingers closed.

"Glorified is my Lord, the Exalted," he recites. "Glory be to Thee Our Lord, and I praise Thee. Our Lord forgive me my sins."

In southern India the Hindus also make full-body prostrations, with eight parts of the body (*ashtanga:* "eight limbs") in contact with the ground to symbolize their utter surrender and submission to Almighty God.

In my own Episcopalian tradition we did not kneel to God but leaned grudgingly against the pew in front, chin propped on fist, elbow on one knee: chin, fist, elbow, knee. Nonetheless, there is great power in *kneeling,* as in full-body prostrations. I don't pretend to understand it; it's as though we have acupuncture points on the kneecaps that send the message more powerfully to the universe. But of course you don't kneel when swaying on the strap of a rush-hour bus, your mind in prayer. You fling all ritual aside. *Intention* is what matters. A ritual provides a form by which to hold the intention, that's all, but a ritual performed without prayerful intention is no more than a dry and desiccated, useless shell.

The Serenity Prayer[1]

God, grant me the Serenity to accept the things I cannot
   change;
Courage to change the things I can;
And wisdom to know the difference. . . .
Living one day at a time;
Enjoying one moment at a time;
Accepting hardships as the pathway to peace;
Taking, as He did, this sinful world as it is,
Not as I would have it;
Trusting that He will make all things right if I surren-
   der to His will;
That I may be reasonably happy in this life and
   supremely happy with Him, forever, in the next.

Chapter 13

The Principles of Petition

ount Leo Tolstoy tells the story. Once, long ago, two Christian monks, sailing along a coastline, came to a remote island. As they beached their boat, three hermits came running down the hillside toward them, their rags flapping about their knees. They kissed the newcomers' hands, weeping in welcoming delight at this visit from the two robed, saintly men.

"Now you can teach us how to pray," they said; for, not knowing how to make a proper prayer, the three friends in their simplicity had made one up. "We are a threesome. You are a threesome. Have mercy on us."

The visiting monks blessed the wild, mad hermits and smiled at one another, smug in their ability to teach the proper Christian ways, including the great Lord's Prayer. They wound their way up to their little hut, shared a meager supper, and later by the bead of a weak oil lamp, they instructed the hermits in the art of how to pray. They told them that if they followed directions diligently, with great discipline, and if their hearts were really settled in the right place, they might one day, after years of practice, even be able perhaps to perform the miracles of Christ: give sight to the blind and limbs to the lame! But the hermits would have to practice faithfully, they emphasized, to acquire any benefits. The hermits thanked them copiously, bowing to the earth, hands lifted in inexpressible gratitude for this teaching. The two monks promised to return in a year, to instruct them further in their prayers.

The next morning they provisioned their boat, bade the three hermits farewell, and unfurled the sail, sending the little boat seaward, skimming over the glittering water, when suddenly they heard a voice calling behind them.

"Wait! Wait!" They looked behind, and here came one of the hermits, skirts lifted, running full tilt over the waves.

"Wait! I've forgotten how to pray!"

Everyone knows how to pray. Stab anyone, and he will pray. A cry of outrage is a prayer. A whimper. A plea for help. The shaking of your fist at God. The one thing is . . . it's heartfelt, short, and real. There are many books on prayer, and many souls more qualified than I to speak of how to pray. But I will set down what I have come to understand over the years, by experience and observation, and perhaps it will be helpful to someone on the path.

You begin with the rudimentary one, the prayer of petition and need.

When you have a fire in your house, you do not call the fire department and explain, "The curtains in the bedroom are on fire, and I think you are going to need a truck and a number-two hose, and—oh, dear, the fire has spread to the rugs. You'd better bring some foam."

THE PATH OF PRAYER

No, you run to the phone and yell, "Fire! Help!"

So the first rule of *asking* in prayer is to be short. The second is sincerity—to be as simple and innocent as a child.

Not long ago I met a beautiful and deeply spiritual woman, Karen, whose fifteen-year-old son had been diagnosed with a form of autism, with its characteristic developmental delays. As a single parent, Karen is protective of Adam, who has experienced ridicule and isolation both by his peers and by adults who misinterpret his behavior.

But it turns out the boy has special gifts.

One day a colleague at work invited Karen and her two children to dinner. After spending an evening with them, this colleague dropped into Karen's office next day to tell her how delightful her son was. She said that perhaps Karen didn't know that he was a teacher.

"What do you mean?" Karen asked.

"Well, he didn't have to come in this time."

"Come in?"

"Into this lifetime. All the qualities that most people on this plane are trying to master—trust, honesty, unconditional love—he has already mastered, and I believe," she continued, "that he is here to teach others how to learn."

This was Karen's first indication that Adam might be special.

Karen's mother had also noticed it. Karen's mother never took much care of herself. At the age of 83 she learned that she had not only an intestinal obstruction but arteriosclerosis. She needed a colostomy, which would leave her with a colon bag, but because of the atrophied blood vessels and very small blood flow to her legs, there was also the threat that one or both legs might have to be amputated.

There was a 75 percent chance she would not survive the surgery. But if she did, she could look forward to the C-bag, nursing care, and the agony of being bed-bound for the rest of her life. Now she asked her daughter if Adam would say a special prayer for her when the little family met at bedtime for prayers.

Karen explained to her son in simple terms what would happen to his grandmother and asked him to pray for her during the two or three days before the operation.

His prayer was innocent. "God, please don't let my grandma have a bag of poop on her belly, and please don't cut off her legs. She wants to go back to her house on the beach and be able to look out at the ocean."

For the next three days they prayed each night. "My grandma doesn't want this bag. . . . My grandma wants her legs. . . ."

When it was time for the surgery, the doctors found they could do a section without a colostomy. Neither did they have to amputate her legs, because for some reason her blood was flowing in her legs just fine!

She stayed in the hospital for three months, and later she went a rehab center to learn to walk again. Adam visited her, they prayed together, and she continued to ask him for his nightly prayers. Within three weeks she was discharged and sent back home.

But a change had taken place. Formerly a negative woman, Karen's mother is now happy, caring for others, inquiring about her grandchildren, aware and grateful for everything she has and for the four children who support her. All this came suddenly out of her distress.

But that's not all.

Two months afterward, one Friday afternoon, Karen's

sister, Sue, went to the doctor, who confirmed a lump in her breast. The surgeon said it was significant enough to operate immediately, and he scheduled surgery for Monday. He completed the imaging workup that same Friday afternoon, marking the exact spot on her breast for surgery three days later.

"I'm not going to give you a good weekend," said the doctor.

Sue called Karen and asked Adam to pray for her. Again Karen took her son aside and explained about the lump that had been found in his aunt's breast and how she might have to have one breast removed. "And you know how she likes to wear open blouses. I think her breasts are important to her, don't you?"

Adam prayed. "God, Aunt Sue has a bubble in her breast. We need you to take it away, because Aunt Sue's breasts are very important to her and we don't want you to take one off."

Over the weekend they repeated the prayer in different words. On Monday, Adam's Aunt Sue drove to the hospital, entered the operating room . . . and was told that the doctors could find no lump!

"Please don't put me through this again."

But the surgeon said, "Look, I can't operate on you blindly. I'm not going to go in with a knife, not knowing where I'm going. Come back in a month."

A month later, when she returned, no lump could be found. Since then Adam's prayers have produced more miracles.

Oh, if only we *all* had an Adam praying for us! If only we *all* could pray with the innocence of a child! If you want to know how to pray, that's the trick: You pray with perfect faith and simpleness. Unfortunately, innocence is not easy to acquire. Which is why, as adults, we undertake the disciplines that children do not need to do—of praying for ourselves, to forgive ourselves, to have souls clear as glass. Illuminated. Filled. Then, sometimes, we experience those moments when man, and all else, is known to be divine.

"If you do not make yourself equal to God," wrote Joseph Campbell in *Occidental Mythology,* "you cannot apprehend God; for like is known by like." He was quoting from the gnostic *Corpus Hermeticum.* How can we manage except by prayer?

I said earlier that scientific experiments with seedlings indicate that undirected prayer is twice as effective as directed prayer. From this we might conclude that we should never ask for what we want. The fact is, we can't help ourselves. Jesus himself told us to ask for what we need.

"Put me to the test, says the Lord of hosts, if I will not open the windows of heaven for you and pour down for you an overflowing blessing." (Malachi 3:10)

We are enjoined again and again to ask. We can pray for *anything!*

"For whatever you ask in my name, I will do it . . . if you ask anything in my name, I will do it," says John 13:13,14; and Luke: "Fear not, little flock, for it is your Father's good pleasure to give you the kingdom."

Prayer is a law of the universe, like gravity. You don't even have to believe in God to ask, but there are certain principles, and although they can be bent, we might as well respect and use them if we can. I have written of this in other books. Imagine that there is a giant radio station out in space, beyond the stars, a receiving station, and all you have to do is to beam your desire to that station. If it is received clearly, without static, the answer will come pouring down in abundance, with insights, comfort, miracles, and help.

So the question is how to send that thought in such a way it can be heard?

- You ask.
- You notice when the answer comes.
- You say thank you, and then you pass the gift along.

Asking

There are four rules to asking, and they are similar to those concerning affirmations.

First, you use the present tense, for the universe does not understand the past or future. It has no concept of time. All things happen simultaneously at a spiritual level, and Spirit knows only *now.*

Second, you phrase your prayer in a positive voice, for again the universe has no conception of "not." There is no "lack" or "absence" in the spiritual world, but only possibility—and therefore no recognition of what's negative.

Many people do not know this, so that the mother may be praying on her knees, with all the yearning of her heart, "Don't let my baby die." But there are two negatives in her prayer—the "not" of "don't" and the word "die." Does the universe receive the cruel whisper, "Let my baby die"?

Much better for the mother to voice what her heart is longing for: "Let my baby live!" Or even better, to express thanks and gratitude for what has already come to pass, since the universe has no concept of time. "Thank you that my baby lives!" Give thanks! Give praise!

It is imperative that we guard the language of our

thoughts. If we pray, "Don't let my baby die," we are, against our very will, imagining the future loss and already grieving and mourning it.

Nonetheless, I have to admit, even if the mother prays "Don't let my baby die," her heart may be speaking its own silent language, demanding that her baby live, and what is received by that radio station, therefore, out on the far fringes of space, may represent her heartfelt prayer, her desire having overpowered fear. Remember that Adam prayed in his innocence that his aunt's breast *not* be removed or his grandmother's legs cut off!

Amen, you say. Amen.

Does everyone know that "amen" means "so be it"? Or, with absolute confidence, *It is so!* With the word "amen," we claim our prayer! We cry out. *Yes!* and *It is done!*

This brings us to this matter of belief. Or doubt. Some people pray correctly on their knees and in submission and with the proper language. They are careful to articulate in gratitude their desire for having the wishes of their hearts fulfilled—and then they are swept by doubt. *What am I doing? Here I am sitting on my knees! Thank God no one can see me here. This is absurd, there isn't any God. My*

*Therefore, I say unto you, if you have faith and doubt not . . .
whatever you ask in prayer, believing, you shall receive.*

—Matthew 21:21,22

At an acceptable time, O God, in the abundance of your steadfast love, answer me.

—Psalm 69

prayer is not going to be answered! What is received is static, the fervent prayer, followed by the negation of the same, expressed in "I disbelieve, prayers aren't answered."

To which thought should a loving universe attend?

If the doubt and negation are stronger than the longing heart, the universe will give you doubt, so willing is Providence to provide everything, even pain and doubt and despair and isolation and alienation and fear, if that is what we want.

Fourth, after holding in your attention *even for a few seconds* the idea of the completed, answered prayer, having remained in this state of prayerfulness and perhaps even having fallen into the light, in which you know the prayer was heard, then you release the need. Open your hand to acceptance of life. "Thy will be done!" you add, or "This or something better, for the highest good of all."

We release it, because God knows more about what is best for us than we do ourselves, which is why folk wisdom advises us to be careful what we pray for—lest we receive our wish.

Noticing

The second requirement of prayer is to notice when it has been answered, and again many people receive the answers to their prayers and then ignore or deny them, because the answers did not come in the expected way or time frame. We're like children when the ice cream truck comes by ringing its bell, and we run inside to our mothers saying, "Mom, Mom, can I have an ice cream?"

"Not now," she says, "it's almost dinnertime. You can have one after dinner."

"No," says the child, "I want it *now*."

Or she says, "Yes, but that ice cream is too expensive, I have a quart in the freezer. Have some of that."

"No!" cries the child. "I want the ice cream from the *truck*."

Or her mother says, "Yes, here is a dollar."

In each case she gave her child an ice cream, but the child believes she gave it only in the last example.

That's how it is with prayer. Many times we refuse to see the answer. I think that this step of recognition is the one that most eludes extreme rationalists—those who admit the existence of nothing beyond the material world—and perhaps it frightens them as well, challenging, as it does, that voice of skepticism and scorn, rebellion, fear, and need to control that resides in all of us. I think this step of recognition is the most difficult hurdle to prayer. The alternative, after all, is terrifying. What if we are not in command at all? What if we're utterly alone? Most of us, however, as we get older, come to the realization that there is more out there than we can readily explain. We aren't in control of anything. I have yet to meet an atheist who at the moment of peril, against his will, does not cry out, "Oh, help!"

Responding

The final act of prayer is to respond. Once we have noticed that the answer has been given, this last step comes naturally. You accept the gift with all wonder, joy, and gratitude, saying "Thank you," humbly, and then *you*

THE PATH OF PRAYER

Give, and it will be given to you. A good measure, pressed down, shaken together, running over, will be put into your lap. . . .

—Luke 6:38

pass it on. The reason you pass the gift along is that the energy must circulate, and gratitude requires that you give away your delight.

I know a man who, on learning that his son would survive an operation, walked to the hospital blood bank and donated a pint of blood in gratitude for answered prayer. A woman, receiving the relationship she wanted with her mate, phoned a friend to report her answered prayer. Another woman wrote a check to charity in gratitude for answered prayer. We find different ways to demonstrate our thanks and love, and when we do, the very universe tilts with joy, for Spirit loves to be thanked, and, once thanked, I promise you, it pours more blessings forth, abundance falling on our heads, anointing us with oil.

A Hindu Prayer

(Shanti path—hymn of peace)

There is peace in the heavenly region, there is peace in
the atmosphere; peace reigns on the earth; there is
coolness in the water, the medicinal herbs are healing;
the plants are peace-giving; there is harmony in the
celestial objects and perfection in eternal knowledge;
everything in the universe is peaceful; peace
pervades everywhere. May that peace come to me!

May there be peace, peace, peace.

Chapter 14

The Prayers of Light

The Bhagavad Gita, the Hindu sacred text, notes that four kinds of people direct their prayers to God.

1. Those with wishes, desires, needs
2. Those in grief
3. Those seeking knowledge
4. Enlightened beings

Of these, the prayers of the enlightened being are most powerful, because that person lives like Adam, innocent as a child in the bliss of God, right there in the middle of the source of love. I don't know if enlightened beings pray without ever *asking,* but asking is what we lesser beings do, if only to build up reservoirs of faith. We'll need the trust and faith in difficult times; we'll need a bank account to draw upon. But there are other prayers besides petition, and many ways to make a prayer, and so we come to the following suggestions for cleansing and empowering yourself in order that you can, like an enlightened master, become a vehicle of prayer yourself. It's not impossible; it's what we're supposed to do. These prayers can be done on your knees or sitting comfortably, as you choose.

Because they take concentration, however, I recommend that you do not practice them while walking down the street or driving a car or traveling on the subway, where you need all your wits about you.

Beginning

You begin with yourself.

Remember the story of the little girl who prayed, "Lord Jesus Christ, have mercy on *me-ee*"? There is no sense in praying for someone else if you do not have the power and inner resources to send out strength for them. We forget this fact. We pray for the healing of a cancer-ridden child and forget to pray for the parents to find the courage to bear her illness and her loss. Or we pray for restoration of our broken love relationship and neglect to pray for our own happiness. We are overcome by doubt and pray to push our own solution through, forgetting to ask to have our doubts removed. Or faith restored. We forget to *ask* to be shown that something there is on our side.

I think it's important to begin prayers with yourself, praying for help, praying for understanding and insight, praying for all the qualities and clarity you think you need, in order that you may be a clear and light-strewn vessel for the use of God, in order that your prayers for others will have more weight. How? There are several ways, from the simplest heartfelt request to long meditations. Here is only one. Read through it, adjust it to your own lifestyle, use it as you will:

First, ground and center yourself. You sit comfortably,

your feet resting flat on the floor or on a stool to steady you—because to pray requires energy at the same time that it gives you energy. You must be balanced, stable. Imagine that there are roots growing from the soles of your feet deep into the earth, grounding, steadying you; imagine that the energy of the earth is moving up these roots and into you. Put your attention on your breath. Watch two or three breaths, as they pass in and out of your nostrils. Breathe. *In . . . out.*

Scan your body, moving upward from the ground. Relax your feet. Relax the calves of your legs. Relax your thighs. Scan your hips and stomach, the trunk of your body, feel your sit-bones on the chair. Notice the right angle your body makes with your thighs. Watch your breathing. *In . . . out.* Relax.

Drop your shoulders, relax your arms and hands, relax your neck. Feel your head floating on the column of your neck. Relax your face, relax your cheeks, your tongue, your jaw, your eyes.

Now visualize a column of white light entering the crown of your head, moving down into your body, flooding you with light. It pours into your skull, your mouth, around your eyes, out your nostrils, down your neck, into your shoulders, into your chest—the whole trunk of your body is filled with light. From your feet you receive earth energy. From your crown you receive the light of heaven. Feel yourself disappear into the light. Now allow your compassion to touch anyplace in you that hurts, emo-

There is only love or illness, and if you do not love, you will get ill.

—Sigmund Freud

THE PRAYERS OF LIGHT

tionally or physically. Send the light to any sore or fear or uncertainty, the light of love.

Now let your awareness move out gently toward one whom you love. Surround her—or him—with light. Ask nothing, for the organism will always reach toward the highest good. Hold your loved one in the light.

Using the Light

Not long ago at a workshop in Texas, a woman asked how you hold someone in the light. I was surprised. I had to stop and think how to respond, for I consider this a basic principle of prayer. I don't know if she was satisfied with my answer. But I'll set down here the exercise we did. You'll notice how close it is to the first instruction, in praying for yourself.

As in that earlier direction, you begin by grounding or centering yourself. You scan your body. Watch your breathing, calm your thoughts, and fill yourself with a sense of the beauty around you, the presence of the Holy Spirit. Now draw white light into the crown of your head and allow it to flood your body, as in the prayer above.

Now visualize or name the person you are praying for.

You are surrounded by the light. Spread it outward to enfold the other, too. Now both of you are encapsulated by the light.

Ask the Source, "Dear God, what would you have me pray for?" Now allow yourself to move into a wordless silence. . . .

Perhaps the light is so clear and bright that you disappear in it. Perhaps it comes only as a soft gray mist. Perhaps it reveals itself as a gentle nudging toward some action, a word, an unexpected understanding of something you must do. You hold the person in this light of love until the prayer releases you, then open your eyes and move about your day.

But there is another way to pray the light. Jim Gore, a graduate of the U.S. Naval Academy who worked after World War II with the Atomic Energy Commission, became concerned in the 1960s by the threat of nuclear war. He quit his job to devote his life to prayer. He founded United Research, based in North Carolina, and developed what he called Effective Prayer, releasing all negative fears, then announcing oneself a being of light, a carrier of light, radiating light. Here is the prayer he taught:

1. *I release all of my past, negatives, fears, human relationships, self-image, future, human desires, concepts of sex and money, judgment and communication to the Light.*
2. *I am a Light Being.*
3. *I radiate the Light from my Light Center throughout my being.*
4. *I radiate the Light from my Light Center to everyone.*
5. *I radiate the Light from my Light Center to everything.*
6. *I am in a bubble of Light and only Light can come to me and only Light can be here.*
7. *Thank you, God, for everything, for everyone and for me.*

His prayer is similar to the famous one from Unity School of Christianity:

The light of God surrounds us.
The love of God enfolds us.
The power of God protects us.

The presence of God watches over us.
Wherever we are, God is!

Or this one, with its reference to Christ, in which you visualize yourself surrounded by Christ light. Some people substitute "angels" for the Christ, and others, I imagine, use Yahweh, Allah, or whatever name is theirs for goodness, protection, and superior love.

Christ above me,
Christ below me,
Christ to the right of me,
Christ to the left of me,
Christ behind me,
Christ before me,
Surrounded in the Light of Christ.

Forgiveness Prayers

Every religion and every spiritual path maintains that you cannot pray well until you have forgiven your brother, your neighbor, your so-called enemy, for half of praying is merely getting clear, lifting your vibration, and coupling the spiritual connection. The other half is sending thought out toward another, as demonstrated in the preceding section. We forgive in order to be clear and innocent.

I have a friend, Jane, who one day was driving across

"Whenever you stand praying," said Jesus, "forgive, if you have anything against anyone; so that your Father in heaven may also forgive you your trespasses."

—Mark 11:25

*Cleanse the thoughts of our hearts by the inspiration of thy
Holy Spirit, that we may perfectly love thee, and worthily
magnify thy holy name; through Christ Our Lord.*

—"The Collect for Purity," The Book of Common Prayer

the Potomac River and past the Lincoln Memorial on her
way to work when she was struck with this thought:
What would it be like if I knew I had everything?

The light flickered on the river and flashed against the
white frieze of the memorial.

Why, I could forgive them all! The thought came unbidden—meaning everyone she ever knew or did not know,
herself, the warring parties in the Middle East, her bosses
and co-workers, the driver just then cutting her off—forgive everyone. *She would be free!*

Here is one forgiveness exercise: On a piece of paper
write the names of everyone who has hurt or offended
you, anyone whom you resent, anyone you're angry with.
In another column put down the names of all those
whom you have hurt or offended in any way. You may
find the same names on both lists, because often we hate
the person whom we've hurt. Look over the list. Think!
Each person is a teacher, each situation a gift, an opportunity, a challenge.

Now pray for two weeks for each name on the list (this
includes yourself!). At first this may be so hard that you
can only mouth distastefully, "God, give the bastard
what he deserves!" That's all right to start. But as you
continue to pray each day, you'll find your intention
changing, softening, as does your attitude toward your
enemy. Watch what happens as happiness begins to flood
your heart.

I am told that the Buddha spent two hours a day praying the *metta* or forgiveness prayer found on pages 201–204. As with the prayers above, the *metta* prayer begins with oneself and expands outward, until it encompasses all beings, known and unknown, visible and invisible, in all dimensions and on all worlds. Try it. By the time you finish, you'll feel wonderful! Did the Buddha practice this forgiveness prayer because he was so pure, or because the daily confusions of life splash mud even on enlightened souls, so that we must constantly keep washing the windows clean?

I have a friend, John Sack, a gorgeous writer, who has written several books on hate and war. In one *Esquire* article he described hatred and what it does to you:

> Let's say I'm in love with someone, I don't tell myself, Uh-oh, I've got inside of me two pounds of love, and if I love her and *love* her, then I'll use all of my love up—I'll be out of love. No, I understand and we all understand that love is a paradoxical thing, that the more we send out, the more we've got. So, why don't we understand that about hate? If we hate, and we act on that hate, then we hate even more later on. If we spit out a drop of hate, we stimulate the saliva glands and we produce . . . a drop and a half, then two drops, three, a teaspoon, tablespoon, a Mount Saint Helens. The more we send out, the more we've got, until we are perpetual-motion machines, sending out hate and hate until we've created a holocaust. . . . Hate . . . is a muscle, and if we want to be monsters, all we have to do is exercise it. To hate the Germans, to hate the Arabs, to hate the Jews. The longer we exercise it, the bigger it gets, as if every day we curl forty pounds and, far from being worn out, in time we are curling fifty, sixty, we are the Mr. Universe of Hate. . . . We can de-

Self–scrutiny is a stark and shattering experience. It pul–
verizes the stoutest ego. But true self–analysis mathematically
operates to produce seers. The way of "self–expression," individual
acknowledgments, results in egotists, sure of the right to their private
interpretations of God and the universe.

—Paramahansa Yogananda

stroy the people we hate, *maybe,* but we surely destroy
ourselves.[1]

"Hate" is a strong word. Maybe we don't *hate.* But we
all get irritated by a neighbor's construction project, or
by the way our mother or wife or husband (the person
closest to us) offers advice. We all get our feelings hurt. It
helps to pray for help in forgiving these minor annoy-
ances. Moreover, our irritation requires that we look at
our own behavior and attitudes—and who can bear to do
this without help? Surely we must pray for ourselves as
well. We need to forgive ourselves.

The curious thing is that forgiveness *always* comes
when you ask for it, and it always comes full-fledged and
fine. There's enough to go around! Forgiveness is like
sunlight pouring down, the warmth of which is not diminished or used up no matter how many people are sitting in the light. In the parable of the laborers (such a
difficult text!), Jesus recounts how the owner of a field
goes out to the labor pool one morning and hires laborers
to harvest his fields. He agrees to pay them a certain
price. At noon he sees that he needs more men and again
walks down to the market, where the unemployed workers are lounging against the wall, smoking, gossiping,
and bored. He signs up more men and sends them to the

fields, *agreeing to pay them the same amount of money as the men who've been working there since dawn.* At three in the afternoon he goes a final time to the labor pool and sweeps up every man he can find. He sends them into the fields to work, and he pays them *the same amount as the other two groups.* Not the same hourly wage but the same total sum!

Everything about this parable offends our Western ethic. It's not fair.

It's against our principles to pay a man who worked for two hours the same as a man who worked for ten (unless he's the CEO, in which case he may be paid ten thousand times more than the employee). But that's how it is with forgiveness and God's grace. There's enough for everybody, the same uncounted and generous amount. Stand in the sunlight and you will be warmed. Kneel in the pool of forgiveness and you will be cleansed; there's enough for everyone to wash.

If you cannot pray to forgive—or if you cannot forgive yourself—then pray for the *willingness* to forgive.

I used to be a little afraid of the Lord's Prayer, with its cautionary counsel: *"Forgive us our trespasses, as we forgive those who trespass against us."* "No, no!" I wanted to cry. "Forgive me better than that! Forgive me with all your grace, for I am so poor at forgiving others, it's so hard." Yet all the time I knew that unless I could forgive completely everyone whom I disliked, I could not receive full grace—the light, the light! There would always be this ink spot staining the pearl of my soul. Eventually I learned to pray to acquire the willingness and strength and courage to forgive, and eventually I learned also that I had to make these efforts at forgiveness every day. It's a never-ending task, for every day there is someone else who irritates or upsets me—the salesclerk who moves too slowly for my selfish needs, the neighbor using a noisy leaf blower, or the family member who bumps up against an ancient childhood sore. *If I am forgiven only to the degree that I forgive others . . . then I'm lost! Dear God, I beg for mercy, grace.*

Forgiving is one of the hardest things to do, but it's another of those laws of the universe expounded and laid out clearly by Jesus. Condemn and judge and you'll feel nasty, condemned, and judged; forgive and you'll feel forgiven. Give, and measureless bounty will be poured on you.

The question is, how to do it?

The Buddhist Metta or Forgiveness Prayer

This last exercise is difficult to do all by yourself until you have memorized the text. I recommend that you first work it together with another person—or, better yet, in a prayer circle. Allow a good twenty minutes. One person should be designated as the "reader," allowing enough time between phrases so the others can repeat each phrase silently, breathing compassion into space.

Later you will be able to practice this forgiveness prayer by yourself, but it is always more powerful in a group. Go very slowly. Take your time. Return constantly to awareness of your breath.

You begin by going into a quiet meditative state.

Sit quietly. Center yourself. Relax. Scan your body. Breathe. Allow your thoughts to grow calm. Put your awareness on your nostrils, watching as the breath moves in and out the portals of the body. Just watch your breath. Make no effort to control it. Soon the person reading will slowly begin the prayer, taking her time, pausing at each set of dots long enough for you to repeat the phrase just heard silently to yourself, to let it resonate, to take another breath. . . .

The prayer begins with yourself.

———

May I be forgiven for all offenses that I have committed . . . knowingly and unknowingly . . . by thought, word, and deed. . . . May I be forgiven for them all. (Breathe.)

May I forgive all those who have offended me . . . knowingly and unknowingly . . . by thought, word, or deed. . . . May I forgive them all. (Breathe.)

May I be well and happy . . . free of suffering and pain . . . liberated. (Breathe.)

(Here the word "liberated" means "reached full enlightenment"—liberated from self-seeking, the illusions and deceptions of ego. It means to be liberated into truth. Joy. Peace. Love.)

———

Extend your awareness outward to encompass someone you love without reservation—this is not a lover or relationship partner but someone (even an animal) whom you love unconditionally:

May this person be forgiven for all offenses that he has committed . . . knowingly and unknowingly . . . by thought, word, or deed. . . . May he be forgiven for them all. (Breathe.)

May he forgive all those who have offended him . . . knowingly and unknowingly . . . by thought, word, or deed. . . . May he forgive them all. (Breathe.) *May he be well and happy . . . free of suffering and pain . . . liberated.* (Breathe.)

———

Extend your awareness to a total stranger—the bus driver, perhaps, or the waiter at a restaurant.

May this stranger be forgiven of all offenses she has commit-

ted . . . knowingly and unknowingly . . . by thought, word, or deed. . . . May this person be forgiven for them all. (Breathe.)

May this person forgive all those who have offended her . . . knowingly and unknowingly . . . by thought, word, or deed. . . . May she forgive them all. (Breathe.)

May she be well and happy . . . free of suffering and pain . . . liberated. (Breathe.)

This next segment takes practice: *Put your awareness on someone who has hurt or angered you. Repeat the formula for that person, breathing out forgiveness, compassion, and well-being on your so-called enemy.* If this part is too difficult to do at first, you may skip this discipline until your practice is more strongly developed. Move now to all those in your house.

Extend your awareness to all beings in your house or apartment complex.

May all those in this house be forgiven for all offenses they have committed . . . knowingly or unknowingly . . . by thought, word, or deed. . . .

May all those in this house forgive all those who have offended them . . . knowingly or unknowingly . . . by thought, word, or deed. . . . May they forgive them all. . . . (Breathe.) *May they be well and happy . . . free of suffering and pain . . . liberated.* (Breathe.)

Extend your awareness outward to encompass your entire block or geographical area, and repeat the prayer. . . .

Extend outward to all beings in your city or county. . . .

Extend your awareness to include all living beings in your nation. . . .

Then all beings in this hemisphere. . . .

Now wrap your awareness around this little globe floating through the immensity of space and stars. *May all beings on this planet be forgiven. . . .*

Now send your awareness out to the farthest reaches of
the universe, beyond the stars, to all beings visible and
invisible. . . .

*May all beings known and unknown, in all dimensions, visible
and invisible . . . be forgiven for any offenses they have committed . . . knowingly or unknowingly by thought, word, or
deed. . . . May they be forgiven of them all. . . .* (Breathe.)

*May all beings known and unknown, visible and
invisible . . . be forgiven of any offenses they have committed . . .
knowingly or unknowingly . . . by thought, word, or deed.*
(Breathe.)

*May all beings be well and happy, free of suffering and
pain. . . . May they all be liberated.* (Breathe.)

Now rest in the center of this globe of forgiveness,
breathing love and forgiveness everywhere!

When and How Long to Pray

Once the Dalai Lama was asked how long a busy person
should spend in prayer. He thought a moment, scratching his ear and squirming, as he does, then lifted his eyes
with a brilliant smile.

"I don't think anyone needs to pray for more than four
hours a day," he said brightly.

The Dalai Lama, who considers himself an ordinary
monk, rises each day at 3:00 A.M. to spend "four leisurely
hours," as he puts it, in prayer and meditation. I can

attest to the power of that predawn time, when the salty silence of black night quivers to your thoughts. Meditation seems deeper then, prayers stronger. But I like to think there's no bad time to pray.

Nonetheless, it's helpful to have a daily discipline. Some people practice morning or evening prayer or, like medieval monks, they organize their waking lives into seven periods of prayer or, like devout Muslims, into five or more. These aren't long prayers—five minutes, ten—but for those moments the forward march of time, *chronos,* is overlaid with broader *kairos,* God's eternal and immortal timelessness. Without your noticing, things in your life will shift.

To a certain extent the *form* of your prayer will determine when you do it and for how long. Are you praying with words out loud? Are you writing them down in a struggle to express your truth? Are you sitting in silence, simply listening for God's response? Sometimes you decide to nurture your relationship by committing yourself to praying for a month, a year, or more in a particular place each day for a predetermined length of time. At other times you pray until you feel it's done. How do you know it's done? At a certain moment you'll feel a *click,* like a lock on a box, and you know your prayer is complete; then you rise and go about your day in calm serenity. For if you practice, if you pray in a disciplined way, you will remain in a prayerful state even in distraction. I think of Martin Luther claiming that he couldn't possibly get everything done with less than three hours of prayer a day. That's why the Dalai Lama or the nuns of Mother Teresa spend hours in prayer: They're building up a bank account to draw upon during the rest of the day.

THE PRAYERS OF LIGHT

When You Cannot Pray

Yet still there are those times when your heart rebels. Sometimes, no matter what we do, we cannot pray. I have gone through long periods when, to my dismay, it has been impossible to pray. My tongue cleaves to the roof of my mouth. Everything in me rebels! I want to run away and play! Well, you know what? That's what should be done. I think that God loves us when we sing and dance. I think God loves our romping with our children or the dogs, just loving everything that love created on this earth. Aren't these prayers, too? What I do in such times is to loosen the reins and just stop forcing discipline. There's a delicate balance to be maintained. The need and desire to pray will come back in its own time.

Or else you change the way you pray. St. Teresa of Ávila advised her nuns to use Scripture reading to jump-start prayer in these times of difficulty.

"When a fire is going down," she wrote, "you toss twigs on it, not a tree. Take just a phrase, just a small story, to build up the fire of your prayer."

When you cannot pray, then gently tend the fire of your prayers. Be patient with yourself as well, and give yourself some room. It's not supposed to be a chore. A horse will fight the bit that holds his head too tight. Loosen up the reins. Be playful in your prayers.

A Muslim Prayer

O God, give me the light in my heart and light in my tongue and light in my hearing and light in my sight and light in my feeling and light in all my body and light before me and light behind me.

Give me, I pray Thee, light on my right hand and light on my left hand and light above me and light beneath me, O Lord. Increase light within me and in light illuminate me.

Chapter 15

Some Prayers to Practice On

It is important as we move between the various stages of prayer, exploring our own paths, that we do it without guilt. No fault. No wrong. Just as a mother with ten children loves each one differently and each with equal love, so is the relationship of God to each one of us individual and rich, but always it is delivered as the path to your own soul, to "home," to perfect satisfaction, and to love. Find your own way on the spiritual path, whether in church or temple or outdoors in nature, in the cathedral of God. Worship however you can. But for those who may not know how even to begin this search, or who want to test their strength on new trails, leading to the center, to their souls, to love, here are some time-honored ones to practice on.

Reducing the Words

Take any prayer you like. Think about it. Cut it down to three or four words. For example, if you choose the Lord's Prayer, reduce it to: "Feed me, forgive me, guard me" (you are free to choose your own few words). You may decide you prefer "Give, forgive, protect" or "Father, bread, power." This will be your prayer. Repeat it for a week as often as you like.

Now reduce it to one word. Which word do you choose? Perhaps the word "Father" or "Daddy." Perhaps you select "forgive" or "give" or "guard" or "help" or "adore" or "yes." Pray on this one word for several days, a week.

Now cut out that word.

Pray without words.

Centering Prayer

"Nothing in all creation," wrote Meister Eckhart, "is so like God as stillness." The challenge becomes to calm our restless thoughts and rest in the stillness of God.

Father Thomas Keating in his beautiful book *Open Mind, Open Heart* describes the practice of centering prayer, or resting in God.

Place yourself in a quiet holy space, either a physical or interior one. With an empty mind, leave your troubles. The ancient, age-old method of achieving this stillness is by repeating a mantra, a sacred word or phrase.

I think that it's best to receive a mantra from an illumined being, because such a holy one can choose the mantra that matches your individual soul and he (or she) will "enliven it" by the shuddering electrical spiritual power known as *shakti*. Then the very sound brings peace and calm to your soul. But if you have no such privilege, follow the example of Father Keating. Sit quietly someplace where you cannot be disturbed. Decide to remain for a certain amount of time—10 minutes, 20 minutes, more if you are accustomed to this practice.

SOME PRAYERS TO PRACTICE ON

Choose any sacred word or phrase—"grace," perhaps, or "hallelujah" or "angels above." Perhaps you might choose a phrase from one of the Psalms: "My shepherd." Repeat it silently to yourself. I guarantee that in seconds your restless mind will flip off, haring after another idea. Gently nudge your roving mind back to the sacred word. You are training the mind toward stillness.

Another method of achieving stillness is to watch your breathing. In . . . (you notice) . . . out. . . . This is the Buddhist practice. With each breath, think, *Breath of God.* This is itself a mantra. *Breath of God.* And *God is breathing in you.* When your mind runs away, bring it gently home to the breath, to God, and this you do again and again, with neither anger nor annoyance (since it's the function of the mind to run about). Gradually you will train the mind, like a good dog, to enjoy just sitting still. To be alert, aware. To remain centered on God.

Remember that you may begin on one path of prayer and in a while feel drawn to another, then find that as the weeks or the years pass that you want to go back to the first. The soul will tell you what it needs. The universe will call you by its grace. All you have to do is remain open to the invitation, and when in doubt . . . just *ask!*

The Prayer of Silence

I think our forebears had an easier time of it than we have today, assaulted as we are by radio, television, movies, cars, phones, faxes, Internet, e-mail. But when your soul longs for silence, you must pay attention to the call. Silence is the way of the mystic, and our present life does not always give us time to slow down, grow still enough to hear the whispered guidance of our hearts. Have you ever considered going on a media fast? Stop reading the

You have made us for yourself, O Lord,
And our hearts are restless until they rest in you.

—Augustine of Hippo

newspapers for a week, don't watch TV or listen to your CDs or the radio. Listen to the silence of just being. At first you may find it hard, but soon you'll notice that you are growing happier and happier! Count your blessings, make your gratitude lists. You'll be amazed at how the world continues to turn without your attention focused on it. As you move toward your natural interior rhythms, you touch your soul. Then even corporate worship may feel like a distraction from your joy in God.

For years I have found the Sunday services at the Episcopal church, the church of my cradle religion, too noisy to attend. There wasn't any time to *pray!* We were constantly opening and closing books, standing, kneeling, singing, chanting, or responding to the minister, who would no sooner have begun one prayer (in an irritating Episcopalian singsong clip) than he'd moved on to the next: prayers for the church, for the bishop, for the president of the United States, for people suffering in wars. . . ."Hear our prayer," the congregation intones, as if God needed that. Or "Lord, have mercy on us." Where was the timeless silence in which to enfold each prayer and send it out on loving wings?

For years I avoided church. But recently I have found how to let these corporate book-prayers wash over me, while I enter prayerful emptiness. It's hard to describe. I don't try to stumble after the prayers anymore, reading them with the rest of the congregation. Instead I drift into an interior space. I become a kind of antenna and

SOME PRAYERS TO PRACTICE ON

then beam or vibrate energy out toward the prayers of the congregation. I am *present,* but silently emitting prayerful light, while the minister and congregation rattle through the book. Practicing in the silence of your home makes it easier to do in public, and sometimes practicing in your sacred space can also help.

Building Sacred Space

Not everyone maintains a formal altar in the home, but most people who take prayer seriously at least have one special place where they like to pray or meditate. It is the sunporch settee where Janet goes to pray for her Johns Hopkins patients. It is the chair that Charles Fillmore rocked in every morning, as he taught himself to train his mind. It can be a corner of the bedroom, nothing special. Or it can be an elaborate meditation or prayer nook, complete with table, altar, and precious holy things of great meaning to you. But because what happens there is prayer, your mind is ready when you approach it, and urged toward sacredness.

Build an altar. Take your time. Make this sacred space beautiful. Let it reflect beauty and peace, so that each time you approach that space you feel yourself grow quiet and still. Place on your altar a candle, a flower, perhaps an incense holder, a picture of your teacher or of a holy figure, and finally a pretty bell to ring in order to begin and end your silent time (after a while the sound of the bell will sooth you instantly, bringing your attention into prayer). Perhaps you want no objects or images, but only a clean, pure, white cloth that suits your soul.

Each day at the same time sit at your altar. This is holy space. Close your eyes. Breathe. Say your mantra, reflect on a single word, or practice meditation. Rest in stillness. You are alive, alert, awake. Now pray. Pour blessings on all those you love and on our little world.

The God Box

When I first heard about a God Box, it delighted me. It can be as precious as an antique ivory coffer or as plain as a brown paper bag. You may place it on your altar in your sacred space or keep it on the kitchen counter—it doesn't matter where it sits! Scribble down your prayers, place them in the God Box, and leave them there. Now you've put your problems in the hands of God. Every month or two open the box, go through your prayers, and see with pleasure (and thanks!) which have been answered and can be taken from the box and tossed.

You don't have to pray these all the time. You don't have to keep on asking, begging, suffering over them. The universe knows what's in the box, and by forgetting your demands you avoid the prayers of worrying and doubt.

Constant Prayer

But if God knows our needs, if we drop prayers into a God Box like letters in the mail slot, if we are admonished to let go, stop badgering, then what of that other scriptural injunction to pray constantly, to implore the universe like the obdurate woman wearing down the judge? Aren't we advised in all traditions to "pray without ceasing"? The Benedictine monk Brother David Steindl-Rast speaks about praying even in our sleep, even in our dreams, so that we wake up in the middle of the night and find ourselves in prayer.

There is a lovely little book called *The Way of the Pil-*

grim, with a sequel called *The Pilgrim Continues His Way.* First translated into English in 1930 by R. M. French, they are considered the most penetrating personal look into the soul of Eastern Christianity. They tell of a Russian peasant who in the 1850s wondered what was meant by the phase in 1 Thessalonians to "Rejoice always. Pray constantly." He was thirty-three years old when the question came to mind. His name is lost to us. All we know is that he was literate, widowed, physically disabled, and that in his spiritual quest, taking the admonition literally, he began to walk, each footstep a prayer. His task was to pray constantly. He walked across Russia, through forests and open country, on roads or off them. At every step he repeated the Jesus Prayer: "Lord Jesus Christ, have mercy on me, a poor sinner." As he prayed, he found himself growing happier and happier . . . and then he discovered that praying makes you happy!

But how can you pray constantly when you have work at the office and marketing to do? How do you pray constantly and still have any social life? Is it possible, or even *desirable,* to spend your life in prayer?

Once I was driving from Washington D.C., to New York. This is a five-hour drive, and I spent the entire five hours repeating the Lord's Prayer out loud, listening to the words. "Our Father, who art in heaven. . . ." Over and over again I repeated the words, concentrating, thinking, puzzling over them. What did they *mean?* "Our Father, who—"

What did that mean, "Our Father"? What did I think of fathers? Where is heaven? What does "hallowed" mean? What is my daily bread? With each run-through of the prayer, its meaning deepened, until after four hours the entire prayer had taken on new coloration.

It opens with utter adoration. "Our Father, who art in heaven, hallowed be Thy name." *Sacred, holy, hallowed thou art (Kadesh, kadesh, kadesh!)* As the miles passed, I could feel my heart opening in recognition of this sacred mystery. *I* was hallowed by this adoration!

The prayer then asks for three things. Three things only do we ask: Feed us, forgive us, protect us. That's all it says, before closing with a final adoration.

But I found difficulties. What does it mean, "Lead us not into temptation"? Why would a loving God lead us into temptation? Even if you substitute the Aramaic words to "keep us from the time of trial," the plea seems equally strange.

C. S. Lewis, musing on the "festoons" of the Lord's Prayer in his book *Letters to Malcolm,* tasting the Greek word for "trial" or "trying circumstances," offered as the meaning: "Make straight our paths. Spare us, where possible, from all crises, whether of temptation or affliction." It's as if we said (he says), "In my ignorance I have asked for A, B, and C. But don't give me them if you foresee that they would in reality be to me either snares or sorrows."[1]

But I did not have C. S. Lewis's book with me in the car. I had only my own intuition and the whispers of the voice of God. "Lead us not into temptation. . . ." As the hours passed, as the road rolled under my car, as the words resonated in my ears, my mind, my heart, a different conclusion came to me. (I wasn't arguing or defending Lewis's position, but only pondering the words.) Driving along, I decided that the prayer had left out one simple praising pronoun: You! "*You* feed us. *You* deliver us from evil. *You* lead us not into temptation! *You* forgive us our trespasses. . . ."

SOME PRAYERS TO PRACTICE ON

By the end of five hours of driving and thinking about each word of this ancient prayer, by the time I was moving along the Brooklyn-Queens Expressway, the towers of New York City ahead of me, I was so happy I was flying! I understood how joyful it must be to pray the rosary. You are not just mumbling through the beads by rote, but *listening,* with the ears of God, for once again (I keep insisting), prayer is the path by which we rush into rapture. We're in love, swept up in union.

The words of the Lord's Prayer in Western languages may be far removed from those spoken by Jesus in the original Aramaic. Aramaic is a language of subtleties. We don't know what Christ actually said, for the prayer comes down to us through Greek, the language of the early Gospel writers. But not long ago several different scholars translated our version back into Syriac Aramaic and then from the Aramaic into English again in an attempt to maintain some of the Aramaic rhythms and nuances of meaning in a language where "heaven" means the universe, where "kingdom" is related to the word for Great Mother, and "daily bread" derives from roots for the divine feminine or holy wisdom—Sophia. Here is one transliteration of the prayer that Jesus spoke, as rendered by Neil Douglas-Klotz. Would any of us recognize it?

O Breathing Life, your Name shines everywhere!
Release a space to plant your Presence here.
Envision your "I Can" now.
Embody your desire in every light and form.
Grow through us this moment's bread and wisdom.
Untie the knots of failure binding us, as we release the
strands we hold of others' faults.
Help us not to forget our Source, yet free us from not
being in the Present.

THE PATH OF PRAYER

> *From you arises every vision, power, and song, from*
> *gathering to gathering*
> *Amen: May our future actions grow from here![2]*

And here is another translation, so different you wonder where the words so familiar to us today first came from! Yet each one makes sense. Each one adds layers of meaning to the prayer.

1. *O Thou, the Breath, the Light of All*
2. *Focus your light within us.*
3. *Create your reign of unity now.*
4. *Your One Desire then acts with ours, as in all light, so in all forms.*
5. *Grant what we need each day, in bread and insight.*
6. *Loose the cords of mistakes binding us, as we release the strands we hold of others' guilt.*
7. *Don't let surface things delude us.*
8. *But free us from what holds us back.*
9. *To you belongs the ruling mind, the power and the life to do, the song that beautifies all, from age to age it renews.*
10. *In faith I will be true.[3]*

1. *Our Father who art in Heaven*
2. *Hallowed be thy name*
3. *Thy kingdom come, thy will be done*
4. *On earth as it is in heaven*
5. *Give us this day our daily bread*
6. *And forgive us our trespasses, as we forgive those who trespass against us*
7. *Lead us not into temptation*
8. *But deliver us from evil*
9. *For thine is the Power and the Kingdom and the Glory, for ever and ever*

SOME PRAYERS TO PRACTICE ON

How Not to Pray

Any cry delivered from your heart is a prayer. The important thing is to speak it in your own voice, spontaneously and with passion. Here is how *not* to pray:

1. *Lip-service prayers.* Your lips are moving while your mind is roaming elsewhere in the fields of your imagination. Forget it! Go do something else. You're wasting your time, murmuring your memorized prayers or whirling your prayer wheel without attention. If you are mumbling meaningless prayers, then sit back and ask yourself why you're there. These aren't prayers at all.

2. *Show-off prayers.* These are the prayers designed to demonstrate your piety to others. You are worshipping in church or temple or mosque, repeating the prayers you learned by rote, but you are saying them out of pride and vanity or out of duty. These are the prayers that Jesus warned against—the prayers of the hypocrite who stands before the altar beating his breast and making a noisy display of his own sanctity. True prayer arises from a desire to be seen by God, heard by the Holy Spirit and no one else.

3. *Harmful prayers.* These are prayers of vengeance, anger, violence. You must never pray for harm to befall another person—and this in spite of the ferocious Judeo-Christian Psalms that call on the Lord to wipe out our enemies; or that dance with joy because He has extinguished them. (I take "enemies" to mean our fears.) Such prayers bring no relief from anger, fear, hurt, and in fact they may twist around to hurt the one who prays; for whatever thoughts we

THE PATH OF PRAYER

send out will come back onto our heads. "What goes around comes around." Curses and voodoo can be yours, but the price is terrible. It is better, if you have been badly hurt and are afraid, to pray for the so-called enemy. If you cannot do that, then pray for the willingness to pray for him. Gradually, by probing self-examination, you will find yourself relieved of whatever is causing you to hurt, whatever stands in the way of your relationship to the highest possibilities.

4. *Prayers of worry and doubt.* It's important to come before the Holy Spirit in confidence and joy, presenting yourself with simplicity and making known your longings and your need without concerning yourself with how God works things out. If you are consumed by fear and worry, therefore, pray first to have your fear removed (your enemies). Pray for yourself. When trapped by doubt, just call out "Help!" Then relax, handing over all concerns to the Beloved. Thus you move from the problem into the solution, for trust and faith eliminate all fear.

Chapter 16

Surrender and Relinquishment

Someone once said there are only three necessary prayers and each has only three words:

"Lord, have mercy"
"Thee, I adore"
"Into Thy Hands."

I once asked my Hindu teacher in Jaipur what is the best way to pray. As usual, he answered with a story. He likes to speak in parables.

Once there was a dog, he said (and immediately I visualized one of those stringy black curs that slink along the gutters in India), who was set upon by a pack of wild dogs, snarling, biting. He fought his way free, his jaw broken, one foot crushed. He limped home, bleeding, and there he dragged himself to his owner's feet, thumping his tail in the dust. And what does the owner do? He picks up his dog, carries him indoors. He takes him to the vet, who washes his wounds, sets his broken bones, gives him antibiotics. Every day the owner feeds his dog, gives him water, medications, a soft bed. He changes his bandages, and soon the dog gets well. The dog did not ask for anything. The dog merely presented himself.

"For if you ask for a shirt," said my teacher, "you will get a shirt, and if you ask for a pair of trousers, you will get a pair of trousers. But if you simply present yourself, every blessing will be yours."

That is how you pray, he said.

In India there is often an easygoing relationship with God. Here is the ancient song of the Vedic singer, who stands on such familiar footing with his deities that he teases Indra like a family member, and in return he expects a wealth of cows and hero sons:

> *If I, Indra, like thee,*
> *Were the sole lord of all goods,*
> *The singer of my praise*
> *Would never be without cows.*
>
> *I would aid him gladly;*
> *Give the wise singer his due:*
> *If, O Bounteous God, I*
> *Were, like thee, the Lord of Cows.*[1]

Our formal Christian prayers are less lighthearted, although as we get older we realize something is working things out, even in our deepest grief. One day we may say with the lovely 13th-century mystic and anchorite Julian of Norwich that "we shall thank and bless our Lord, endlessly rejoicing that we ever suffered woe; and that will be because of a property of the blessed love which we shall know in God, which we might never have known without woe preceeding it."[2]

SURRENDER AND RELINQUISHMENT

The Structure of Prayer

The rules for making up your own prayers are simple. You pray for yourself. Ask for anything you want for others. Ask for the highest good for all concerned. As you proceed, your prayer will automatically fall into a simple structure:

Adoration
The body of the prayer
The closing thanks

But at a certain point in our prayer path, we lose even the body of the prayer. We ask for nothing.

Nothing?

Nothing, because the Holy Spirit already knows the longings of our heart.

Listen: It's hard to tread the path of prayer. You begin with baby steps, by memorizing rote prayers. Slowly the memorized passages seep drop by drop into your soul. Later you will cast them out in defiant hurt and anger. Perhaps you don't want to pray at all! Yet still the soul refuses to stop, praying against your very will, until you reach the point of absolute abandon.

Asking for Nothing

One day you find you're no longer even asking for anything. You have given your life into the care of a loving universe. This is the prayer of surrender and relinquishment.

"Into Your hands I place myself," you say, *"knowing that that which is for my highest good will come to me."*

Mother Teresa called herself "a pencil in the hand of

God," and St. Francis said he was God's donkey. Hildegard of Bingen referred to herself as "a feather on the breath of God," and Thérèse of Lisieux, "The Little Flower," was "a ball in the hands of child Jesus." There is enormous freedom in giving up, being guided by a higher power. Someone else is the chauffeur, and you're just a passenger, going along for the ride.

Nonetheless, actually letting go and surrendering your will takes practice. It's not easy. A priest once told me that the hardest thing to learn is, "you're not God." The 11th step of the Alcoholics Anonymous 12-step program advises prayer "only for the knowledge of God's will and the power to carry that out." *Only?* Perhaps it's more an ideal than a possibility. In the beginning, as I set out on the path of prayer and first heard this principle, I didn't even try! Instead I went ahead and told God, the Holy Spirit, the Creative Principle, my Beloved, what I wanted, needed. I explained exactly how to achieve it, describing how things should come out. Only after I'd gotten everything off my chest could I practice surrendering or letting go. But I've never felt I had to be such a saint as to pray *only* for knowledge of God's will. I still pray for things I want!

But afterward I place the outcome in the hands of God and sit back to watch with curious anticipation to see how things work out.

So how do you make a prayer of surrender? I think you begin with baby steps, first memorizing such a prayer, repeating it until it is engraved on your heart, and then, whenever you are afraid, it will rise automatically to your lips—as well as the urgent heartfelt cries of "Help!"

The first is the prayer from the 12-step Alcoholics Anonymous program.

The 12 Steps of the Anonymous Programs

1. We admitted we were powerless over [people, places, addictions]—that our lives had become unmanageable.

2. Came to believe that a Power greater than ourselves could restore us to sanity.

3. Made a decision to turn our will and our lives over to the care of God *as we understood Him.*

4. Made a fearless and searching moral inventory of ourselves.

5. Admitted to God, to ourselves, and to another human being the exact nature of our wrongs.

6. Became entirely ready to have God remove all these defects of character.

7. Humbly asked Him to remove our shortcomings.

8. Made a list of all persons we had harmed and became willing to make amends to them all.

9. Made direct amends to such people wherever possible, except when to do so would injure them or others.

10. Continued to take personal inventory and when we were wrong promptly admitted it.

11. Sought through prayer and meditation to increase our conscious contact with God *as we understood Him,* praying only for knowledge of His will for us and the power to carry that out.

12. Having had a spiritual awakening as a result of these steps, we tried to carry this message to [others], and to practice these principles in all our affairs.

> *God, I offer myself to thee, to build with me and to do*
> *with me as thou wilt.*
> *Relieve me of the bondage of Self that I may better do*
> *thy will.*
> *Take away my difficulties, that victory over them may*
> *bear witness to those I would help of thy power, thy*
> *love, thy way of life.*
> *May I do thy will always.*

Note that you have asked for almost nothing except to extinguish ego and to help others. It's slightly different from that earlier prayer of surrender, "Into Your hands I place myself and all of my affairs. . . ." It has taken things to a deeper level. Now you have asked to serve.

Here is a prayer of surrender that I first heard at the Healing Services of the Washington National Cathedral and that so touched me that I still murmur it as I drive in the car or walk down the street, the words reminding me that I've given my life away. If you cannot pray in the name of Jesus Christ, delete the name of the Christian deity. Or add one of the thousand other names of God.

> *Almighty and Eternal God, so draw our hearts to*
> *you, so guide our minds, so fill our imaginations, so*
> *control our wills, that we may be wholly yours,*
> *utterly dedicated to you, and then use us, we pray, as*
> *you will. And always to your glory and the welfare of*
> *your people. In the name of our Lord and Savior Jesus*
> *Christ. Amen.*

Amen, and it is so!

Would you like a third surrender prayer? Twelve years ago, when I first heard this last one, John Wesley's Covenant, I had to force myself to utter these terrifying phrases, and even as my lips rambled over the words, my soul shied from them like a panicked horse, refusing the jump! It took months before I began to *mean* the prayer. I have kept the first "thine" for the sake of the rhyme, but I've changed the other "thee"s and "thou"s to the more intimate "you" of our modern times; for three hundred years ago "thee" was the informal, tender voice that a mother used when crooning to her baby. It was the address of a child to his papa, of a gentle husband to his wife. These days, however, "thee" and "thou" have taken on a distancing and formal usage, reserved for God-Almighty-in-Heaven, who is too far away for us to address except with doubt and awe. Look at this prayer of relinquishment, and you'll see why it struck me with fear.

> *Almighty God, I am not mine but thine.*
> *Do with me as you will.*
> *Let me be employed by you, laid aside by you,*
> *Exalted by you, laid low by you,*
> *Give me everything, give me nothing,*
> *Put me to doing, put me to suffering,*
> *Let me be full, let me be empty.*
> *I utterly and wholeheartedly release all things into*
>   *your care and pleasure,*
> *In the name of the Father, Son, and Holy Spirit*
>   *So be it.*
> *And now, O most beloved Lord,*
> *You are mine and I am thine!*
> *And this covenant that I have made on earth*
> *May it be ratified in Heaven.*
>   *Amen.*

Who can say these words without hesitation? *"Let me be employed by you, laid aside by you."* Wait a minute! What does "laid aside" exactly mean?

THE PATH OF PRAYER

"Laid low by you." Oh, no! I want to be exalted only.

"Give me everything, give me nothing?" Can I bear nothing?

"Let me be full, let me be empty." Wait! I want only to be full.

Just to make matters worse, there is the line that so gagged me that I could hardly utter it: *"Put me to doing, put me to suffering."* Put me to suffering? Are you mad? What good would that serve? I can accept pain, but why extended suffering? There's nothing spiritual about suffering! Besides, (I thought) suffering is not the opposite of doing. I dropped this line, therefore, until it was pointed out to me that in this case the word was used in the sense of "patiently tolerating" while doing nothing: Put me to action, put me to waiting.

Gradually the awareness crept over me that a glass must be empty before it can be filled. One day I could affirm that, yes, I wanted to be empty of my petty self, this overloaded ego, in order to be full with God. When I have nothing, I am rich. (When I have everything, I am also rich, but what is "everything"? How much does one need?) What difference does it make—exalted or laid low? For these are human judgments. What's important is how I feel about myself.

"I utterly and wholeheartedly release all things into your care and pleasure." One day I meant it. With relief I realized Someone Else can take care of me. Nonetheless, this prayer did not come easily to my lips, and it took a long time before my heart leaped at the precious words *"And*

The person who knows she has enough is rich.

—Anonymous

SURRENDER AND RELINQUISHMENT

now, O most beloved Lord, / you are mine and I am thine!" Like lovers, inextricably entwined.

A Medley of Practical Prayers

Years ago, when I was first learning to talk with my spirit guides or angels, I asked many questions about how to pray. Some of what they had to teach, I've already passed on in the pages of this book. But sometimes the angels gave me the very words I needed to say. "God, how do You wish for me to pray?" I asked.

"Dear God, what do You want me to pray for in this time of crisis?"

You don't need to be afraid. I find that if the words that rise into your mind are sweet and gentle, full of relinquishment, they come truly from the angels of God; and if they are filled with hatred, vengeance, power-driven thoughts, as sure as night follows day, they come from a dark energy or from the base nature of the self. For an angel—the spirit and messenger of God—has no thoughts except those expressing tenderness and love. Since their eyes are always turned to God, the Beloved, the Majesty and Master, they do not fear, and their words are sensible, intelligent.

Even when praying for a particular person or event, an outcome, peace, for a healing or cleansing, for comfort and help, you can pray with surrender and relinquishment. The prayers below may sound too romantic for your taste, their language too extravagant. But they have served me well, and the exaggerated expressions of their loving relationship have time after time reminded me of my place in the affections of my Lord, my Mother, my Home. The Goddess is in these words, the Christ, Allah, Brahma, the Atman, Jehovah, Yahweh, and all the spirits of a loving force for which we have no words. The extravagant wording arises from the soul, which knows no boundaries to love—it would leap into music if it could! Or poetry. So don't toss out these prayers because they offend good taste; they have nothing to do with the miserly, orderly nature of structured intellect. They are songs lifted by the soul in love.

FOR A BROKEN RELATIONSHIP

Dear God, O Most Beloved and Adored, I thank You with all my heart for Your great goodness in times of trouble and sorrow. O my Joy, my dearest love, my Lord, my master, mother, Beloved one. I am Yours. I kneel before You, O my Desire, and give myself to You, and [name of the one involved in this relationship] *and* [name a third party, if involved]. *Take us, and do with us as You will.*

Notice that in relinquishment you have not asked for anything, for God knows already what you want. If you wish to outline your loneliness and sorrow, the *need* for healing, you may do so, but that is not the prayer. If you wish to add your desire—*"Heal our broken relationship"*— you may do so, but the prayer alone will suffice. Say this prayer three times a day, and see if abundance is not showered on you all.

Here is another way to express the same idea.

In the stillness of God's presence, we turn to the power within, releasing all anxiety and troubles, knowing that God is present in every person. God's radiance fills [name]. *God works in and through* [name] *to attract in her life all that will give her happiness. She is blessed with a holy relationship and with the fulfillment of the desires of her heart. Her heart responds with joy and gratitude. We pray this in the name of the living Christ. Amen.*

FOR YOUR CREATIVE WORK

Each time you begin, offer yourself and your work to God, asking for talent, strength, courage, and help in your creative vision—asking to be emptied, in order to serve as a vessel of the highest good.

Each time you finish, give thanks for the work done through you that day.

O most Glorious and Blessed God, I present myself and this work into Your hands. Do with it as You will. Guide my thoughts. Hold my hands, that You alone are writing {painting, carving} through me, producing whatever You wish me to say. And now, O my Beloved and my Joy, I prostrate myself into Your most loving embrace in thanks that You give me talent, inspiration, discipline to do Your work. Amen. So be it.

FOR PEACE

Do you wish to pray for peace in Ireland, the Middle East, the Sudan, Pakistan, or any other war-torn area, including your own home, including any zone of environmental destruction? Then try this or variations of this prayer:

O most Beloved Lord, O Thou, my friend in all: We turn to You and ask Your Light, O my Delight, Our Joy, to spread throughout this earth, and especially in [place]. O Lord, we turn to You for Peace and Calm and Light, for Serenity and Your Holy Riches poured upon us all, upon [place]. And thank You, Lord. Amen.

Now send light. Do this three times a day.

A CHILD'S PRAYER

I have an agnostic friend whose little children could not be calmed down at night to go to bed. "Do you pray with them?" I asked. She looked at me with a puzzled expression. "No." She'd never thought of that and, being herself the child of Jewish and Protestant parents, had never been taught a child's prayer. I offered her a prayer and suggested that she kneel at their bedside and say it with them. Within a week she reported with surprise and delight that both children were going quietly to sleep, now feeling safe in the night.

A child needs a prayer to memorize, and every word must be the same each time. No disorderly made-up prayers! The prayer must be very simple. This one, accommodated for my agnostic-Jewish friend, substitutes the names of the four archangels for the Gospel writers:

There are four corners on my bed,
There are four angels at my head.
Raphael, Gabriel, Michael, and Uriel,
Bless the bed I sleep on.

FOR BLESSING A HOME

To enter a new home, knowing that it will be yours, is a special moment, and if it is your first apartment or house, the place where you expect to remain for a while or raise a family, it is a joyful enterprise. Most people know intuitively how to fashion the blessing that will suit themselves and their home; they don't need a book to suggest that friends gather to celebrate, or that a priest or shaman walk with their friends through the rooms, blessing and praying for their happiness and well-being

SURRENDER AND RELINQUISHMENT

in these new surroundings. Blessings are made with flowers, food, and dancing, with prayer and invocation to the spiritual world, with drums and flutes, guitars and song, with incense and candles, with dreams, and finally with a rich and thankful heart:

Bless this house, Lord God. Bring joy and happiness into this room. Bless all who enter these doors — may they find serenity, peace, calm and wisdom, love.

Now stand in the middle of your new home. Extend your blessing outward to encompass the entire property (should you be lucky enough to have acreage) and then the property of your neighbors, thinking in all four directions as well as up and down.

Bless all around, O God: bless to the north, bless to the south, bless to the east, bless to the west . . . bless the ground below, bless the skies above.

Now stand in the center of this six-pointed star and allow your blessing to flow to everything around. Now feast or fast in celebration of your home.

Don't be afraid to make up your own ceremony.

Listen to your intuition. You'll know what to do, so long as it is always done in love.

FOR CLEANSING A HOME

Let's say that you have moved into a new home where you feel an anxious energy, an unclean or grieving, dark vibration. Perhaps one room gives you the creeps. Take holy water. This water either may come from a place of miracles, like Lourdes or Medjugorje, or else been blessed by any shaman, imam, priestess, or holy man. If you have neither sacred water nor a priest to bless it, then bless the water yourself, with your prayers. A simple one suffices:

Almighty Spirit, enter this water, purify it, make it holy, in order that whatever it touches is cleansed and purified. In Your holy name, for the Highest Good. . . .

Now, standing in the center of the room, fill yourself with light. Directions to this practice have been given previously, and I shall not repeat the method here. Breathe in the light, asking that you may be pure and clean, a suitable channel for the work of God. Once filled with energy, send it outward, calling on the God of your understanding, by whatever name you use. Sprinkle the water in each corner, on each wall, and on all windows and doors, and with each sprinkling of the holy water you say a prayer. Since I pray to the light of Christ, I myself would say something like this:

Lord Jesus Christ, we thank You with all our hearts for Your Presence in this room. Come to us now and fill this space with light. Fill us with light. Send light into every crack and corner of this dwelling place. We thank You, Lord, that You cast out all darkness, disease, despair, all discouragement and grief . . . that this room is filled with Your love, peace, freedom, and serenity. That this room is purified and cleansed. In the name of all that is holy, we give thanks. . . .

Move through the entire house, cleansing every room in this manner, or in whatever words you choose.

If Christianity is not your tradition, use whatever name for God inspires love, goodness, and power for you. Feel free to make up the words yourself, because the intensity of feeling, your confidence, is what delivers prayer.

In the name of God, we send all dark energies into the light. Let this room resonate with good, that all who enter here may be touched by calm, peace, wisdom, light, joy, love. . . .

As you speak, remember to breathe and beam these qualities from your heart out into the room.

FOR HEALING SOMEONE

Sit quietly. Pray first for your own courage and strength in this time of stress, for freedom from anxiety and fear. Draw up the image of the one in need. Imagine her surrounded by a flame of healing light. Now pray to the mother-god of health; here, unlike in the earlier prayers, do not hesitate to ask for healing of all sorts—only in your heart be aware that the healing may take place spiritually rather than physically, as you might wish. Remember, nothing is impossible to God, not even miraculous healings (we hear of them all the time), and why should one not come to this person whom you love?

Of course you need no words to send this prayer, but if you did use words, they might go something like this:

O God, my darling one, in trust and love I come to You. Take [say the person's name]. *Pour into her Your healing energy. Take her, O my Beloved. Heal her mentally, emotionally, spiritually, and physically. Fill her with Your love. Take her, God, heal her, that she may serve You still by thought, word, deed. And thus we thank You, Lord God, Almighty. . . .*

Rest wordlessly in the prayer, watching with your inner eye as it surrounds your loved one. When you have finished "sending," give thanks for this healing in meekness and humility, adding, "This or something better come to her" or else "This prayer, for the highest good of all concerned."

FOR YOURSELF

Finally, remember always and first to pray for yourself. Hold yourself in the light. Or if you need to, *ask* for what you need, whether it be strength and courage or some blessing only you may know. The finest prayer is to serve God by thought, word, deed. To know His bidding. To do it. To have strength, intuition, clarity to know the will of God. But at some point, no matter how blessed we are, life will deal us a blow. We fall to our knees in anguish.

Lord God, I'm Yours. . . . O God, please help!

Other times we fall to our knees in love.

O God, my all, O God, my love!

The Simplest Prayer

Now we come to the close of this book. What is it we should remember or take away with us? I think it's very simple.

When I was a child, my sister and I knelt with our mother beside our beds at night and said the prayer that told us we were safe.

There are four corners on my bed,
There are four angels at my head. . . .

Then we said the Lord's Prayer and finally the Child's Prayer, ancient as time:

Now I lay me down to sleep,
I pray thee, Lord, my soul to keep.

If I should die before I wake,
I pray thee, Lord, my soul to take.

Later, as a young mother, I looked back at this image with horror! What kind of prayer was that to teach a baby? Now, years later still, I turn to this simple prayer with a sense that perhaps it is the single most important and beautiful prayer that can be made. What does it say?

"Keep me, love me, take me when I die."

What else is there for anyone to say?

An Islamic Prayer

O Allah! Give us steadfastness in obedience and keep us from sin. Give us sincerity in intention, and knowledge of that which is sacred; bestow on us guidance and constancy; seal our tongues with reason and wisdom; fill our hearts with knowledge and learning; keep us clean from within from what is forbidden and from those things of which we are uncertain; keep our hands from oppression and stealing; hide from our eyes immorality and treachery, and close our ears to foolish talk and calumny. Grant this through Thy Overflowing Generosity and Thy Mercy, O Merciful and Compassionate!

(The Holy Qur'an)

Epilogue

Once I was in India visiting my teacher, as the only Western woman in the group. I was taken to a holy site, and I was finding things very, very hard. Everyone was painfully attentive and nice to me, but I simply could not throw off my mean, little, bitchy mood. Or just accept, *enjoy* these lovely men and women (they did not appear lovely to me!) who made such efforts over me. The women picked their way across the dry grass, their silk saris dragging in the yellow dust, and the men leaped ahead to hold back a branch or help me over a hillock, while I frowned in annoyance—at *myself* as much as at them. I didn't want to be there. Everything in me felt bitter and irritable.

The holy site lay off in a woods and across a meadow, where we had to jump a small ditch and then walk farther; and all the time my Indian hosts were trying gallantly to cheer me up. After a while we came to a gully, a kind of shallow crevasse. They pointed to a painted orange rock down in the hole.

"That's it?" A painted orange rock.

"This is the *lingam* of Lord Shiva. You can make any wish, any prayer, and touch this rock, and you will get your wish." They were nodding and smiling their encouragement, prancing in excitement. "Lean down and touch it."

It was no easy task. The orange rock lay deep in its cavern. Well, what the heck! They expected some response. My reluctant wish was that I get back to center and enjoy myself, that I stop being as nervous, irritable, and mean-spirited as I was feeling then, delighting in neither myself nor my surroundings, much less the people in this group. I was to be five weeks in India. At least it could be enjoyable.

I had to drop to my knees to lean into this chasm (inadvertent surrender), and even then I had to hold on to the grass, to keep from falling into the hole. I had to reach with the full length of my arm to touch the painted orange rock. Everyone applauded: I didn't fall.

Now, this was not my culture and not my ritual, and certainly I expected nothing to happen. But when I touched that rock and silently spoke my prayer, an electric charge ran through me, up my arm and down my spine, covering me. I wanted to weep. I stood up trembling, queered. I felt undone—and when I came to my feet, a little dizzy, I looked about in wonderment: Suddenly everyone was beautiful! They were shining and goodhearted, and the place itself, this barren, dusty grotto with its dry yellow grass, was as lovely as any site on earth! Indeed, my trip to India was the most perfect blessing I could have been given.

I felt jubilant. My mean spirits had vanished. My heart was singing. I wanted to touch the rock again. I wanted to know everything about the people I was with. I went to many holy sites on that wonderful trip to India, but I fell in love with that orange rock.

But what are we to make of it? I think there are holy

sites, places so spiritually attuned that people sense their high vibrations, and then these places become so imbued with their footsteps and prayers that each person who comes after is spiritually touched in turn. Nonetheless, when approaching such a place it helps to stand in prayer. I once made a pilgrimage to Santiago di Compostela in Spain and placed my fingers inside the curved carved pillar of the great cathedral . . . and felt nothing whatsoever! Why? Because I came almost as a tourist. I did not approach it in a prayerful state.

Whatever your practice, tradition, or ritual, it takes constancy to achieve the fruits. In that word lies the true purpose of ritual or form. The rituals have been with us since the beginning of time. They are designed to help us hold and fix our attention, to guide the soul back home.

The Egyptians burned incense and made food offerings to the gods. The ancient peoples of the Middle East, including the later Greeks and Romans, made blood sacrifices of bulls, goats, sheep, doves, and then, leaving the sinew and bones for the gods, they ate the good roast meat! According to myth, the division of good meat from bad was determined by the cunning of Prometheus, who cheated the gods on behalf of his beloved people.

Don't think you can attain total awareness and whole enlightenment without proper discipline and practice. This is egomania. Appropriate rituals channel your emotions and life energy toward the light. Without the discipline to practice, then, you will tumble constantly backwards into darkness.

—Lao-tzu

I will praise the name of God with a song; I will magnify him with thanksgiving. This will please the Lord more than an ox or a bull with horns and hoofs.

—Psalm 69

Prometheus wrapped the useless bones and fat into a succulent-looking packet. He made a second packet of the edible flesh and rolled it in muck and ashes, disguised it as foul trash, then asked Zeus, king of the gods, to choose which would be the sacrifice to the Gods. Zeus, poor dolt, chose wrong! The humans took the good roast goat or beef for themselves, leaving bones and guts to the gods. The crafty Greeks. They were superstitious, but they didn't take their gods too seriously.

Today, generally, we are no longer propitiating hungry gods. Few religions demand blood sacrifice, although Islam asks each Muslim once a year to sacrifice an animal—a camel, sheep, or goat to commemorate the sacrifice of Isaac—and a messy business it is, I'm told, when you live in a Paris or Lyon apartment, the slaughter performed ritually in a bathtub and the French authorities opposed to the religious practice.[1]

We don't sacrifice virgins or young men anymore, as the Aztecs did, but some people still undertake ascetic practices, as do the *penitentes,* who still operate secretly in New Mexico and South America. They reenact the Crucifixion, complete with whippings, thorns, and sometimes living bodies lifted to the cross. The ceremonies may be similar in intent to those of the Native American sundance rituals, in which the spiritual aspirant pierces his chest with pins or thorns and hangs by them on ropes attached to a tree. The eagle dancers hang for four days under a broiling sun, with no water and no food. The "pledges," those new to the dance, commit themselves to hang, praying, for anywhere from one four-day dance to four years of four-day ceremonies, but old-hand sundancers have the option of determining how long they will perform the ceremony and whether they will fast or pierce their flesh. The dance is intended as a way of life, and the point is not so much to reach a spiritual ecstasy as to make as many prayers as can be packed in, praying for others and for the world, in order to be of maximum service to God and fellows and to earth.[2]

Your body becomes the offering to God.

In China the offerings are smoke and incense, and elsewhere people offer fruit and flowers. In any Christian church you'll find flowers on the altar, holy symbols of our worship.

Even *darshan,* while sitting in devotion at the feet of a saint or enlightened being, becomes a form of prayer. Even walking in the cathedral of nature. Even doing the dishes, attending to your work, weeding the garden, sanding the windowsill, repairing the roof. Surely life itself is nothing but a prayer.

It's not the ritual or technique itself that matters; it's the attention you give to it, the openness of your heart! Ritual is one path to the silent, light-struck point, which (paradoxically) you can reach either through your senses (music, incense, dance, food) or through the practice of abolishing the sensory world by asceticism and certain kinds of meditation.

But if you merge your attention with the activity, then the ritual itself becomes a prayer—the prayer of clashing cymbals, dance, timbrels, psalteries, sistrums, horns, and gongs.

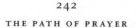

The prayer of silence.
The prayer of touch.
The prayer of action.

When engaged in the prayer of action, you find yourself working effortless, joyfully for another person. You fold the laundry, you put oil in the car. Surely nurses and doctors in hospitals are engaged in the prayer of action—if they can remember in the frenzied rush that their work is prayer. Trash collectors, police, firefighters, government bureaucrats, roofers, builders, musicians, artists—if they are performing their work in a prayerful state as service to others and if they are aware of themselves at work—are involved in the prayer of action.

Here is a French prayer, found in the chapel at Charles de Gaulle Airport:

> *I need your hands*
>
> *Since I rose to heaven*
> *I have had no hands to work on earth*
> *Nor feet to run on roads*
> *Nor arms to embrace the children.*
> *So I have need of you.*
>
> *With your hands I want to touch your brothers*
> *With your eyes I want to see their soul*
> *With your feet I want to walk and contemplate my*
> *father's heaven.*
> . . .
> *With your compassion I want to heal the wounded*
> *With your presence I want to comfort the afflicted*
> *With your prayers I want to free troubled spirits and*
> *hearts.*
> . . .
> *Tell me, can I count on you?*

I used to think that if I found the right prayer path or followed the right ritual, all would be well. I didn't know it was only a road, and that all the rituals take us to the same place. Imagine there is a giant wheel, and each of the spokes is a different religion leading to the center hub, to God, the same God by whatever religion's name—Islam, Christianity, Hinduism, Judaism, Baha'i, Zoroastrianism, the worship of Druids—as many religions and pagan rituals as can be named. The rituals of any spoke, followed with constancy, will lead you to the hub. Or you can walk around the circumference, scorning and deprecating the various spokes; or perhaps you start down one spoke, testing out one tradition, then change your mind when the road gets rough and, reversing your decision, return to the circumference, only to dodge down another spoke, trying out the rituals of another tradition before changing your mind again. In that case, all you're doing is walking around the rim; you'll never reach the center of the wheel. Your God.

I'm not saying that you cannot attend the services of another religion and find solace in it as well. I'm not saying that you cannot experiment with different forms of prayer. What I'm saying is that prayer takes constancy to show results. It takes determination, decision, dedication. It takes ambition, longing, a certain persistence in the face of difficulties.

And then the results come seeping like groundwater up into your soul, and you are watered with such joy and love that you understand the meaning of this strange word "God." You understand that the soul itself—you, at your deepest core—are *composed of* love, your very atoms, and there is nothing but love surrounding you. You see that although terrible things happen in this pretty little world—great sorrows, suffering, death, and often misery—in spite of all . . . you are cared for, loved. You care for others, as you are loved yourself, and then the goodness of love is passed like spiritual honey around the hive of populations, the ambrosia of God, discovered and drunk up by prayer.

I keep coming back to this one important point: The spiritual dimension is a template waiting to receive your call. Send forth your intention with all the passion and longing at your disposal, and Spirit will deliver your desire. With our thoughts we make reality. If we concentrate on happy, loving, optimistic thoughts, then love and happiness are ours. If our thoughts are of failure, despair, depression, distaste, dislike, disturbance—all the things that bring dissatisfaction and dis-ease—then so loving is the universe, so utterly dedicated to fulfilling our desires, that it will bring us these. Whatever we think strongly about, that is what we are praying, whether we use that word or not. *Thought, intention, surrender.* What will bring happiness? It is ours to choose. Only, pray.

A Christian Prayer

May the peace of God that passeth understanding be with you now and evermore.

Amen.

Sources

Epigraph

George Bernanos, *Diary of a Country Priest.* New York: Doubleday, 1954, reissued 1974.

The Simple Prayer of St. Nicholas of Flüe

1. A card.

A Jain Prayer for Peace

1. From "All in Good Faith," words of Satish Kumar, member of the Jain community, Prayer for Peace movement, 1981.

Chapter 2: What Is Prayer?

1. "Sadhana—a Way to God," in *Writings* by Anthony de Mello, selected with an introduction by William Dych, S.J. Maryknoll, New York: Modern Spiritual Masters Series Orbis Books, 1999.

Chapter 3: What God Do You Pray To?

1. Matthew, 7:9–11. Also, Luke, 11:11.

A Hebrew Prayer

1. *Gates of Prayer: The New Union Prayerbook.* Published by the Central Conference of American Rabbis, New York, 1975.

Chapter 4: Looking into the Terror

1. Joseph Campbell, *The Masks of God: Oriental Mythology.* New York: Penguin Arkana, 1962, 1991, pp. 9–10. From Brihadaranyaka Upanishad 1. 4.1–5. Ref 519.

2. Ibid., p. 5.

3. Convent of St. Onuphrious.

4. *The Washington Post,* Sunday, August 29, 1999, Style Section, pp. F1, F5.

5. See Isaiah 54:5–10.

6. *The Choice Is Always Ours: The Classic Anthology on the Spiritual Way,* Dorothy B. Phillips et al., eds. San Francisco: HarperCollins, 1989, p. 120.

A Hindu Prayer

1. "All in Good Faith," words of Satish Kumar, member of the Jain community, Prayer for Peace movement, 1981, p. 109.

A Buddhist Prayer

1. "Shantideva: Guide to the Bodhisattva's Way of Life," 10:34, 35, 55. From "All in Good Faith," p. 146.

Chapter 6: The Four Stair-Steps of Prayer

1. Lama Surya Das, *Awakening to the Sacred: Creating a Spiritual Life from Scratch.* New York: Broadway, 1999, p. 258.

2. Richard Foster, *Prayer: Finding the Heart's True Home.* San Francisco: HarperSanFrancisco, 1992.

Chapter 7: Pleading and Petitioning

1. Larry Dossey, M.D., *Healing Words.* San Francisco: HarperSanFrancisco, 1993, pp. 30–31, 257.

Chapter 8: Three Ways to Ask in Prayer

1. Larry Dossey, *Healing Words.* San Francisco: HarperSanFrancisco, 1993, pp. 97, 181.

2. Paramahansa Yogananda, *Autobiography of a Yogi.* Los Angeles: Self-Realization Fellowship, (1946) 1985, p. 105. And the next story, pp. 112–121.

Chapter 9: Loosing in Heaven, Binding on Earth

1. James Dillet Freeman, *The Story of Silent Unity.* Unity Village, MO: Unity Books, pp. 47–49.

2. Rosemary Ellen Guiley, *Miracle of Prayer.* New York: Pocket Books, 1995, p. 63.

3. Silent Unity, 1901 NW Blue Parkway, Unity Village, MO 64065-0001; or call 816-969-2000; online www.unityworldhq. org, and if you have no means of paying: 800-669-7729.

4. Walter Weston, *How Prayer Heals: A Scientific Approach.* Charlottesville, VA: Hampton Roads Publishing Co., 1998, p. 315.

Chapter 10: The Mystery of Unanswered Prayer

1. C. S. Lewis, *Letters to Malcolm: Chiefly on Prayer.* New York: Harvest/HBJ, 1964, p. 58.

2. Joseph Campbell, *The Masks of God: Oriental Mythology.* New York: Penguin Arkana, 1962, pp. 140–141.

3. Ibid., p. 143.

4. C. S. Lewis, *Letters to Malcolm,* p. 47.

5. Tenzin Gyatso, the 14th Dalai Lama. Foreword to *Meaning of Life,* Jeffrey Hopkins, ed. Boston: Wisdom Publications, 1992.

Chapter 11: The Prayer of Touch

1. He is now professor and research director at the Institute of Transpersonal Psychology in Palo Alto, California, and codirector of the institute's William James Center for Consciousness Studies.

2. Larry Dossey, *Healing Words.* San Francisco: HarperSanFrancisco, 1993, p. 200.

A Buddhist Prayer

1. "A sample of healing prayers and readings from various religions," Mayo clinic newsletter; Women's resource.

Chapter 12: A Hundred Ways to Pray

1. *The Washington Post,* December 22, 2000, p. A-20.

2. Thich Nhat Hanh, *Touching Peace: Practicing the Art of Mindful Living.* Berkeley, CA: Parallax Press, 1992, p. 11.

3. Aeschylus, *The Oresteia,* a new translation by Ted Hughes. New York: Farrar, Straus, & Giroux, 1999, p. 165.

The Serenity Prayer

1. Written by Reinhold Niebuhr, American theologian, 1892–1971.

Chapter 14: The Prayers of Light

1. John Sack, "Inside the Bunker," *Esquire,* February 2001, p. 140.

Chapter 15: Some Prayers to Practice On

1. Lewis, *Letters to Malcolm: Chiefly on Prayer.* New York: Harvest/ HBJ, 1964, p. 28.

2. Neil Douglas-Klotz from *Original Prayer* (audio tape), Boulder, CO: Sounds True, 2002.

3. *Prayers of the Cosmos: Meditations on the Aramaic Words of Jesus,* translated and with commentary by Neil Douglas-Klotz. San Francisco: HarperSanFrancisco, 1990, p. 41. See also www.NeilDouglas-Klotz.com

Chapter 16: Surrender and Relinquishment

1. Joseph Campbell, *The Masks of God: Oriental Mythology.* New York: Penguin Arkana, 1962. Chapter 4, ftnt 43, OR: Ft 43: citing *Rg Veda* VIII. 14, 1–2.

2. Mary Jo Meadow, "A Psychological Understanding of Selected Women Mystics," paper presented at the annual meeting of the American Academy of Religion, New York City, 1979.

Epilogue

1. Id ad-Adha, Id al-Qurban, or al-Id al-Kabir (Feast of the Sacrifice) forms part of the ceremony of the hajj or pilgrimage, and is carried out at Mina, near Mecca, on the tenth day of Dhul-Hijja, which is the last day of the Muslim calendar. Muslims all over the world sacrifice an animal on this day. Generally part of the meat is eaten by those making the sacrifice and part is given to the poor.

2. The pins may be disconnected from the ropes in order to allow the aspirant to walk around, go urinate. Eventually in a few hours, the pins will break free and then must be reattached.

Twayne's United States Authors Series

Sylvia E. Bowman, *Editor*

INDIANA UNIVERSITY

George Washington Harris

GEORGE WASHINGTON HARRIS

by **MILTON RICKELS**
University of Southwestern Louisiana

Twayne Publishers, Inc.   ::   New York

For
My Mother and Father

Preface

THE QUALITY of George Washington Harris' work is only now being discovered. During his lifetime and for sixty years after his death, even the best-educated American readers never heard his name. Now, mid-twentieth-century readers discover a new interest in his low comic defiance of civilized life, in the thick texture of his difficult style, and in the complex variety of his meanings.

This present work is the first book-length treatment of his writing. Because the facts of Harris' life are little known and contrast sharply with his comic world, the opening biographical chapter includes most of what we now know about the busy public man. Next, his comic sketches are surveyed in three chapters to trace the development of his ideas, to define his leading themes, and to examine his literary techniques and their sources, both English and American.

The materials for the study include Harris' one published volume, *Sut Lovingood's Yarns,* and all the newspaper sketches now identified as his in various New York, Tennessee, and other journals. Some of these tales have been republished; most are accessible only in rare journals. The frequent quotations from these various sources, which cover a long span of time, will follow their numerous inconsistencies of form—including the spelling Lovingood with either an *e* or an *i*. This writing is of varying quality and significance, but a broad survey indicates the range of concerns Harris attempted to express in fiction.

After the life and the overview of Harris' production from 1843-67, four other topics are considered. A chapter on the making of his book studies his revisions, not heretofore examined; his most obvious humorous conventions; and his comic symbolism in its extreme implications. Following chapters present his final writings, his use of the traditional fool as a comic point of view, the quality of his language, and, finally, the major critical responses to his work.

Harris' work repays the careful reader because underneath the surfaces of his comic world lies an abyss of strange meanings—powerful, incompatible presences so complicated, formless, and even unutterable that it seemed to Harris only comedy could express them. Comedy covers a wider range of meanings than romance or tragedy, and it is more pervasively human. In its lower reaches it descends into the animal; in its upper, into spiritual, even ethical yearnings.

Harris' comedy invites the modern reader's attention both in its primitive and in its sophisticated aspects. His comedy is primitive in its creation of scapegoats and in its expression of the demonic impulses of cruelty and hatred, impulses which he creates with esthetic power and without any intrusion of the intellectual or ethical desire to rise above them in order to understand or to control them. His comedy is sophisticated in its exploration of the human creature's modes of masking reality, in its expression of the yearning for complete freedom, and especially in its language. Its spirit, whether high or low, is always fierce; its meanings complex.

Harris' revival may be attributed in part to the extending interest in our national culture—the whole American Studies movement; surely in part it can be attributed to the expanding consciousness of our age, for truly, as Søren Kierkegaard has said, "The more thoroughly and substantially a human being exists, the more he will discover the comical."

MILTON RICKELS

University of Southwestern Louisiana
Lafayette, Louisiana

Acknowledgments

Obligations incurred in research projects are a pleasure to acknowledge, and for help with this book I am indebted to many persons for their kind assistance. Franklin Meine generously packaged the large collection of notes, letters, and typescripts of legal records he had accumulated for his own projected biography of Harris and mailed them to me with the invitation to study them as long as I needed. If my biographical chapter is in any degree helpful, it is so largely thanks to Mr. Meine's pioneering research and continuing generosity to students of Harris' work.

To many of my colleagues I am indebted for a variety of favors: to Brom Weber for encouragement to examine Harris' themes, for reading and generously commenting on my manuscript, and for the use of the file of reviews which Grove Press collected following Weber's edition of Harris; to Walter Blair for his reminders that Harris is a comic writer; to Hennig Cohen, and to folklorists Herbert Halpert and Richard Wagner for information about American and European fools and fool killers; to Ben Harris McClary (founder of the Sut Society) for many items of information; to M. Thomas Inge for typescripts of new sketches by Harris as he discovered them in preparing his edition of Harris' work for Twayne's United States Classics Series, and for the use of his bibliography of Harris' writing; to the late Miss Flannery O'Connor for her comments on Harris' work both by letter and in conversation; to Ray D. Smith for items from his index to the *Confederate Veteran* magazine; to Warren C. Sledd for photocopies from Rutgers University Library's holdings of *Yankee Notions*; to Robert W. Hill of the New York Public Library for tracing the history of Dick & Fitzgerald Publishing Company; to Robert T. Quarles and William T. Alderson of the Tennessee Historical Society and William J. Griffin of the Tennessee Folklore Society for information and comments; to John Q. and Loraine Anderson for bibliographical items; and to many others who kindly replied to my letters, including Nancy Agnew, William W. Bass, William H. Thomas, Virginia Pride

Binger, Josephine B. Wingfield, and many more. To Arlin Turner and Lewis P. Simpson I owe special thanks for their long continuing and generous encouragement.

Ida Belle Blanchet of the Dupré Library at the University of Southwestern Louisiana, who hopes to find her name in another book someday, is here thanked for ordering many volumes from many places for me. My thanks are due also to the Graduate Council Committee on Faculty Research at the University of Southwestern Louisiana for a grant to purchase photocopies of Harris' newspaper work.

Charles Chester Martin, M.D., and C. Marston McClure, M.D., both read the accounts of Harris' death that I had collected and patiently explored possible causes with me.

Thanks are due the following publishers for permission to quote: Chandler Publishing Company for quotations from Walter Blair's *Native American Humor;* Faber & Faber for quotations from Enid Welsford's *The Fool;* Harcourt, Brace & World for quotations from Constance Rourke's *American Humor;* Alfred A. Knopf for quotations from H. L. Mencken's *The American Language;* W. W. Norton for quotations from José Ortega y Gasset's *Meditations on Quixote,* particularly a translation appearing in the notes of a passage from Miguel de Unamuno's *Del sentimiento trágico de la vida;* Little, Brown and Company for quotations from Kenneth Lynn's *Mark Twain and Southwestern Humor;* Oxford University Press for quotations from F. O. Matthiessen's *American Renaissance* and Edmund Wilson's *Patriotic Gore;* The Viking Press for quotations from William Faulkner appearing in Malcolm Cowley, editor, *Writers at Work: The PARIS REVIEW Interviews.*

All scholars owe special gratitude to members of the American Association of University Presses for their policy of encouraging authors to quote from their publications, within the doctrine of fair use, without prior permission. From this group my thanks are due the University of North Carolina Press for passages from R. E. Barclay's *Ducktown back in Raht's Time;* and the Princeton University Press for quotations from Northrop Frye's *Anatomy of Criticism.* The following individual holders of copyright gave permission to quote their work: Brom Weber allowed use of a passage from his introduction to *Sut Lovingood,* and

Acknowledgments

Wylie Sypher for phrases from his essay "The Meaning of Comedy," appearing in his book *Comedy*. The editors of *American Literature* kindly gave permission for me to reprint portions of my "The Imagery of George Washington Harris" which first appeared in their journal, May, 1959.

My greatest thanks go to my wife, Patricia Kennedy Rickels, who read and wrote with me throughout this work so extensively that she deserves to be acknowledged its co-author. She has declined until after the reviews. Finally I wish to express my gratitude to my son Gordon, who is very understanding about the time it takes to make a book.

Contents

Chronology

1814   March 20, George Washington Harris born in Allegheny City, Pennsylvania.

1819   Harris' half-brother, Samuel Bell, takes the child southwest to Knoxville, Tennessee.

1826   Harris builds working model of a steamboat; serves as apprentice metalworker in Samuel Bell's shop.

1835   His metalworking apprenticeship completed, and already captain of the steamboat *Knoxville*, Harris marries Mary Emeline Nance.

1839   Harris buys 375 acres of land in Blount County, in Tucaleeche Cove at the gateway to the Great Smoky Mountains; contributes political articles to the Knoxville *Argus*.

1843   Harris leaves his farm, returns to Knoxville to open a metalworking shop; Knoxville papers praise him as man of "remarkable genius" in metals, and as a man of many skills. Contributes "sporting epistles" to William T. Porter's New York *Spirit of the Times* under the pseudonym of Mr. Free.

1845   Harris contributes "The Knob Dance—A Tennessee Frolic" to the *Spirit*, a re-creation of the joy of life in the Tennessee hills. Plans to collaborate on a book "illustrative of manners and customs of East Tennessee."

1849   Harris superintends Holston Glass Works; continues practicing the art of silversmithing.

1854   Works in the coppermining community of Ducktown in southeastern Tennessee mountains; meets Sut Miller, source of his best-known character. Contributes first of the Lovingood tales, "Sut Lovengood's Daddy 'Acting Horse'" to the *Spirit*.

1856   Serves as delegate to the Southern Commercial Convention at Savannah, Georgia—generally a secessionist group.

Meets William Tappan Thompson, author of *Major Jones's Courtship* (1843) and other books. Writes first political satire, "Playing Old Sledge for the Presidency." Elected alderman, Fourth Ward, Knoxville.

1857 Appointed postmaster of Knoxville; retains office only seven months.

1858 Writes several Sut sketches for the Nashville *Union & American;* plans collection of Lovingood stories.

1859 Leaves Unionist Knoxville for Nashville. Elected to Democratic State Central Committee.

1861 Contributes three anti-Lincoln sketches to Nashville *Union & American,* pro-secessionist, pro-war in intent.

1862- Flees Nashville with family before Union troops. Lives
1865 in several Southern cities during the war.

1866 Resumes anti-Republican, anti-Yankee newspaper writing. Works for Wills Valley Railroad.

1867 In April appears Harris' one book, *Sut Lovingood's Yarns.* His wife dies.

1869 In October, marries Jane E. Pride in Decatur, Alabama. In December, on railroad business, takes manuscript of another book, *High Times and Hard Times,* to Lynchburg, Virginia, to arrange publication; dies on return trip in Knoxville.

George Washington Harris

CHAPTER 1

'A Craftsman of the Kind Thoreau Admired'

—MATTHIESSEN, *American Renaissance*

I

THE SEARCH for George Washington Harris' ancestors has hardly begun. Harris himself traced his line to Sir George Harris of Brentwood, near London, and neatly wrote out the family genealogy for his children.[1] But as far as independent verification goes, in length of line and multiplicity of forebears, he is, as Mark Twain wrote of himself, as poor as Jesus: no grandfather. According to family tradition his father's name was also George W. Harris and his mother's Margaret Glover.[2]

Margaret Glover was married first to Samuel Bell, to whom she bore a son, also named Samuel, about 1798. Where the family lived is not known: perhaps North Carolina or Virginia. After a time the family moved to Allegheny City, now a part of Pittsburgh, Pennsylvania. There Samuel Bell died, and his widow married George W. Harris, who had been an associate of her husband's for some years. In Allegheny City, on March 30, 1814, to Margaret Glover Bell Harris and George W. Harris, of whom nothing further is known, was born a son, George Washington Harris.[3]

Probably in Allegheny City, young Samuel Bell, a skillful worker, was apprenticed to an arms factory, where he made swords for the War of 1812.[4] In 1819, his apprenticeship completed, Bell traveled into the Southwest, seeking a new location. After some searching, he decided to settle in the tiny village of

Knoxville in the foothills of the Chilhowee and Clinch mountains, where the confluence of the Holston and the French Broad rivers forms the Tennessee, offering traffic routes and power for industrialization.

His arrangements made, Bell returned to Allegheny City and married an English girl, whose first name only, Elizabeth, is known.[5] When the couple moved to Knoxville, they brought along Bell's young half-brother, George Washington Harris. Whether Harris' parents were alive or dead, or whether they too came to Knoxville or remained in Allegheny City, is not known.

Samuel Bell kept a metalworking shop in Knoxville in his house at the corner of Main and Prince streets. Many years after his death, the Knoxville historian George F. Mellen wrote of Bell's work: "The skill he exhibited as a workman with precious metals was equally displayed in the fashioning of pistols, swords, dirks and other weapons. Old Tennessee families still have in their possession specimens of his handiwork to which they refer with pride. The impress of Sam Bell's on any article was a guarantee of its genuineness and durability."[6]

In this shop Samuel Bell apprenticed his half-brother to metalworking. Bell taught his own sons these skills too, and took other apprentices, who, after the manner of the time, lived in the house with the family.[7] Thus from his childhood George Washington Harris learned to work ingeniously in many metals: gold and silver, steel, iron, and brass. He learned to make jewelry and silverware; to repair clocks and watches, rifles and pistols; to build and repair a variety of machines and mechanical models.[8] This training in skills requiring painstaking attention to detail may well have had its influence on his later craftsmanship as a writer. Of formal schooling Harris had but little, perhaps only eighteen months; but probably there was some reading, at least of a technical nature, in Bell's large, industrious household.

In 1826, when George was twelve, the first steamboat reached Knoxville. The complex craft inspired the boy to build a mechanical model, which he sailed successfully on the flag pond at the foot of town and thus gained his first acclaim from the townspeople.[9] The arrival of the little *Atlas* also led a group of Knoxville citizens to form a company to buy their own steamer and to begin regular service on the Tennessee River. In time

W. B. A. Ramsey was sent to Cincinnati to contract for a boat, and sometime before 1831 the *Knoxville* ascended treacherous Muscle Shoals and arrived at the town.[10]

II

Steamboats and steamboat captains were part of the romantic dreams of glory of every river-town boy in those days, but for Harris the dream came true. When, at the age of nineteen, he finished his apprenticeship with Samuel Bell, he became captain of the *Knoxville*[11] and, perhaps, the envy of every boy in town. As an old man Harris enjoyed recalling his adventures on the river to the delight of his children. Whether he kept aloof from the temptations of the straggling river towns or whether he roistered in places like Waterloo, Alabama, described in a contemporary account as a "hamlet of doggeries & of brothels, got up to entertain the low and sensual tastes of the boatmen who navigate the rivers,"[12] is unrecorded. Probably a sense of social separation from the "lower orders," reinforced by strict Presbyterian upbringing, had already produced a reserved, sedate, rather formal character.

When he was twenty-one, Harris took a wife. He married, on September 3, 1835, Mary Emeline Nance, daughter of Pryor Nance, for many years surveyor and inspector of the port of Knoxville. Besides their interest in navigation, Harris and his new father-in-law had something else in common: Mr. Nance was proprietor of the Knoxville race track,[13] and Harris had a life-long interest in horse racing, having taken advantage of his small stature to ride as a jockey in quarter races when he was fifteen.[14]

As late as 1838 Harris was still on the river. During that year he took part in the genocidal forced removal of the Cherokees, when they were driven from their ancestral lands and transported, some by river boat, to regions west of the Mississippi. Many years after Harris' death, legends of his part in the event lingered in Knoxville. One records him as keeping whiskey from the Indians on his boat; another has him refusing to allow General Winfield Scott, who was in charge of the Indian removal, to give orders on board his vessel. Both of the shadowy legends show the young man as a strict disciplinarian, jealous of his authority.[15]

During the years on the river, Harris' household was growing; about two years after his marriage, his first child was born, named Pryor Nance after his grandfather. The event was celebrated by a Southern custom often observed in families that could afford to do so: a slave was bought to grow up as companion and servant to the white child. On October 16, 1836, Harris bought, according to the bill of sale, "a certain Negro boy child named Jasper, aged about eight months, it being the descendant of a woman . . . called Neoming. . . ."[16] He was making long-range plans for genteel living.

Shortly after the Indian Removal, Harris left steamboating in favor of a more stable, gentlemanly way of life. In June, 1839, in nearby Blount County, east of the town of Maryville in the foothills of the Great Smoky Mountains, Harris bought 375 acres of land "on a branch of Nails Creek waters of Little River."[17] The land, in three parcels, had springs, creeks, and fields; woods of hickory, black oak, post oak, and pine; and was large enough to give him boundaries with a dozen neighboring farms. Harris bought the land from David Newman (or Neiman) for $2,000, paying about one-fourth down and signing four notes for the balance, one due each year.

Although the Scotch-Irish had settled in large numbers in East Tennessee, the names of Harris' neighbors sound as if he lived among English farmers: Phillips, Knight, Nicholson, Logan, Young, Harvey, Caldwell, along with three Neimans and Archibald Murphy. Many farms in East Tennessee afforded the most marginal existence, but Harris' neighbors in Blount County were, judging by his first writing, members of a hard-working, productive yeomanry, fond of music, dancing, hunting, and horse racing.

Harris' own family was established in a comfortable, well-furnished dwelling. When the census taker visited the Harrises in 1840, the household numbered eight people: Harris and his wife, both in their mid-twenties; three children (only the oldest son, Pryor Nance, was destined to survive the next ten years); a young girl of about fifteen, perhaps to help Mary Emeline Harris; two adult slaves, and the child slave Jasper. The house was elegantly furnished. The Harrises owned a dozen Windsor chairs and thirty-two yards of fine carpet. A delicate wire fender graced the main fireplace, and the smaller fireplaces had their screens and tools. Fine looking glasses, three dressing tables, seven bedsteads, trunks, bureaus, corner cupboards, and a tin safe for the kitchen suggest a very comfortable beginning for the new life.

For himself, Harris owned a wall map of the world and a book case with seventy-five books, plus, for this Presbyterian, one Bible. The books were an unusual luxury for the time and place, and they show Harris' strong interest in literature. Except for the Bible, the titles are unknown. Later references in his work, however, show he read Shakespeare; Congreve; much Dickens, who was popular throughout Harris' lifetime; Robert Burns; Byron; Pope; Longfellow, whose sentimentalism Harris satirized frequently; and others. Harris also read widely in the newspapers and magazines of his time. He was not altogether bookish, though. He owned, in addition to his farm horses, a fine bay mare and a rifle.

Harris was not a farmer. The heavy debt he contracted to buy land may have grown out of an image he had of the good life of a country squire, the Southern ideal of the gentleman planter. If he were experimenting in land speculation, he did not stake his family's fortunes altogether on such enterprises, for the 1840 Census lists him as engaged in "manufacturing and trade." It may be supposed that he continued in his craft of metalworking during the years in Blount County.

III

While he was living on his Tennessee Land, Harris did his first writing: political comment for a Democratic newspaper. Blount County is not far from Knoxville, and Harris kept ties of friendship there, where he had met Elbridge Gerry Eastman, editor of the Knoxville *Argus*. A native of Bridgewater, New Hampshire, Eastman had been apprenticed to learn the printing trade and had then migrated to Washington, D. C., to read proof for the *Globe*. He somehow met James K. Polk, who encouraged him to establish a Democratic newspaper in Knoxville. So Eastman moved to Knoxville, where he edited the *Argus* and published the *Yeoman*. Not wholly concerned with politics, he was interested in frontier life, and his papers printed many sketches of life in early New England.[18] But he was always a supporter of the Democrats, and in 1839 he supported Polk, who left the House of Representatives to run for the governorship of Tennessee against the Whig incumbent, Newton Cannon.[19] Which of the *Argus'* political polemics, all aggressive and fiery, were written by Harris, Professor Donald Day, who has examined the files of the *Argus,* cannot say.[20] Long after Eastman's death, Harris remembered with affection the encouragement to write that Eastman had been the first to give him.[21]

Omens of disaster for Harris' rural life in his cove of the Great Smokies quickly appeared. In December, 1840, the Southwestern Railroad Bank at Knoxville protested one of Harris' notes, endorsed by his father-in-law, Pryor Nance, and by Nance's brother Peter, owner of the Mansion House in Knoxville. On December 23, 1840, Harris made an indenture on his household goods and livestock to secure the note.[22] From this unhappy inventory comes the list of Harris' furniture, tools, and books. The same week he executed other indentures on his slave Jasper and on his bay mare to secure indebtednesses to Maryville merchants and to William Swan, who held his note for $100.[23] Whether some personal disaster had struck, or whether—which seems more likely—Harris had merely overextended his credit, he managed to weather this storm, and remained in Blount County at least until February, 1842, when he was forced to sell Jasper. Within a year from that date, he left his farm. The failure to succeed as a gentleman landowner was only the first of many thwartings of Harris' ambitions and desires.

Harris must have rescued a fair amount of capital from his farming venture, for by February, 1843, he was established back in Knoxville, corner of Prince and Cumberland Streets, in a metalworking shop with tools and large machinery elaborate enough, for example, to cut screws from eight to sixty-five threads per inch and as long as five feet. Harris' advertisement ran for many years offering to do every variety of turning in steel, iron, or brass; to make copperplate and wood engraving, county and corporation seals; to sink dies; to make models of "new inventions for the Patent office or exhibition . . . Surgeons' and Dentists' instruments, mathematical and philosophical ditto; model steam-engines for Colleges"; to work in jewelry and silverware; to make racing cups "from the latest English models, in gold or silver"; and to repair guns, clocks, and watches.[24] The advertisement presents a shop cheerfully devoting mechanical ingenuity to the service of beauty and utility.

Harris had a guildsman's feeling for protecting his professional interests. In July, 1843, he was chairman of a committee to draft a public letter to "The Mechanics of East Tennessee" protesting competition from state penitentiary products.[25] He was a member of the Mechanics' Library Association, and treasurer of the Young Men's Literary Society, then busy collecting a library of "Standard works" and items for a small museum.[26]

Harris seems always to have been a devoted husband and father. For the silver to make a gift for his wife, he bought a saddle from a Dr. Black of Amsterdam (once the saddle of the Sultan of Mysore, said Dr. Black). Harris engraved stamps for spoons, and his colleague David Hope made a dozen which Harris then engraved with his wife's initials, "M. E. H." for a Christmas gift. After the death of Mary Emeline Harris in 1866, the spoons were divided among the children, and Harris' last surviving daughter, Amanda Pillow Harris Raymond of Austin, Texas, showed Donald Day one of them in the early 1940's.[27]

IV

After Harris' first published writing, about 1839, he seems never to have lost interest in practicing the art; and, with the passage of years, he bestowed on his work the craftsman's meticulous attention to the smallest detail. Although his friend Eastman still edited Knoxville's Democratic paper, Harris wanted to try some form other than political polemics. He chose to write next for a national journal, the New York *Spirit of the Times,* edited by the genial, urbane William Trotter Porter. A chronicle "of the Turf, Agriculture, Field Sports, Literature, and the Stage," it offered Harris no pay other than Porter's praise and advice and a national, even international audience; for it circulated in England and in the British possessions overseas.[28]

Harris' first contribution (almost certainly his) was a series of letters describing the quarter racing, hunting, and other outdoor sports of the East Tennessee mountains.[29] The fourth letter, dated September 2, 1843, moves from a description of sports to a semi-dramatic presentation of the rural customs of log-rolling, dancing, and the quilting bee. The partly formed characters are a happy yeomanry rather than the coarse backwoodsmen or degenerate poor-whites satirized by A. B. Longstreet in his *Georgia Scenes* (1835). The letters are a somewhat uncertain version of the ideal pastoral life, signed with the symbolic pen name, Mr. Free.

The next work identified as Harris' was published in the *Spirit of the Times* in the summer of 1845; is experimental in form; and marks a considerable technical advance over the conventional letters of two years earlier. "The Knob Dance, A Tennessee Frolic" is an effort to re-create the sound, rhythm, and imagery of the rural dialect, and to create a mood of wild joy, almost free of restraint. What dialect the Bells and Harrises spoke is unknown, but possibly theirs and certainly the English-born Elizabeth Bell's and his friend Eastman's would have called to Harris' attention the varieties of speech in Knoxville. Harris signed this sketch "Sugartail," abandoning his earlier pseudonym "Mr. Free." This second *nom de plume* he sometimes disguised further as "S——l, of Tennessee," hinting at a possible indecency. For ten years Harris contributed irregularly to the *Spirit*. Although Porter was liberal in the degree of realism he allowed and even encouraged—printing sketches which alluded to backwoods fornications, adulteries, and un-Victorian nakedness—he once refused one of Harris' sketches as "too highly seasoned to be published as it is."[30]

As "The Knob Dance" indicates, by the time Harris was thirty, the difference was growing between the quiet Presbyterian businessman who was the public George Washington Harris, and the intense, sometimes fierce artistic creations of his writing.

Throughout the 1840's Harris' writing is varied and experimental. He tried political analysis, Addisonian moralizing, and character sketches, elegiac and nostalgic epistles, somewhat condescending descriptions of backwoods life, and, in the growing tradition of Porter's *Spirit*, re-creations of the folk art of the oral tale, particularly as told by the unlettered backwoodsman, sometimes written in a framework which contrasted idioms and points of view.

As family man and as public man, Harris is remembered as dignified, formal, and generally kind.[31] In appearance, "a little fellow, whose steps measured about fifteen inches," he was quick and nervous in his manner.[32] More revealing of the man's public personality is an exchange of letters published in the *Spirit* in 1848 jesting about the formality of Harris' religious life. One of Harris' friends wrote the *Spirit* a letter, denouncing another for reading the journal on Sundays. The second replied with a denial, "like 'S——l,' I am a church going man." The writer of the first letter, a Knoxville physician, reiterated the accusation; then, turning to another topic, said he troubled the *Spirit's* editor only in the hope of getting Harris to contribute more sketches. But Harris' failure to write, he continued, was excusable because the man was so busy making and repairing every variety of machine that he had no spare minute, "unless he should write on Sunday (to do which he is too 'square up an old Blue.')"[33] The blue Presbyterian was one notable for the strictness of his life at a time when the ordinary Presbyterian sabbath meant morning and afternoon church services—the prayers long; the sermons, dry and logical.

In the light of Harris' other church activities, his friend's classification of him as a "blue" Presbyterian seems more than half serious. The Harris family had its own pew in the First Presbyterian Church of Knoxville, where for many years Harris was an elder. Harris' fourth son, James Park, was named for the Reverend Dr. James Park, for over forty years pastor of the First Presbyterian Church.[34] Harris' last surviving daughter recalled that Dr. Park had baptized all the Harris children. The formality of Harris' public life, his Sabbatarianism, and his "blue" orthodoxy contrast sharply with the increasingly broad, coarse humor of his writing. He wrote in a newspaper tradition of harsh vituperation and of frankly physical masculine humor; but even within these latitudes his work is extreme in its realism, as well as in its skill of comic fantasy.

Though, as his friend said, "he worked so hard that he had no spare minute," Harris' metalworking shop apparently did not

bring him the income he desired. By 1849 he was associated
with a new factory, the Holston Glass Works, where he was
superintendent, a position which may have demanded only a
part of his time since he listed himself for the 1850 Census as a
silversmith. His household in that year consisted of himself, his
wife Mary, his son Pryor Nance, thirteen (two of his children
had died); a daughter Mary, three; and a one year-old-son named
for his father. Also in the household were two young craftsmen
who worked at the glass factory: James D. Lilley, a glass cutter,
and Nicholas Hackett, a glass blower, both from New Jersey.
Servants in the household were two mulattoes: twelve-year-old
Allen Scott and a cook, Henry Steel. Harris also employed a
washerwoman. The number of servants in the house was as
great as it had been ten years earlier, and their presence
indicated that Mary Nance Harris did not do her own housework. In contrast, the prudent Samuel Bell, who had reared
Harris, listed his wife, five children, and one apprentice, but no
servants at all. It seems as if George Washington Harris' family
lived as gentlefolk, but Harris had to hold two jobs and take
in boarders to manage it.

V

In 1854 Harris was captain of a new steamboat on the
Tennessee, the *Alida,* but not for long. Probably later in that
year he traveled to Polk County, in the extreme southeast corner
of Tennessee, to superintend the surveying of the Ducktown
copper mines.[35] Here in the mountains where the ore had once
been packed out on mule back, he observed mining-town life,
which impressed him with its fighting and hard drinking; some
of the men seemed to Harris "wild mountaineers." The people
of this remote, isolated mountain country at once engaged
Harris' imagination. Like most of Porter's contributors, he was
sensitive to unusual local patterns of life, character, and language. He quickly wrote a comic fantasy of a mountain family
so poverty-stricken that the father had himself harnessed to plow
the corn patch to keep the family from starving. Harris presented
the sketch as told in vivid, ribald dialect by the son, Sut
Lovingood.

Perhaps the story is the retelling or re-creation of a tale Harris heard told. His narrator seems based on a real local personage, Sut Miller, which accounts for the strange first name (though not for the erotic implications of the last name).[36] Sut tells his tale to a crowd of mountaineers in front of Pat Nash's doggery; Nash, too, was real, a saloonkeeper who died on September 12, 1854, and whose unsavory reputation still lingers in the Copper Basin.[37]

But if setting and narrator were real, the actual Sut Miller, farmer and occasional laborer, was only a beginning. For the rest of Harris' life, his imagination circled around the creation of a creature called "Sut." In 1857 and 1858, several years after his first appearance, Sut becomes under Harris' slowly shaping hand something of a traditional fool. Sut's character and adventures are in the tradition of the *Spirit's* country clowns; and they recall, more remotely, the European folk tradition embodied in Till Eulenspiegel.[38] Sut's surfaces are those of realism, comic fantasy, and local color. As an esthetic concept, Sut also seems to owe something to the fools of Shakespeare: Launcelot Gobbo, Touchstone, and the Fool in *Lear*.

Throughout his life Harris used Sut in a variety of ways: sometimes Sut is mouthpiece for Harris, although rarely; sometimes he is a political observer in the tradition of the Crackerbox Philosophers;[39] but by the time Harris published his only book in 1867, Sut as a fool has come to dominate Harris' slowly crystallizing concept. By extensive revision of and by addition to his newspaper tales, Harris creates the most complex and fully realized point of view to be found in any of the Southwestern humorists. Not a simple, heroic child of nature like Thomas Bangs Thorpe's masterful Big Bear of Arkansas, not a comic rogue like Johnson Jones Hooper's Simon Suggs, Sut is the fool as truthteller—wild, knowing, and free. As a complex, esthetically coherent point of view, Sut is the most skillful creation to appear in the tradition before Mark Twain's Huckleberry Finn.

How long Harris remained in Ducktown is unknown. By 1855 he was back in Knoxville, planning to construct a sawmill. Beginning early in 1856, he began serving as alderman for the Fourth Ward in Knoxville.[40] In the same year he wrote some political propaganda and analysis for the Nashville *Union &*

American, now owned and edited by his friend Eastman. In the fall he went to Savannah, Georgia, as a delegate to the Southern Commercial Convention. These conventions, ostensibly to promote Southern economic independence, were already hotbeds of secessionist sentiments; Harris' presence indicates that he was one of the political extremists in his section. Harris had long been a Democrat. During these same years, however, his half-brother Samuel Bell remained a Whig, served as mayor of Knoxville, and was so staunch a Union man that during the Civil War he wore in public an American flag.[41] This strong political opposition between Harris and Bell, who had stood in the place of a father during Harris' early life, might, if we knew more, help explain Harris' very mixed feelings toward father-figures and all symbols of authority.

While in Savannah for the convention, Harris met William Tappan Thompson, another humorist, a contributor to William Trotter Porter's *Spirit,* the author of *Major Jones's Courtship* (1843) and other volumes, and at the time editor of the Savannah *Morning News.* Shortly after his return home, Harris sent Thompson a story for his paper titled "Sut Lovengood Blown Up," a variation on one of Thompson's own stories. It was a reworking of gentle, decent Major Jones's courtship as Sut's ill-fated attempt to seduce beautiful Sicily Burns.

In the summer of 1857 Harris was appointed postmaster of Knoxville, but his appointment terminated in a few months. In September, Howell Cobb, Secretary of the Treasury under President James Buchanan, appointed Harris, J. G. M. Ramsey, and Thomas C. Lyon commissioners to receive proposals for a new federal building to be erected in Knoxville.[42] Harris had supported Buchanan, and the appointments seem minor political rewards.

Early in 1858, E. G. Eastman wrote in the Nashville *Union & American* that Harris was planning to publish his Sut Lovingood sketches in a book, and in the summer of that year Harris went to New York, probably to see if he could find a publisher. He was unsuccessful, but 1858 was a year of great literary productivity for him. He wrote three stories about Sut's vengeful pranks on Sicily Burns and her family, plus at least seven other sketches and letters.

Beneath the exaggerated, grotesque action of some of these sketches, additional underlying attitudes begin to emerge in Harris' work. The argument seems political at first glance, but political categories are too narrow for all the work in and after 1858. In images of great energy and extravagance, Harris actualizes anti-Northern feelings which are not only against Abolitionists but also against industrialization (which Harris promoted in Knoxville), against temperance, against reform, and against the age's speculative, experimental, self-examining mood. Harris' surface tone of coarse fun seems to some degree self-consciously and defiantly shocking. Much of the writing is witty and at times revealing of human incongruity; but behind the mask of comedy from time to time the creator's face seems to darken and twist in splenetic fantasies of power and dreams of fear. Hard humor in the manner of Tobias Smollett's *Roderick Random* (1748) alternates with an occasional jarring sentimentality. Even within the brief form of the mock-oral tale, Harris occasionally loses control of his effect. Wisely, he did not reprint many of his 1858 sketches. The work hints at a variety of inner tensions which perhaps not a few of the Secessionists felt. Further, Harris' economic life seems to have been growing less stable.

By 1859, Harris was devoting a considerable amount of his time to politics. In March he attended the state Democratic convention in Nashville. He was elected by the convention to the Democratic State Central Committee, and he remained a few months in Nashville. During the spring he contributed several satiric attacks on the Opposition party to Eastman's *Union & American*.[43] By October he was working as conductor on the Nashville and Chattanooga Railroad.[44] November 23, 1859, Harris' friend Eastman died suddenly, just after another of the paper's editors was shot and killed in a dispute over the paper's policy. During 1860-61 Harris worked as freight agent for the Nashville and Chattanooga.

In February and March, 1861, Harris contributed three sketches to the *Union & American* lampooning Abraham Lincoln, the newly elected President. Harris' presence in Nashville probably indicates that he moved his family out of Knoxville, perhaps finding the city uncomfortable for one of his politics. In the special election of June 8, 1861, pro-Union Eastern Tennessee voted heavily against secession, although middle and west Tennessee voted for it, and it carried.[45] So strong was the Unionist feeling that East Tennessee attempted to secede from the Secessionists. On June 17, a convention of anti-Secessionists was held at Greenville with 292 delegates from twenty-nine East Tennessee counties; the convention petitioned the state legislature for permission to separate itself and form a new state. The legislature refused, and Confederate troops were soon in the area. Harris never returned to Knoxville to live.

Harris' sons were as ardent for the Confederate cause as he. Pryor Nance left his job as salesman for L. B. and T. D. Fite, wholesale drygoods merchants of Nashville, to form and become captain of the Harris Guards, Fourth Tennessee Cavalry, C.S.A.[46] Harris' second son, before he was fifteen, joined Walthall's division and fought under General Joseph E. Johnston at the Battle of Kenesaw Mountain in the spring of 1864.[47]

However, when the war that Harris so eagerly supported broke out, only Pryor Nance was old enough to care for himself. For Harris, his wife, and four children, the war years were years of wandering. They fled Nashville in February, 1862, and during the next four years they lived in Chattanooga; Decatur, Alabama; Trenton, Georgia; and perhaps other places.[48] If Harris did any writing during the war years, which seems probable, it has not been discovered.

VI

After the war Harris bought the right-of-way for the Wills Valley Railroad being built by the pro-Unionist William Crutchfield, who had in 1861 called Jefferson Davis a traitor when Davis spoke briefly in Chattanooga on his way back from the United States Senate to his home in Mississippi.[49] Only the screams of Mrs. Davis and Mrs. Crutchfield, some eyewitnesses reported, averted a duel.[50] Crutchfield was not the only friend of Harris who differed profoundly from him on important issues. Harris could not only tolerate but appreciate Crutchfield's courage, and said of him in one of his two serious dedications of the *Yarns* that he was "brave enough to be true, and true enough to be singular; one who says what he thinks" (xiv). For all the intemperance of Harris' political satires, the man himself possessed sufficient intelligence and urbanity to separate people's political affiliations from their other human values.

During 1866 Haris wrote at least five sketches for the un-reconstructed Nashville *Union & American:* violent attacks on General Sherman, on an unidentified Wisconsin newspaperman, on "the Puritan Yankee," and on local pedigree hunters. He was also revising his old sketches and writing new ones in an effort once again to publish a volume. For a national audience, Harris omitted the personal satires he had written. The manuscript was accepted and published by Dick & Fitzgerald of New York City, in the spring of 1867, as *Sut Lovingood. Yarns Spun by a "Nat'ral Born Durn'd Fool.*["]

Concentrating on complex practical jokes, on the comic and symbolic possibilities of the fool's point of view, and on the comedy of language, Harris produced a vigorous, intense, cruel minor comic masterpiece which has caused Professor Brom Weber to call Harris a pivotal figure in the analysis of American and Southern culture,[51] and Edmund Wilson to say of the *Yarns,* that, as far as his experience goes, "it is by far the most repellent book of any real literary merit in American literature."[52] Young Mark Twain, reviewing the book for the *Alta California,* enjoyed the humor but predicted the "East" would find it coarse.[53] According to the *United States Catalogue* and other sources, the book remained in print and for sale by the various successors of Dick & Fitzgerald until the last stock was sold by the Walter H. Baker Company of Boston to Charles Olson, Nashville bookseller, in 1960.[54]

In the spring of 1867 Harris' wife died, and shortly after, fearing she might be "talked about," the housekeeper left. To his sister-in-law, Mrs. Fouche, whose husband was a Knoxville dentist, Harris poured out his troubles:

> What course to pursue now, I cannot determine; I have no earthly desire to marry, and if I had and had even found a person suited to me, unless I was *absolutely* sure that she would be a kind mother to my poor motherless children, no consideration would induce me even to think of it. . . . We are in a most *delightful* country but have fewer women in the right sense of that word than any place I ever saw; ignorant, rough, primitive—

I don't know five in the valley whose hands I would trust Pillow's [Amanda Pillow Harris] future—and they all have homes of their own. . . . Suppose I were to marry some one and she proved unkind to them or unfit to raise them, why I risk all on one throw of the cards and *lose all.*[55]

During the latter part of 1867 and into the next spring Harris wrote sketches for the Chattanooga *Daily American Union.* The tales, not much concerned with politics, are among the coarsest and broadest in their sexual comedy of any of Harris' work. In April he returned to political satire for the Knoxville *Press and Messenger* with two burlesques of Jesse R. Grant's biography of his son Ulysses S. Grant, which was then being printed in the New York *Ledger* as a part of Grant's presidential compaign.[56]

Harris remarried on October 19, 1869, at Decatur, Alabama. His second wife was a widow, Mrs. Jane E. Pride, a tall, beautiful, blonde woman renowned locally as a witty conversationalist; the two "proved quite a match for each other at the dinner table."[57]

VII

When, two months after his marriage, in December, 1869, Harris had to go to Lynchburg, Virginia, on business for the railroad, he took along the manuscript of another book to see if it could be printed there. The title, echoing Dickens' *Hard Times* (1854) as well as describing postwar Alabama, was to be *High Times and Hard Times.* He attended to his railroad business, asked at the printing office of the Lynchburg *Republican* about the cost of setting his manuscript. Then on Friday, December 10, 1869, he boarded the Virginia and Tennessee for the trip home. He became ill on the train and was transferred at Bristol while he was unconscious. Both conductors thought he was drunk, and he traveled through the night and next morning lying in two seats, wrapped in his overcoat. Finally the conductor managed to rouse him momentarily, and he replied "yes" when asked if he wanted to be taken off at Knoxville.[58]

At 1:00 P.M., he was carried to a room in the Atkin House at Knoxville; and Dr. Kraus, called to attend him, diagnosed his condition as apoplexy. At 9:00, Dr. Fouche, Harris' brother-in-law was sent for and arrived shortly thereafter, accompanied by Dr. McIntosh: "They found the sufferer in a critical condition, his eyes set in glassy stare, and breathing heavily. Dr. Fouche was recognized a moment, and then Harris lost all consciousness."[59] Harris rallied again about 10:00, "recognized a few friends and replied in answer to a question of one of the physicians, the word, 'poisoned.' "[60]

Toward midnight he died.

The verdict at the inquest was that Harris died "by some unknown cause." No post mortem examination was made. To the *Press & Herald* questions, Dr. Kraus said he believed Harris died of apoplexy; "The other physicians ascribe his death to morphia."[61]

The *Press & Herald* subtitled its story "Sudden and Mysterious Death," and repeated at the end that Harris' was a "most mysterious death." Four of the five physicians present, including Harris' brother-in-law, ascribed the death to "morphia"; but what they meant is obscure. At the time, the term was a general synonym for morphine. The narcotic was easily obtained and widely used; patent medicine and drug companies long fought successfully all sales regulation. The doctors might have known that Harris used the drug; they might have known Kraus had treated Harris with the drug; there are other possibilities, all remote.

The newspaper's mystery-making seems unconscionable journalism, a mystery based on Harris' own whispered "poisoned." As for this self-diagnosis (not strange from a man who hated the food and ways of innkeepers all his life), if a very ill, semiconscious man says only one word, it would probably not be clearly understandable. If it were, it would rarely be significant, in view of the mental impairment present. Finally, the common poisons, such as arsenic or cyanide, produce characteristic symptoms; and the victim's decline is progressive and inexorable. The coroner's jury saw no reason to order a post-mortem examination.

If Harris were an addict or an experimenter with morphine, the possibility of death from an overdose, intentional or not, is remote if he died with "his eyes set in a glassy stare, and breathing heavily." An overdose of morphine causes respiratory depression, with slow, shallow breathing, and the characteristic pinpoint pupils. Dr. Kraus' diagnosis of apoplexy remains the most tenable. The victim of a cerebral vascular accident may suffer his attack unexpectedly, lose consciousness, be mistaken for a drunken man, rally, and because the rally causes more bleeding into the brain, lose consciousness and die.[62]

Mary Blanchard, Harris' daughter, believed that the manuscript her father had been carrying remained in the possession of Mrs. Jane E. Pride Harris and her children. She tried for many years to locate it.[63] Both Franklin Meine and Donald Day have tried without success to trace the manuscript.

CHAPTER 2

Tennessee Pastoral

I

FOR HIS 1843 contributions to Porter's New York *Spirit of the Times,* Harris had followed the practice of most of Porter's gentleman amateurs in choosing a pseudonym, Mr. Free. Whatever Harris meant by it, the name foreshadows one of his most basic fictional motifs: a yearning for freedom from all limitations underlies most of his writing throughout the coming years. An accompanying sober knowledge that freedom is impossible provides an ever-present tension.

At first, however, Mr. Free is a fictional gentleman of leisure, free to enjoy quarter races, cock fights, and hunting trips. The first epistle, rambling in form, introduces a famous local hunter whose rifle is named "Old Turkey Reacher," described with just a touch of dialect as "the best ever heard tell of," and two incomparable coon dogs, Locksley and Thunderbolt. In Haunted Hollow of Raccoon Valley the dogs tree an old raccoon in a tall chestnut. Old Turkey Reacher fails twice. The hunter, Tom, climbs the tree to fire his pistol at close range; the coon will not fall, and Tom backs down and runs home: "Tom on his homeward march said he believed he had encountered the 'Prince of Darkness' in the shape of a 'coon; and that he had formed the resolution never more to interrupt any of the 'coon family."[1] A second trip shows Mr. Free that the malevolent coon was merely a bump on the trunk of the tree.

The folklore of heroic hunters and fabulous weapons was already common in the *Spirit* and had reached wide circulation in the Crockett books during the 1830's. The devil as animal was common, also. The Big Bear of Arkansas that Jim Doggett hunted through the Western woods in T. B. Thorpe's tale was such a shape shifter that Doggett came to believe he was "hunting the devil himself."[2] Harris' attempts at humor are traditional, too: the hunter backs down the tree like an old she bear and runs home in fear. This literature reveals, as Constance Rourke has demonstrated in *American Humor*, that one of the significant frontier experiences was fear of the supernatural and the mysterious and that laughter was one of the woodsman's most potent psychological weapons. Laughter was not only joy; it was a public ritual to demonstrate that man cared nothing for the malevolence of bears or for the isolation of the forests. Harris' first anecdotes merely signify his interest in American frontier and backwoods life. He has yet no power to evoke the feelings he observes.

The second Mr. Free letter attempts a comic anecdote at the expense of a Hoosier, a description of a quarter race, and a fight, "the combatants gouging and biting each other—all for amusement, of course." Then Harris quotes two Tennessee legislators to demonstrate their lack of schooling. The third letter continues the political satire with an account of a Knox County grand juror who mistook the braying of a jackass for a stampede of circus animals, an unlikely mistake and an indication that at first Harris was less interested in observing country people than he was in constructing clownish villagers with comic possibilities. In command of language and control of plot and character, the touch is unsure but grows perceptibly; perhaps the author read his work in print, first proudly, then more doubtfully.

The last of Mr. Free's letters reports his defeat for a minor local office and then moves to an extended, fairly unified description of local customs. The first is a combined log-rolling and quilting at Captain Hugh Dillon's. The guests are plain, healthy country people, dressed as their grandparents had dressed, with appetites "such as are ever strangers to your city belles and beaux." The women spend the day at the quilts, the men in the woods, felling trees in joy and gaiety. At night the company dances to the shrill fiddle—reels, cotillions, waltzes. Men "cut the pigeon wing," and the mirth grows uproarious.

For his description, Harris borrows phrases from Burns's "Tam O'Shanter," but the ending of the party is calmly pastoral.

Mr. Free's final topic is a corn shucking in Morgan County, a day spent by "maids and men" husking, singing, talking, betting, drinking, "and last, though not least, kissing who, when, and where they please, and as often as they wish for the red ears." The vocabulary and scene echo distantly the eighteenth-century pastoral tradition. The literary tone and the quotations from Shakespeare, Robert Burns, David Garrick, and others show one of the motives of the essays to be the presentation of a gentlemanly narrator. The progression of the letters, however slight, is away from simple self-consciousness. The last anecdotes focus more successfully and objectively on rural customs and attempt to present life in the Great Smokies as easy and joyous. Images of gaiety and abundance imply that the tasks of daily life are play and delight in the Eden of the New World. As Henry Nash Smith has pointed out, the master symbol of the garden with its associated images of fecundity and blissful labor was throughout the nineteenth century a powerful element in the vision of the good life in America.[3]

II

Harris' next contribution to Porter's *Spirit*, "The Knob Dance," shows a considerable advance in technical competence. Although by 1845 Harris was back in Knoxville, his setting is not the village but the hill country. The tale reproduces the dialect and spelling of the semi-literate narrator, Dick Harlan, and evokes the joyous backwoods dance:

> If a regular bilt frolick in the Nobs of "Old Knox," don't beat 'em all blind for fun, then I'm no judge of fun, that's all! I said *fun*, and I say it agin, from a *kiss* that cracks like a wagin-whip up to a *fite* that rouses up all outdoors—and as to laffin, why they *invented* laffin, and the *last* laff will be hearn at a Nob dance about three in the morning!

The characters are a little larger than life, prejudiced, individualistic, fierce seekers after fun. The romantic primitivism of Harris' point of view is illustrated in the character of host Jo

Spraggins, who "hates a circuit rider, a nigger, and a shot gun—loves a woman, old sledge, and sin in eny shape."

But the sins are sins only by the jealous definition of the preachers and the dried-up old women; the activities of the wild dancers are presented as the spontaneous innocence of natural man. Impressionistic cries and conversation rise through Dick Harlan's narrative, and the reader hears the joyful injunction, "Go it while you're young." In one intrusion a little story is completed:

> "Jim Clark has gone to the woods for fat pine, and Peggy Willet is along to take a lite for him—they've been gone a coon's age. Oh, here comes the lost 'babes in the wood,' and no lite!" "Whar's that lite! whar's that torch! I say, Peggy, whar *is* that bundle of lite wood?" "Why, I fell over a log and lost it, and we hunted clar to the foot of the holler for it, and never found it. It's no account, no how—nuthin but a little pine—who cares?"

The bantering assumes that boy and girl do not go out alone merely for light wood. Peggy's easy reply, her play on the ambiguous reference of the "it" she lost, continues the comic tone and symbolically returns the sexual encounter to its prelapsarian innocence. Illicit sexual intercourse is frankly treated in a number of the *Spirit* tales. Harris' friend "Charlie" contributed an anecdote of a man who came home from prayer meeting and by mistake got in bed with a young woman who was visiting his wife. The wife had him "up in church," and his defense was that he thought the girl was Polly, his spouse. When Nancy, the fair visitor, was asked to explain, she testified that "she thought she was Polly, too, until next morning."[4] Realistic and comic treatment of sex grows increasingly common in Harris' work.

The dancing at the Knob frolic soon turns to fighting, and Harris gives some attention to the psychology of winning and losing. Dick Harlan is thrashed. "The lickin he give me made me sorter oneasy and hostile like . . ." he says, "so I begin to look about for a man I *could* lick and no mistake!" As Huizinga points out, cheating (here consciously choosing a weak opponent), never spoils a contest for the primitive player.[5] The play symbolizes one's life, and the joy of strength, power, and victory is one of its basic values; in the modern manner, realistic recognition is the antidote to the bad faith of the enterprise.

The talk, dress, songs, speech, and dances of the Knobs of Old Knox were not for Harris merely passing customs to record, as folkways were for Longstreet. Instead, the attempt of the tale is to evoke a state of ecstasy. The folk and the folkways, recognizably but impressionistically presented, carry the reader outside himself into the comic world where life is complete. The ecstatic condition is symbolized in the compression and extravagance of the language, in the evocations of music and dance, and in the wildness of the action. For the first time, Harris has discovered his means of breaking surfaces—of getting inside, however momentarily, of human life.

Harris' "A Snake-Bit Irishman" of five months later falls off from the intensity of "The Knob Dance" largely because Harris abandons the folk point of view and the vernacular to tell the anecdote himself. Aimed more precisely at Porter's audience, one of the motives of writer and audience is to establish a little community of gentlemen and to exchange felicitations on the pleasure of status. The setting is a camp of deer hunters, the central incident a practical joke on an intruding Irishman. Status symbols are directly given: Judge A——, whose title is twice repeated, is "an ardent sportsman and splendid rifle shot"; the other gentlemen of the party are the "best materials" of society. The gentlemen's superiority lies in money, civic power to punish outsiders or to assist friends, and leisure which is spent in hunting or other outdoor sports. The main values within the group are security, power, and conformity to the pattern of the caste. The point of view in no way transcends the little community it creates. The heavy pride of place is largely that which Wilbur Cash characterized as pride without accomplishment. The pride issues in an easy feeling of competence to judge the lives of others and to act on those lives.

The language reflects the hollowness of the fable. To the Irishman's crude boast (in dialect) of his power as a fighter, the narrator responds to Porter's audience with the trite irony of "Well, all this was very pleasant, and I have no doubt perfectly satisfactory, so far as he individually was concerned, but with his hearers it was quite a different thing; yet still they endured it; but the cup of patience was nearly full, and that night it overflowed, bearing off on its boiling current the 'cause' of the 'rise' to regions far away and unknown." The point of view limits Harris to perfectly correct and almost perfectly vulgar phrasing. In years to come Harris found his cup of patience overflowing with great regularity, but it did not often overflow with so little artistic control.

The joke itself is to coil a length of deer gut in the Irishman's blankets and to let the stock Irishman's stock fear of snakes scare him out of camp. The trick works. The Irishman leaves in an eruption of religious exclamations which Harris thought would be appropriate to a superstitious Catholic. During the decade, "Irishman Jokes" were as abundant in the *Spirit* as Negro jokes in the South (and perhaps the nation) in the 1960's. As Freud has pointed out, such jokes are a slightly masked and hence socially acceptable form of symbolic aggression.

III

From 1846 to 1854 Harris published little. During this time he gave up his metalworking shop in Knoxville. The three sketches he is known to have published seem casual and mark no advance in his work. "A Sleep Walking Incident" of the fall of 1846 is a simple anecdote opening with a nostalgic lamentation for lost youth:

> Dear P.— Many, very many years have taken their turn in making me older, if not more wise, since the sunny days of youth, when there was not a sallow leaf on life's tree—when all was light and glow, and I felt the present, the past unheeded, and the future unknown. Oh, joyous fifteen, that green isle now dimly seen over life's waste of waters, how we look and long to tread thy shores again! But our bark of life is speeding away.

The Wordsworthian recollection of early childhood, the poetic diction, the imagery of sunny days, green isles, and sallow leaves are all exercises in the popular Romanticism of the 1840's.

From October, 1847, to October, 1854, nothing identified as Harris' work appears. By the latter year Harris was captain of the new steamboat *Alida*. He mailed his sketch "How to Marry" to Porter with a letter promising more work and asking for a meeting in New York. Porter replied in his "To Correspondents" column, expressing eagerness to hear more from Harris and to meet him. One possibility is that Harris was hoping Porter would help him get a book published, as he had helped T. B. Thorpe, Johnson Jones Hooper, and other of his correspondents. If so, the hope went unrealized, but Harris' disappointment served to extend his always profitable apprenticeship in the art of writing.

CHAPTER 3

The Mountaineer as Comic Mask

I

IT SEEMS PROBABLE that sometime in 1854 Harris visited the Ducktown copper mines of southeast Tennessee. In 1849 John Caldwell had recognized the richness of the copper deposits of the basin and had called a meeting of the sparse citizenry to encourage building a road through the mountains for exploitation of the mines. Six years later Caldwell wrote:

> Told the people that as soon as the mines could be opened, their condition would be improved, and that civilization, intelligence, comfort and wealth would be the inevitable results. At the conclusion of this remark, a speaker arose in the crowd and informed me that a large portion of the inhabitants had come here to get away from civilization, and that if it followed them, they would run again.[1]

Although the feeling against work and civilization was passionately strong and vocal, by 1853 Caldwell had opened his road; meanwhile he was working the mine and on Sunday teaching Sabbath school, at which one of the local backwoodsmen exclaimed "Good God Almighty! does that old mud-sucker think he can worship Jesus and work a copper mine?"[2]

After his years on the Tennessee River and his years of reading and writing for Porter's *Spirit,* Harris was prepared for the flight from civilization and for the colorful life of the isolated backwoodsman. In November, 1854, the *Spirit* carried Harris' "Sut Lovengood's Daddy 'Acting Horse,'" not a practical joke but a grotesque yarn Harris may well have heard. The touches

of local color are light: in the tradition of the enclosing framework tale, Sut Lovengood, the narrator, is briefly described by
an unidentified gentleman observer, the mines are mentioned as
his refuge, and he tells his tale in front of Pat Nash's grocery
(that is, saloon).[3]

Sut tells how the one horse of this poor mountain family
starved and the father decided to harness himself to the plow
so that the mother and children could plant or not, as they
pleased. The situation is not merely glanced at, as Faulkner does
with the Armstids in *The Hamlet;* the hard folk imagination (or
Harris') transforms it into comedy. Harris develops this feeling
by creating a set of unsympathetic relationships within the
family; by presenting the members as grotesques; by writing the
story in a flow of vivid, exuberant dialect that constantly sur-
prises with its swiftness, color, and vigorous, conceit-like imagery; and, best of all, by the creation of a narrator, the son of
the family, whose unrepressed vitality, capacity for animal joy,
and uninhibited insight transform the occasion into wild play.

Over the years Harris was to work at the creation of Sut, but
for his first appearance he develops just a few of his possibilities.
The framework obtrudes only briefly to describe Sut as "a queer
looking, long-legged, short-bodied, small-headed, white-haired,
hog-eyed, funny sort of a genius, fresh from some bench-legged
Jew's clothing store, and mounted on 'Tearpoke,' a nick-tailed,
bow-necked, long, poor, horse, half dandy, half devil. . . ." The
rest of the tale is Sut's.

Sut's audience at Pat Nash's is a "crowd of wild mountaineers,
full of fight and mean whiskey." Holding his hearers by vivid
language and large gesture, Sut spins from horseback his yarn
of the family plight:

> Well, thar we was—Dad an' me (counting on his fingers)—Dad,
> and me, and Sall, an' Jake (Fool Jake we called him, fur short),
> an' Jonass, an' Phineass, and me, and Callime Jane, and
> Sharlotteean, an' Simeon Saul, an' Cashus Henry Clay, an' Noah
> Dan Webster, an' me, and the twin gals, an' Cathrine Second,
> and Cleopatry Antony, and Jane Lind, and Tom Bullion, an' the
> baby, an' the *prospect,* an' mam herself, all left without ara hoss
> to crap with.

Harris characterizes Sut by his dialect, his clownish counting, the incongruous names of his brothers and sisters, the improper reference to his mother's pregnancy, and the folk obscenity, indicated by the spelling of Jonass and Phineass.

The family wait for a horse, but "dog my cat, ef eny sich luck as that ever cums whar dad is, he's so dratted mean, an' lazy, an' ugly, an' savage." That night Sut hears his father rolling, scratching, snorting, and whispering in bed; and the next morning the old man says, "Sut, I'll tell you what we'll do; I'll be hoss myself, and pull the plough, while you drive me, an' we'll break up corn groun', and then the 'old quilt' (that's mam) an' the brats kin plant or let it alone, jist as they d———n please." Once harnessed, the old man crashes through bushes like a real horse and brings down on himself a hornet's nest. In running away, he rips up the harness, crashes through a fence, tears off his clothing, and leaps over a bluff into the river. From above, Sut eyes his savage father cautiously, and under the guise of advice ventures a taunt: "Arter they go tu roost you cum home and I'll feed ye. I sorter think ye won't *need* eny currien for a week or so." Dad vows to "ruinate" Sut, and Sut replies he had better wish never to see hornets if ever he decides to play horse again. With this last shot, Sut says, "knowin' dad's unmolified natur', I broke from them parts, and sorter cum to the copper mines"— the first of Sut's many flights from retribution.

Sut is not satisfied, however, until he has seen the effect of the wasps. He hides until next morning so that he can ask a traveler what he saw at the cabin by the creek. The stranger replies "Why, nuthin much, only a man was sittin' in his door with nara shirt on, an' a woman was greasin' his back an' arms, an' his hed was about as big as a ten gallon keg, an' he hadn't the fust sign ov an eye—all smooth." Sut's pleasure is to see his dad reduced to a sightless ball of flesh, as smooth and round as Samuel Beckett's *l'Innommable,* helpless as an infant.

Harris' traditional devices of humor include the comic series, incongruous acts and comparisons, the point of view of the backwoodsman, and the uneducated language. Some of the devices are inappropriate for a recorded narration, such as the comic misspelling of *rite* for *right, hed* for *head,* and *strate* for *straight*. The play on the pronunciation of *arse* in the names Jonass and Phineass depends on oral delivery.

The style is comparable to that of the "Knob Dance" in its color and intensity; however, a darker quality enters in the characterization of dad as mean, "an' lazy, an' ugly, an' savage." The darkened tone sometimes carries further reverberations of meaning, as in dad's metaphor for mam: "old quilt." In context the epithet is incongruous. It is ungenteel and also connotes the sexuality of the squalid bed in which the son Sut hears his father "awake all nite, a snortin' an' a rollin', an' a blowin', an' a scratchin', and a whisperin' at mam. . . ." Harris' vernacular is both colorful and controlled enough to carry connotations appropriate to his fable.

The creation of Sut, Sut's dad, and the minor characters marks Harris' first effective control in characterization. Sut's grotesque appearance, his defense of his fantastically caparisoned horse, his sarcastic and taunting replies to his audience's questions—all are descriptive of a forceful personality and appropriate to the power of his story to command attention.

Harris' friend Eastman, William T. Porter, and, years later Mark Twain all spoke of the anecdote as if it stayed in their memories. Their recollections may suggest that one of the achievements of the tale is a comic fantasy with power to stir the hearer psychologically. Out of the archetypal rivalry of fathers and sons arises the son's need to express his jealousy and his yearning to celebrate some ceremony of separation. Sut recalls his flight from the family into the world as a rite of passage from childhood into manhood. Sut's triumph over his father is objectified in his momentary control of the old man in harness and in his seeing his father punished by wasps which, like furies, drive him naked to his fall. Instead of Greek tragic splendor, an American comedy of backwoods squalor masks the sketch's psychological nakedness.

But Sut is the ironic hero. He concludes with a tribute to his dad and with deprecation of himself: "Now, boys, I haint seen dad since, and would be feard to meet him in the next ten years. Let's drink." The crowd follows the new man into the doggery. Through his ironic hero Harris begins also some literary satire. In genteel fiction mother, father, and home were sacred. As Sut is the anti-hero, his father the anti-father, so the Lovingood home is, to borrow William R. Taylor's phrase, the anti-home.[4]

Harris contributed no more to Porter's *Spirit* and, as far as has been discovered, had no work published during the next two years. Then in October, 1856, Eastman's Nashville *Union & American* printed "Playing Old Sledge for the Presidency," with the editorial comment that it was written by "the best delineator of a peculiar class of southwestern characters who ever put pen to paper." Harris, however, was always more interested in Sut as symbolic point of view than as a realistic construction. For this second sketch, Sut is presented in a doggery recounting his dream of a visit to Washington where he watched Fillmore, Frémont, and Buchanan play a game of Old Sledge.

Letting a game of seven-up symbolize a Presidential contest is a passable symbol, but Sut's complaints about bad service and high prices at Willard's violates the illusion of a dream and the impression of Sut as an untraveled countryman. Although not effective as a piece of fiction, the sketch does introduce Harris' second most extensive literary project: the satire of political events and personalities of his time to which roughly one-fourth of Harris' fiction is devoted.

Within a year "Sut Lovegood's Shirt" appeared in *Yankee Notions*, a grotesque New York comic journal of considerably lower literary standards than Porter's paper. In a comedy of backwoods ignorance, Sut's landlady cajoles him into wearing a starched shirt, a fashion new to them both. In her zeal she overstarches it. Sut works in it, sweats in it, and finally climbs into the loft to sleep in it. When he awakens, the shirt is stuck to his skin. Desperate with a free creature's itchy discomfort, he skins out of his trousers, nails the shirttail to the floor of the loft, and leaps through the open trapdoor. When he looks back at the shirt, hanging inside out, Sut sees the cause of his pain. Clinging to the stiff shirt are patches of hair and bloody skin. When the householders return, Bill Carr thinks the parson has shot Sut and hung up his hide to dry.

The central grotesquerie is negligible enough, but the sketch has significance for Harris' work in that he here began to develop Sut as a traditional fool. In introducing his narrative, Sut tells his gentleman friend George: "I reckon I'm the darndest fool out en Utaw, cept my dad, for he acted hoss. . . . I'll drown myself sum day, see ef I don't, just to stop a family dispersition to make darned fools on themselves." Sut's comic despair at discovering himself to be a fool is repeated three times in the sketch as a kind of unifying theme for his character.

Harris presents Sut as a folk artist who understands that telling tales of his own humiliations reduces those humiliations. He can see both himself and others with a cold, hard eye; and the fantasy of his language is both an escape from wretchedness and an expression of power:

> You know I boards with Bill Carr, at his cabin on the mountain, an' pays for sich es I gets when I hev money, an' when I heven't eny, why, he takes one-third of it outen me in cussin'; an' she, that's his wife, Betts, takes out t'other two-thirds with the battlin' stick, and the intrust with her tung, an' the intrust's more than the princip'l—a heap more. She's the cussedest 'oman I ever seed, enyhow. . . . She out-breeds ev'rything on the ruver— an' patterns arter ev'ry fashun she hears tell on, from bussels to briches.

Like a true provincial, Sut blames the outsider, the young lawyer Johnson, for tempting Betts Carr with his elegant ways and starched shirt. But the scapegoat is unimportant; in telling his tale, Sut exorcises his humiliation.

In the fall of 1856 Harris had met William Tappan Thompson, and as a variation of one of Thompson's anecdotes, wrote "Sut Lovengood Blown Up" for that editor's Savannah *Morning News*. Sut's adventure follows his pursuit of sexual experience. He is tempted by a wild mountain girl, Sicily Burns, who is all bosom and buttocks: "She never got in an arm cheer in her life, and you cud lock the top hoop of a churn ur a beeg dog collar round her waist." Sut believes Sicily also finds him attractive, and he tells George: "I was beginin to think I wur just the greatest and comfortablist man on yearth, not exceptin Old Buck [Buchanan] ur Brigham Young. . . ." As a prank, Sicily gives Sut soda powder, which he believes is a love potion; for she has promised him a new sensation. Sut breaks for his horse and rides madly away, foam streaming from his mouth and nose. By telling the joke, Sut objectifies it, reduces its power to crush; instead, he turns it back into the fun it began with for Sicily. By his ability to see the comedy as well as feel the disappointment of his life, Sut expresses the power of humor to restore the balance of existence after defeat.

Harris continues in "Sut Lovengood Blown Up" his creation of minor characters. Not only is Sicily well realized, but a circuit rider and the Yankee peddler who sells Sicily the soda are both sketched in with developing skill. By the irrational processes of scapegoating, Sut decides it was the Yankee who spoiled his prospects for seduction. In the growing sectional strife of the age, Harris uses his situation to satirize the commercialism of the Yankee as a greater evil than Sut's lust or Sicily's deceit:

> Durn him. Durn all Yankee pedlars, and durn their principils and practisis, I say. . . . They aint human, no how. The mint at Filadelfy is thur Heaven, they think that God eats half dimes for breakfus, hashes the leavins for dinner and swallers a cent an a dried apple for supper, sits on a stampin machine fur a throne, sleeps on a crib full ove half dollars, and measures men like money, by count.

Sut's ability to conceptualize and symbolize shows how far Harris had moved from the simple mountaineer. For the moment, Sut is the merest comic mask for Harris' expression of fiercely growing hatred of the North and of the personal tensions his own consuming pursuit of commercial success was producing.

"Sut Lovengood's Lizzards" is a practical joke with Sut as trickster for the first time and with a backwoods preacher the victim. Parson Bullin, discovering Sut in a huckleberry thicket with a girl, first beats him and then makes him promise to attend meeting. Sut comes but brings lizards which he looses up Bullin's trousers. The preacher tears off his clothes and flees naked through his congregation:

> Now old Bullin had nuthin left on him but a par of hevy low quarterd shoes, short woolin socks, an eel skin garters tu keep off the cramp, an his skare wur a growin on him fast. He wur plum crazy, fur he jist spit on his hands an leaped over the frunt ove

the pulpit rite inter the middle ove the pius part of the kongrega-
tion, *kerdiff!* an sot in tu gettin away. He run, or rether went
in a lumberin gallop, heavy, like an ole waggin hoss. . . . He
weighed nigh onto three hundred, hed a black stripe down his
back . . . an his belly looked about the size and culler ove a big
beef paunch, an hit a shakin frum side to side.

The women react to the sight in various ways, all calling attention to the sexual significance of Bullin's nakedness.

Undressing and nakedness are recurrent themes in Harris'
work. The incidents usually occur inadvertently; the victims are
most often the hypocritically pious and respectable. Their nakedness reveals their ugliness and the powerful reality of the flesh.

"Sut Lovengood's Lizzards" was the last of three sketches
Harris published in 1857. With it, the main lines of his development as a writer are established. His plot patterns are generally
anecdotes or practical jokes, which become increasingly elab-
orated in conceit-like structures that emphasize the elements of
fantasy and play. They are drawn from popular lore, some
traceable to folklore, a few apparently original.

His characters are beginning to grow in variety and number.
As American types they are distant parallels to Washington
Irving's creations but are closer to Johnson Jones Hooper's and
other *Spirit* creations. Psychologically and sociologically some of
them show the influence of Charles Dickens, particularly the
grotesque physical types, the evangelical preachers, the coarse
old women.

Harris' most fruitful technical development continued in two
ways: the development of the Fool as point of view, and the
exploitation of the vigor and imagery of the folk language to
carry increasing burdens of comment and meaning. These two
elements are related in that Sut's language both embodies his
vision of the world and at the same time characterizes him. In
the newspaper sketches particularly, Sut is not always a consistent character. He is sometimes comic mask for Harris and
often expresses ideas which, if directly presented, would be
profoundly shocking to Harris' audience. For instance, his attack
on circuit riders is increasingly an attack on institutionalized
Christianity, but veiled and, in the mouth of Sut, ambiguous.

II

In 1858 Harris had at least nine sketches published. The first two are insignificant, but with "Sut Lovengood at Sicily Burns's Wedding" and, linked to it, "Sut Lovengood's Version of Old Burns's Bull Ride," Harris returns to the Frog Mountain ranges and the Ocoee River—misprinted Oconee later in his book. Sicily marries circuit rider Clapshaw, and Sut, in revenge for the soda trick, disrupts the wedding by driving Burns's bull first into the bee hives and then into the house. The bees sting everybody, including Clapshaw and Sicily; and Sut's motive becomes clear: "Sicily an him didnt sleep tugether fur ni onto a week. . . ."

By this time, plot summary gives no idea of content. The language is too compressed; and, for another thing, Harris increasingly explores the freedom of the fool's point of view to mock preachers and fathers, propriety and morality. His father, Sut says, is the biggest fool since Joseph ran from Potiphar's wife: "I used tu think my pint wur like dad's, onmixed fool; but when he acted hoss, I gin in. Maybe when I gits his sperience, an em es old, I kin nock the hons ofen him, an be king fool misef on his pint." In view of the frequency of sexual references, the phallic imagery of the horns is probably not inadvertent.

Sut as a knowing fool begins to develop his philosophy. What he desires is freedom: "Now ef a feller knows what his pint is, he ken get along, allers purvidin he dont swar away his liberty tu a temprance society, ur liv tu fur frum a still-hous, an tu ni a church ur a jail." Like the copper-basin backwoodsman who taunted John Caldwell for trying to mine ore and worship Jesus, Sut sees the threats to his liberty as organized religion and organized society, represented by the church on the one hand and by the sheriff on the other. What Sut desires is freedom to follow his impulses: "Men folks wur made jist tu drink, eat, an fur stayin awake in the yearly part ove nites; an the wimin tu cook the vittils, mix the liquor, and help the men tu du the stayin awake."

By now the wild Sut is superior to the gentleman George of the framework—in knowledge of the world and of the joys of animal life unknown to religious puritans, scientific abstracters, and all men deformed in their professions. With easy condescension the Mask of the Fool turns to George W. Harris, the square, Blue Presbyterian Elder who never wrote on Sundays: "Yer don't onderstand life, George, yet."

Clearly, Harris was not at peace with himself in his rigid church and in his commercial ambitions, increasingly difficult ambitions to realize in the declining economy of the South. Further, in the intensifying political debate, Southern writers were creating the fictional sociology that the South was an aristocratic, non-acquisitive society. This public rationalization withdrew from Harris some source of pride in his middle-class way of life. His reaction was to symbolize in his writing the choice in its most extreme terms, to escape debate in comedy, and to express a yearning for some apocalyptic destruction out of which, somehow, a better life would arise.

The story of "Old Burns's Bull Ride," Harris' next tale, existed in the oral lore of the time and had been retold from 1834 on[5] in several published versions by William Tappan Thompson, Henry Junius Nott, and others. The comedy is the backwoods humor of discomfort and danger, of fear observed from safety, and of wild activity exaggerated into the fantasy of play. Later Mark Twain reworked the anecdote twice.

In the next sketch of the Sicily Burns series, "Sut Lovengood's Chest Story," Sut closes his account with the temptress who blew him up with soda. Hoping for revenge, Sut has watched Sicily and her husband Clapshaw for a year. He discovers she is carrying on an affair with Doctor Fabin, whom "the boys call'd Gut Fatty fur short, and he call'd em 'imperdent onedicated d——d jackasses' fur long. He wur jist four foot fourteen inches high, an wer taller a lyin down than when he wer standin up." One night the watchful Sut sees the doctor's great black horse, "seventeen hans high, an ni ontu seventeen feet long," tied in a sink behind Clapshaw's cabin while Clapshaw is over the mountain collecting debts. Sut ties a joint of cane packed with gunpowder to the horse's tail and then sneaks up to peep in the house. His noise has frightened the guilty pair, and he sees Sicily frantically emptying quilts out of a chest. In jumps the doctor, naked except for his shirt. "She slam'd the lid, turnd the key, an flung on her dress terrectly."

Pretending to be drunk, Sut knocks and asks for supper. As Sicily goes to the kitchen, Sut ties a rope from the horse to the chest. The doctor, thinking he hears only Sicily, asks if the caller has gone. Imitating Sicily's voice, Sut replies that there are signs and wonders in the air, that the two are caught and ruined. When he feels the doctor begin to tremble, Sut snatches fire from the hearth and lights the gunpowder under the horse's tail. The animal drags the bounding chest down the mountain and out of Polk County. As for Sicily afterwards, Sut says she is wearing thin. "She *cant* laugh, an she *wont* cry. Haint hit orful to think ove?" On this unfeeling note, Sut's experience with Sicily ends. Sut has matched cruelty with Sicily. As long as she is free, she wins. When she binds herself with the institutions, she becomes respectable and has a social place to lose. Further, the loss of her voluptuous figure and coquettish ways that had caused Sut so much misery adds relish to his final triumph.

In addition to revenge, Sut's victory over Sicily is part of the struggle he perceives between male and female. A strong-minded woman, Sut says in his flowing rationalization, is able to turn man "inter a kidney worm'd hog what cant raise his bristles in less nor a month." Of all varmints, he says, he is most afraid of women. Not human, they are a mixture of "stud hoss, black snake, goose, peacock britches—and d———d raskil." The reason for the strife is that woman "wants tu be a man; and es they cant, they fixes up thar case by being devils." As woman's discontent is based on an irremediable inferiority, strife is inescapable; and in the male-female relationship one must inevitably enslave the other. This is in part the common Southern anti-feminism which kept women in bondage to their husbands with harsher social and legal controls than did the North or England.[6] However, in all Sut's relationships with others, they seek to assert themselves; and he seeks to assert himself. The mere existence of others impinges on his freedom.[7]

The sketch exhibits another aspect of the ripening power of Harris' imagination: a power of intense and striking fantasy, in this instance the first of several visions of the day of judgment, or the devil, and of hell, all products of Sut's wild or drunken imagination. As he leans over the chest with the half-naked

Fabin inside, Sut replies in Sicily's voice to the doctor's anxious questionings that something terrible is happening, for there are signs and wonders in the air. There are twenty full moons "a hangin in the ar above the comb of the mountin, an they all hes eyes an noses like mister Clapshaw's, an they's a makin dredful mouths et me." After planting in the doctor's mind the fear of the cuckolded husband, Sut frightens Fabin with an apocalyptic vision:

> Thar's a "thousand laig" wum ontu the fence es long es a close line, hits body is red an streaks ove sheet litenin is playin amung hits scales, an hit hev two imiges ove peple in hits mouf, like ontu you an me. I kin see my har a hangin most tu the yearth, an now an then hit gins them a shake an great big drops ove fat comes outen you, an afore they draps tu the groun they ketches fire an burns like tupentine.

The world of pain is made vivid by the graphic description of the eating beast, by the image of Sicily's hanging head and hair, and by the flaming drops falling from Fabin's body. Harris' imagery, in frontier hyperbole, approaches the freedom of myth, and in the animal of great size and in the violence of the eaten bodies, achieves a barbaric, cruel religious vigor.

Harris' tendency to escape the earth in imagination reappears when Sut describes Fabin falling at last from the broken chest: "his har looked like hit had been dipped in thunder and litenin and sky blue. . . . " The Promethean imagery is comparable to that of the anonymous Crockett sketch, "Sunrise in His Pocket." Both the extravagant imagery and the recurring themes of existence as joy and pain emphasize that Harris' real interest was not the "peculiarities of Western life," but the inner world of the spirit where yearning, delight, suffering, hatred, and the struggle for power are the true facts of existence.

III

During the summer of 1858 Harris wrote several inconsequential letters to the *Union & American,* the first of these showing him at his worst as a partisan political writer. Written in his own person, it begins as a denunciation of the abusive and violent political language of the age—and then becomes abusive and violent itself:

> Take an example: Here's the redoubtable prize ox in the human cattle show, Wilson, of Mass, reveling in animal strength, filling the eye with a redundancy of muscle, yet the veriest coward that ever truckled to an inferior foe—sows his insults broadcast, and then simply acts the paltroon. A four year old, well preserved hickory in the hands of a brother blacksmith born south of Mason and Dixon's line, is the true antidote for his grog-house poison.

Provincial and bullying as Harris' tone is here, it is no more intemperate than much of the matter then appearing in the *Union & American*. The same issue contained an editorial denunciation of British policies which quickly turned on other American newspapers:

> There were tories in the Revolution and traitors in the last war. There are such men still whom no insult, no national disgrace can awaken to anger or kindle into resentment. They are men whose craven hearts never felt pride in their country's praise or blushed at her humiliation. Insensible to shame as they are to honor, they submit as readily to private insult as to public infamy. Even the ignominy of the lash cannot stimulate them to resentment. Such are the Editors of the New York *Tribune* and the Louisville *Journal*, and we could not expect that men who are constantly cringing to private insult and disgrace would feel any disposition to vindicate our national honor.

The version of the man of honor as one quick to resent insult was exploited in Eastman's paper to whip up war fever against the North.

Two weeks later the editorial denounced Rutland, Vermont, host to an Abolitionist meeting, as a "moral pest house . . . where all plagues that infest the world have congregated together that they may engender some new and more loathesome leprosy." In Rutland, "Licentiousness scarcely concealing its hideous deformities under the robe of a false and disgusting philosophy" rules the conduct of the assembled reformers; but, happily, these "dangerous and destructive heresies have never flourished in the South. They wither for want of sustenance in the purer moral atmosphere that surrounds them here." Standards of morality, intelligence, and accuracy in newspaper reporting were generally low during this era. Ill-educated readers formed an appreciative audience for propaganda as distorted by community conformity as any produced by the isolating dictatorships of modern Europe.

Harris advises the clubbing of Henry Wilson. A favorite theme of the Secessionists was the supposed cowardice of the North. No vulgar error was more earnestly nourished and, in the provincial South, more firmly believed. The brutality of Harris' expression comes more and more to be expressed comically and not directly, but it never abates. At one time or another, Harris has Sut advocate lynching, shooting, emasculation, and other barbaric modes of dealing with opponents. They are usually offered as fiction and so, mercifully, may be taken as comic exaggeration as well as fantasies of hatred and revenge.

During these weeks in 1858 Harris also contributed two sketches of Sut's adventures in New York to the New York *Atlas*. Somewhat out of character, Sut meets, thrashes, and throws in the river a New York dandy. The comedy plays on affectation and, more strikingly, on the sexlessness of narcissism. Depending on the animal imagery which he exploits with increasing care to provide his meanings, Harris has Sut characterize the city dandy as a castrate: "They [dandies] seems sorter like a strange wether what has seed a heap ove tribulashun among an ekal number ove rams an' yews—they's butted about permiskusly by the one an' is snufft at by t'uther; and as they can't fill or feel the instink ove a man, nur do the juty ove an 'oman, they jest settles on a cross fence atween the two. . . ." The dandy, however, is a symbolic figure; the allegory of his destruction is aimed at Northern effete society and city culture.

In a closing grotesque caricature of Horace Greeley, Sut attributes an essay titled "Free Love an' Human Progress" to Greeley in which he is made to say "he believed that crosses yet would be made atween animals an' varmints, an' sutin mersheans what would perjuce s'thin tu answer in place of humans. . . ." In the opening and closing paragraphs, Sut is mere mask for Harris to express his hatred of progress and his fear that change was perversive or dehumanizing. He seems, like William Gilmore Simms, to have feared that the home and family were endangered by Northern progress. In an essay in the *Southern Quarterly,* September, 1850, Simms had associated the radical, reforming North with the European revolutions of 1848, and in these forces had found a threat of terrifying social chaos. Harris found East Tennessee an unstable, dissolving society in which fierce wills like his own were opposed by the equally fierce wills of Parson Brownlow and his followers. For the next two years Harris' political writings were devoted to the strategy of increasing and focusing the fears of his community in order to unite the people, even if need be in war, and to direct their passions against the North. His technique was to slip the bonds of reason and to use humor's ancient capacity to transform hatred into a feeling of free, triumphant power.

Harris' last sketch for 1858, "Sut Lovengood at Bull's Gap," abandons politics for a terrible comedy of the human creature's eating and sleeping. The yarn has no unity of action or time; it only exists in the free flow of Sut's language. The setting, events, and imagery are all alike—expressions of ugly, physical human activities. The tone at times rises to an almost ecstatic expression of loathsome physical improprieties. The gluttonous Dutchman, whose bedroom Sut shares, dreams he is a bull. Sut claps a chamber pot over his head, and the charging man-beast crashes into the wall and breaks his huge belly open. The fantasy concludes with Sut staring into the open wound to see the paunch, which "looked adzackly like the flesh side of a raw hide," and then sewing up the wound with a dirty bridle rein. In major and minor incidents, human existence is represented as a constant, debasing, ugly struggle to satisfy animal needs.

IV

In the spring of 1859, Harris turned to state politics in a series of reductive satires for Eastman's Nashville *Union & American,* generally titled "Sut Lovingood's Love Feast ove Varmints." The Democratic Party's opposition is rendered comical and contemptible by presenting the politicians then in convention in Nashville as animals: "evry varmint a usin ove his natral wepuns; a ridin wun anuther down stairs, a smellin at people's cotails, a runnin thar fore paws inter the overcoat pockets what wer a hangin ontu a wall, an alookin tuther way al the time."

One of the minor themes of the sketches is the power of the beasts to disguise themselves and change their appearance. Donald Day sees this as expressing Harris' dislike of politicians who shift party allegiance. One of the principal animal shape-shifters is presented in a way to evoke uneasy confusion:

> A varmint then climbed up ontu a box tu make a talk, an durn me ef ever I hev been so bothered in all my life tu make out what hit was. At fust I tuck hit fur a ole billy goat frum hits gray beard an wore-out looks. I happened tu look away fur a minit, an hit hed changed powful; hits har wer es black es a mink, an all slicked up, an hit wer shaped like ontu a coon. In fac hit changed shape an color every time I looked away. Hit gin me a sorter skeer, hit wer so many beasts at once.

Recurrence of this theme suggests that Harris' interest in disguises, masks, and changing appearances goes beyond interest in the political turncoat to a broad attempt to probe through surfaces to some stable reality of being.

Individuals, like communities, seemed dissolving and changing under Harris' troubled view. In 1859 he moved his family from Unionist Knoxville, under what circumstances is unknown, and took up residence in Nashville. In March he served as a delegate to the State Democratic Convention. Here he was elected to the Democratic State Central Committee and served until the elections of the fall of 1859. To support his family, he worked for the Nashville & Chattanooga Railroad, and his son, Pryor Nance, got a job at L. B. and T. D. Fite's wholesale dry-goods store. In mid-November, 1859, one of Eastman's associate editors on the *Union & American* was shot by a rival editor. Five days later, Eastman himself died.

What Seward had called the "irrepressible conflict"—made irrepressible by such fears and propagandizing as Harris'—was moving swiftly toward its climax. Sumner's chair in the Senate was still empty. In the fall of 1859, John Brown's party raided into Virginia; and he was tried and quickly hanged on December

2, 1859. None of Harris' writing during 1860 has been discovered. In November of that year Lincoln was elected President. In December South Carolina seceded from the Union, followed by Mississippi, Florida, Alabama, Georgia, Louisiana, and Texas.

The course of Tennessee still hung in the balance. On February 9 the voters defeated a proposal for a convention to reconsider Tennessee's relation to the Union. By this time the *Union & American* was the leading mouthpiece for the "radical group"—the most ardent Secessionists. The editors brought a great variety of pressures to bear, skillfully and energetically, on their readers: fear of "outsiders," hatred, shame for not fighting; promises of success, power, and happiness. "Our policy will be dictated by our wants," they wrote February 28; "Prosperity and boundless wealth will be the result of this separation." Favorite butts for the paper's unrestrained invective were Winfield Scott, and, of course, Lincoln: "Can an enlightened nation of thirty millions of people be controlled by this half-witted village politician . . . ?"

V

Harris' contribution to the *Union & American's* effort to bring about the secession of Tennessee was three coarse, high-spirited satires on Lincoln. Warned by his friends Ward Hill Lamon and Norman Judd of a plot to assassinate him, Lincoln had, on their advice, gone through Baltimore at night on his way to Washington. The story was started that Lincoln arrived disguised in a Scotch-plaid cap and a long military cloak. Thousands of hostile journals everywhere reported the item in story and cartoon.[8] Harris' version is that the fool Sut disguised Lincoln and smuggled him into Washington. In his parody of the journey as flight, Harris condenses a large number of public issues and actual persons to create a dense, coarse, exuberant, comic texture.

Harris' aim is to satirize, his technique to create around Lincoln an image of ugliness which will symbolize the new President's supposed traits of crafty ignorance and cowardice. Harris' impressionistic caricature chooses a limited number of features to exaggerate for ugliness and to play on for meaning:

"His mouf, his paw, and his footzes am the principal feeters." In the last of a series of reductive images, Sut pictures Lincoln as the reincarnation of a frog he once killed:

> I kotch a ole bull frog once an druv a nail thru his lips inter a post, tied two rocks tu his hine toes and stuck a darnin needil inter his tail tu let out the misture, an lef him there tu dry. I seed him two weeks arterwurds, an when I seed ole ABE I thot hit were an orful retribution cum ontu me, and that hit were the same frog, only stretched a little longer, and had tuck tu warin ove close tu keep me from knowin him; an ketchin him an nailin him up agin, an natral born durn'd fool es I is, I swar I seed the same watry, skeery look in the eyes. . . .

The association of the frog and Lincoln implies, beyond its ugliness and harmlessness, that killing Lincoln would be a perfectly safe business.

In the second sketch Sut spends the night in Lincoln's bedroom. This intimacy provides opportunity to dwell on the incongruous and usually hidden aspects of life. Sut watches the new President stand naked and search painfully through the long legs of his red flannel drawers for fleas. Throughout the night, Lincoln scratches himself—the epitome of comic impropriety and ineffectual human activity.

As the hours pass, Sut explains to Lincoln, in covert threat, the fierce legendary figure of the fool killer. In the South, he says, along with their governors, the people elect a fool killer for every county and furnish him with a gun, arsenic, and a steel trap. The fool killer travels the country one day behind the circuit rider; and, after the preacher has gathered the people together, the fool killer "kills off the stock ove fools tu a considerabil extent every round he takes. Our fool-killers hev dun thar juty, and consekently the South hev seceded." New England is the home of new religions, new social movements, and humanitarianism, Sut believes, both because the fool killer does not do his duty and because the soil and climate produce the "d——d ole cusses" that lead new movements. Harris ridicules Lincoln's humanitarianism by having him propose the elimination of fools by the "more humane way [of] emaxulation." The Texas way is better, says Sut: "give em a black jack an a pece

ove bed cord and that ar all they ax." The symbol of the West
is enlisted in support of lynching. The association of lynch rule
with the fool killer hints that his legendary figure embodies the
primitive dream of community purity through destruction of all
dissidents.

In the third sketch, the two arrive in Baltimore where Lincoln
makes a brief speech praising the Declaration of Independence
and, taken for a fool or a madman, is showered with rotten eggs.
Harris expresses the lowest point of Lincoln's degradation
through an ancient folk motif: the image of the man who befouls
himself through fear. Lincoln, mistaking a trombone player for
Alexander Stephens with a cannon, asks if the cannon has gone
off. No, says Sut, "but you did, you moved yerself." Lincoln defends himself by saying that people are not responsible when
they are scared. Sut agrees and suggests that Lincoln announce
the principle publicly, as it will cover the acts of his whole
administration. On this thematic note of Lincoln's uncon-
trollable fear, Sut delivers the President safely to Willard's in
Washington.

Ortega y Gasset defends the destructive element of comedy as
necessary to the comfort of our normal vulgarity of mind.[9]
Harris' pro-war satire offers us an example of the cost at which
this comfort is sometimes bought. The satirist selects absurd-
ities, as Northrop Frye has pointed out; and the act of selection
is a moral act.[10] By selecting images of the leader without control—ugly, contemptible, filthy, only weakly threatening—Harris,
with some success, was forming and directing those most primitive folk impulses which find in outer ugliness signs of intellectual
or moral deformity. The hatred is accompanied by an illusion of
triumphant strength to slay the hated object. Harris' dramatizing
Lincoln's abilities and relations with the South in this manner
illustrates the power of humor to escape stark reality, to avoid
the work of gathering facts and making analyses. Harris' comedy
here is a flight from thinking, an escape into illusion, a ritual
creation of success.

CHAPTER 4

The Sleep of Reason

I

IF HARRIS did any writing during the years of the war, it has not been discovered. These were wandering years for Harris and his family, who probably left Nashville before it fell to Union soldiers on February 23-24, 1862. Perhaps for a time Harris worked at an armory in Chattanooga. The family also spent time in Decatur, Alabama, and in Trenton, Georgia. Harris' youngest child, Amanda Pillow Harris, remembered in her old age hearing the guns of the battle of Chickamauga, where, she was told, one of her two soldier brothers was fighting.[1] All members of the family survived the war.

During April and May, 1865, the Confederate generals surrendered their armies. Harris emerged from the war undefeated. His first sketches began appearing about a year after its close. The first of these, "Sut Lovengood's Hog Ride," is a folk comedy of the wild, disruptive animal ride. Sut, in a Nashville alley, with his trousers around his ankles, bends over to pull them up and sees between his legs an oncoming sow pursued by a dog. When the dog sees Sut, he is frightened from his chase:

> He sot all his laigs and his tail ahead tu stop hissef, and he slid fifteen feet, whinin pitiful, and lookin monsous wishful back up the alley, the way his hart wer gwin. He hadn't the melt tu venter a secon' look—the fust wun hed run him crazy, an ef he ever sees the likes agin, which I doubts much, I'll bet high he jus gins up the ghost, not wantin tu live anuther minit in a world whar dorgs' souls am tu be harrowed wif sich orful, onnatr'l, onuseful, an tarifine sights.

The sight of Sut's naked posterior and, more specifically, his organs of generation is too harrowing for the dog to bear. The minor theme expresses coarse anti-Semitism.

Some of the materials of the story are traditional. Jim Doggett in Thorpe's "The Big Bear of Arkansas" was caught with his "inexpressibles" down around his ankles when the fabulous bear he had been hunting unexpectedly appeared. To be caught with one's trousers down is a common image of unpreparedness in the American vernacular today. Another element of the tale Harris may have borrowed from Phillip B. January's "That Big Dog Fight at Myers's," where the sight of a man's behind breaks a dog's heart, more clearly implying jealousy.[2] Such incidents, plus scraps of songs, and many phrases make up a large body of allusions to and use of obscene folk humor. Without a motif index of erotic and scatological English and American humor, it is impossible to tell how much of Harris' material is traditional.[8]

The following spring Harris returned to the columns of the *Union & American* with "Sut Lovingood Come to Life," provoked by a series of letters over the penname "Sunstroke" appearing in the Wisconsin *State Journal*. These letters called for stricter measures against the South; and Harris replied in a grotesquely misspelled "Orfishul Dokymint" written by Sut after his appointment as Fool Killer General. This creation of the folk imagination embodies the image of the tribal executioner of dissent in a figure of implacable ferocity and power. The figure had engaged Harris' imagination since the 1858 "Sut Lovengood's Chest Story" as a regulator of community morals. Sut's letter to "Sunstroke" is Harris' most extended effort to provide a fable for the fool killer.

Sut's document announces he is on his way to execute "Sunstroke." Meanwhile he demands an account of "Sunstroke's" activities, and outlines matters to be included in the report. "Sunstroke" is ordered to confess his stealing in the South during the war. Among the categories he must account for stealing are pianos, quilts, frocks, daguerreotypes of people's dead relatives, packets of love letters, and the dead baby's shoes. The series mixes comic incongruity with sentimentalism. Although Harris perceived the false in sentimentalism—and its growing weakness to stir the reader—he uses the mode himself occasionally in times of stress. Its use generally signifies loss of artistic control.

After reporting his stealing, "Sunstroke" is required to confess whether he has been the ruin of any females. He must enumerate them and give the number of legs—if over two. Then the ruined females are to be classified by color, and the categories allow only for Negro women and animals. This charge of buggery is gratuitous. The final section abandons even the flimsy fable of a report and is a fierce direct denunciation, full of images of skunks, dogs, spittle, whores, and suicide.

This sort of comedy, as Northrop Frye notes, approaches the lower limit of art. It brings us "the figure of the scapegoat ritual and the nightmare dream, the human symbol that concentrates our fears and hates."[4] Sut's document implies that New England women do not believe in the permanence of marriage and do believe in sexual promiscuity. More extreme is the reference to human-animal sexual contacts. The sketch has almost no ideas, but it abounds in images which are products of dark instincts and hatreds and are expressed in references to illegal or furtive sexuality, cruelty, and suicidal despair. This aspect of extreme despair in the post-war South is perhaps best exemplified in the conclusion of the Virginia Secessionist Edmund Ruffin's career. After years of urging the necessity of secession and the might of Southern power, he saw his plantation Beechwood destroyed and was, in his old age, called upon to digest the news of Appomattox. He first carefully entered in his diary his "unmitigated hatred" of the Yankee race, lamented he could not create this hatred in every Southerner, and then he propped up the butt of his silver mounted rifle, put the muzzle in his mouth, and tripped the trigger with a forked stick.[5] The despair that Ruffin expressed by action, Harris attempted to express in words.

"Sut Lovengood's Big Dinner Story" returns to the wild humor of Sut's practical jokes. The small satire is of a village social climber. Old Mrs. Jerrold gives a pretentious dinner for her daughter's suitor. The prankster Sut puts frogs and a blacksnake into the dishes. After the traditional violent disruption of the dinner, the snake gets inside the collar of the young lawyer suitor, crawls down his back, doun the dark, greasey, pimply holler, along that legul back bone, ontil he cum to the forks ove the road; then he would roun' the turn, a leavin' a laig on his right, an a laig on his left, an' started up hill agin, along the legul belly, aimin' fur a little sink-hole, jist onder the waisbun buttons ove the crazy, frighten'd cuss, but afore he got thar, he seed a streak ove day light an poked out ni onto a foot ove hissef to 'zamine the open country a little.

The lawyer has both hands behind his neck pulling at the snake's tail so desperately that he fears it has cut him in two, for he feels what seems to be "hot links ove [his] intrals down bof laigs ove [his] britches." With ironic solicitude, Sut reports his fear that the sight of one foot of a blacksnake sticking out of the young lawyer's fly will ruin his chances for marriage with old Jerrold's "bud of promise." The story contains internal evidence that Harris wrote the sketch to satirize an actual woman who had complained about his intransigent political writing.

II

In the fall of 1866 and in the spring of 1867, as Reconstruction got under way, unreconstructed Harris produced two more pieces in the mood of "Sut Lovingood Come to Life." These three represent his Disasters of War—and for Harris, as for Goya, "El sueño de la razón produce monstruos," unrestrained dreams of hatred and vengeance. "Sut Lovingood on the Puritan Yankee" begins directly with Sut speaking, without any framework of explanation. It is a swift, chaotic outpouring of passionate anti-Yankee sentiments.

The piece opens with a description of the ugliness of Yankee babies, as if by choosing the customary symbol of innocence Harris could best express the intoxication of hatred: "The rale, pure puritan, yankee baby, has a naik like a gourd, a foot like a glut, an a belly like a mildew'd drum head." The central charge is that every Yankee is a cheater from birth: "As the dorg vomits, as the mink sucks blood, as the snail shines, as the possum shams death, so dus the yankee cheat, *for every varmint has hits gif*." Sut's flow of language roils up denunciations of the Yankee from birth to death. His deceitful life is symbolized in two conceit-like images, the first of a clock. In addition to the connotation of the inexorable flow of life, the continual movement, "never restin, never missin ontil the clock's wore out an the cords broke" symbolizes the mechanical regularity of the Yankee's cheating. The Yankee grandfather clock reintroduced at the end of the sketch is the Yankee with a window in his breast, "showin all his inside, springs, traps, an' triggers." This is "A YANKEE nakid," his heart and soul exposed for all the world to see.

The second image, the tumble bug with his ball of dung, is an attempt to evoke disgust at the Yankee. He lives within his cheating as the young bug grows in his ball of dung: "he lives on hit, wallers in hit, rolls hit, an' at las' is buried in hit." The degrading image is darkly memorable.

The sketch abounds in filthy and scatological image and detail: the dog's vomit; the blood-sucking mink; the throwing of cow-dung; the leg with "guts in hit"; the Yankee as "moril disease"; the Indian with "grub worm oder." Yet, for all the energy of the imagery, the Yankee object has no fictional reality. The failure to create character, to explain Sut's speech, or to motivate his hatred is not only evidence of Harris' loss of control of his material; it is also evidence that he was writing for the "little community." He depended on shared community feelings to bridge the gaps of omission and to leap at once to the experience of hatred.

"Sut Lovingood's Dream," of early 1867, is somewhat more successful in giving form to hatred. The fiction is that Sut drank too much green whiskey, fell in the dog fennel, and dreamed he had gone to hell for voting the Radical ticket. The device of the dream allows Harris' hatred ecstatic freedom.

Sut's visions in hell open with a Dantean scene. A vast sluice of newly dead pour into hell, all Radicals, some with ropes around their necks and running nooses under their ears; some with holes in their heads; and some with "a big gill cut under their chins." That is, all had been shot or lynched or had their throats cut. The dead include Stevens, Sumner, Wade, Butler, Wendell Phillips, and others.

The action, as usual, is simple. The Radicals explain their presence to the devil by saying that "the Constitution people has riz"—the old invocation of the Constitution, the old dream of solution by violence. Sitting in a boat on the lake of fire, the devil sorts the newcomers out. He takes a needle as big as a harpoon, threads it with trace chain, and then strings the common Radicals on it, running the needle in their mouths and out their rectums, and drops them over the side into the brimstone: "Jehosophat! how they sizzled, an' sloshed, an' dove, an' sprinkled hot iron about wif thar tailes."

While the devil arranges punishment for the small fry, the great Radicals begin to repeat their earthly life. Wendell Phillips tries to turn the boat around to make hell run backwards. Enraged, the devil cries that the Radicals cannot stay in hell. To get rid of them, he loads them into a huge mortar and fires them out the hatch of the ship, all except Phillips who hides and manages to stay in hell to threaten its orderly continuance.

Much of the humor turns on the physical suffering or deformities of Northern politicians. Remembering Preston Brooks's beating of Charles Sumner with a cane on the floor of the Senate, Harris has Sumner ask the devil at once if Brooks is in hell. At the devil's "no," Sumner brightens in relief. Benjamin "Beast" Butler's alleged spoon stealing is alluded to as well as the cast in his eye when Sut observes that Butler kept "one eye sot on the devil, an' tother on me." Later, when Butler is fired out of the mortar, instead of flying out the hatch, "he followed the line of his cock eyes, and busted into a million pieces agin the wall." Thaddeus Stevens claims kinship with the devil by comparing his twisted foot with Satan's hoof. When Stevens is fired out the mortar, Sut catches a glimpse of "Thad's hooked foot scrapin a splinter off the hatch combin." Upon awakening, Sut meditates on Stevens, alone without his Negro mistress, "as he roams through nuthin forever."

Both "Sut Lovingood on the Puritan Yankee" and "Sut Lovingood's Dream" contain pleas for social order. However, the dream of social order is a primitive one without room for growth, without exercise of self-discipline, without responsibility toward others—indeed, without room for any but conforming or subservient beings. The dream is the yearning of the will to impose itself on others without inner or outer restraints. For example, the Negro woman presented as Stevens' mistress is reduced from human status to object status, a simple object of control. When Stevens asks that she be loaded in the mortar with him, the devil with sardonic understatement says "no," "I think we can manage her arter you is gone." There is no pretense of responsibility, patriarchal concern, or other commonplace rationalizations, only the ironic promise to "manage" the Negro. Ironically, Harris thought he was attacking the danger of the unchecked will in the Radicals.

The three sketches are not political in the sense that they attempt to define, defend, or rationalize any possible social procedures. Like the masks of primitive art, they give form to the unseen. Primarily they objectify hatred in a rapid flow of language and in an imagery full, intense, teeming with prohibited desires.

CHAPTER 5

The Making of a Book

I

THE VOLUME Harris had hoped for twenty years to see in print appeared in the spring of 1867; published by Dick & Fitzgerald of New York, it bore the title *Sut Lovingood. Yarns Spun by a "Nat'ral Born Durn'd Fool["]. Warped and Wove for Public Wear*. The text is bad, containing typographical errors and misreadings of Harris' handwriting, but just how bad cannot now be determined.

Of the roughly thirty sketches he had already published, Harris chose to include in his volume only eight. To these he added sixteen to make up a three-hundred-page volume. When the newspaper versions of the eight republished sketches are compared to their versions in the *Yarns*, all show the effects of careful and extensive revisions. These changes reveal the degree of conscious artistry with which Harris worked and the quality of his techniques. The skill and intelligence of the revisions permits the generalization that Harris was the most self-conscious and the most resourceful craftsman of all the humorists of the Old Southwest, a point first suggested by Professor Walter Blair in the 1930's.

Of these eight sketches, "Sut Lovingood's Dog" is the least revised, yet even for it the changes are significant. The original seven paragraphs are broken into nineteen to lighten the movement of the story. Apostrophes are extensively added to make slightly easier the reader's task of interpreting Sut's dialect. Spelling errors are corrected, and changes are made to increase the accuracy of Sut's dialect: for example, *with* and *both* become *wif* and *bof* in revision.

In the rest of the sketches revisions are so extensive that they average several to each line of text. The largest changes are structural revisions to cut out long blocks of material. The original "Sut Lovengood Blown Up" had a long paragraph on Yankee women and peddlers with the memorable image of their God who "eats half dimes for breakfus." Satisfying to Harris' prejudices as the attack was, he cut it out completely and reduced the paragraph by one-half. The result tightens the structure and focuses more clearly on the characterization of Sicily and Sut. A three-hundred and fifty word digression is cut from "Old Burns's Bull Ride" to speed up the pace of Burns's comic ride through the mountains. Generally the cutting reduces the amount of mere self-expression and improves the esthetic focus. In his earlier work, Harris had often depended on digressions to express his personal feelings; in revision, he depends increasingly on imagery.

With digressions pared away, the simple linear, picaresque plot structure of the sketches is even more apparent. Either Harris could not construct a plot, or, more probably, his primary interest lay in Sut's character. R. W. B. Lewis has hypothesized that creating an imitation of significant psychological or moral change was a central problem for American writers because their primary interest in character led them to create protagonists outside the relations of society.[1] To a large extent, Sut is an outsider propelled by self-generated energy. In revision, Harris improves, clarifies, but does not alter the nature of his simple lines of action.

Harris' most significant changes are in language. Sentences are frequently changed, sometimes lengthened, more often shortened. Phrases are added or subtracted to improve the speech-like rhythms of Sut's language or to increase its compression. In "Sicily Burns's Wedding," Sut says of the girl, now pregnant, "Durn her, she's down on her heels now, and walks flat-footed at that." In revision Sut is made to say "Durn her, she's down on her heels flat-footed now." The rhythm is improved, and particularly the compression adds force to the sentence.

Throughout, individual words are changed. A word may be substituted or dropped. Instead of having Sut say Bullen's pockets contained "sum copper ore speciments," in revision Harris corrects to "sum copper ore," omitting the inappropriate "speciments." However, Harris was not primarily interested in the accuracy of the dialectal vocabulary. The value of the word itself takes precedence over its propriety for Sut's speech. Within this order of value, Harris makes many changes to regularize, improve, or correct Sut's dialect. Although the dialect is not absolutely consistent, one comes to appreciate, after examining the changes, how extensive Harris' task was and how faithfully he listened, learned, and revised to improve his version of the mountain speech.

Harris worked carefully over his imagery to increase the frequency of metaphor and simile and to add to their denotative and connotative power. For example, in describing the fight between the Burns and the Mills bulls, Sut tells George that afterwards Mills's bull "sought hissef anuther suckit," and added in revision "an' becum es morril es a draft-steer." On the surface the impropriety of applying concepts of moral conduct to a chastened bull is comic. With the added witty simile revealing a further congruity between the conduct of bulls and men, Harris extends his comparison in the direction of the conceit. The result in both form and content is to increase the element of surprise and thereby the element of comedy. Working within the genre of the mock-oral tale, Harris moves away from its traditional digression and toward intensity to increase the plenitude of his meanings.

The revisions sometimes show the craftsman posing and solving the problems of his material. In the original "Sut Lovengood Blown Up," Sut says of Sicily's figure, "Oh sich a buzum—but thar aint no use trying to describe her." In revision Harris solves his problem with "Sich a buzzim! Jis' think ove two snow balls wif a strawberry stuck but-ainded intu bof on em" (75). By the change Harris not only adds startling color; he also introduces a more obvious impropriety and, as Bernard DeVoto has suggested, a little literary satire on the ballad cliché of the snow-white breast.

Another revision of imagery in the same sketch sets up unusual reverberations of sexual connotation, frequent in Harris' effects.

The first version of Sut's wooing and Sicily's apparent willingness
begins with

> an in spite ove my long legs, appetite fur whiskey, my shurt
> scrape an dad's actin hoss, she sorter leaned tu me, an I was
> beginin to think I wur just the greatest and comfortablist man
> on yearth, not exceptin Old Buck [James Buchanan], ur Brigham
> Young with all his saddil cullered wrinkled wimmen, cradles
> full of babies, and his Big Salt Lake thrown in.

The revision not only cuts the dated political reference, but
sharpens the focus on the sensual experience:

> an' in spite ove these yere laigs, an' my appertite fur whisky,
> that ar shut-skinin bisness, an' dad's actin hoss, she sorter
> lean'd tu me, jis' a scrimpshun, sorter like a keerful man salts
> uther pepil's cattil in the mountin, barly enuf tu bring em back
> tu the lick-log [misprinted as lick-bog] sum day—that's the way
> she salted me, an' I 'tended the lick-log es reg'lar es the old bell
> cow; *an'* I wer jis' beginin tu think I wer ontu the rite trail tu
> es much cumfurt, an' stayin awake a-purpus, es ole Brigham
> Young wif all his saddil-culler'd wimen . . . (78-79).

The lick-log image is added a third time some three hundred
words later. Following as it does the strawberry image for
Sicily's nipples, the metaphor carries connotations of sensual
activity quite startling if read against the proprieties of genteel
Victorian literature. Finally, the image of skillful tempting
emphasizes Sicily's malicious delight in the power of her
sexuality.

II

The revisions of the book's first sketch may serve to illustrate
the scope of Harris' changes. He chose "Sut Lovengood's Daddy
'Acting Horse'" from the 1854 *Spirit of the Times* to open his
collections. His revisions were intended to increase the effectiveness of the sketch and to set the tone of the whole book. He
was aware, therefore, that within the book the sketches would
react on one another by setting up reverberations of feeling
and meaning.

The opening paragraph of the original is broken into two paragraphs. The first is a series of mocking sarcasms cast at Sut by a crowd of mountaineers standing around the door of a backwoods doggery. In revision their comments are enlarged by the addition of four sentences. Two of these call scornfull attention to the long legs of the yet unintroduced protagonist.

The second paragraph cuts four words and adds four. The original describes Sut reined up "among a crowd of wild mountaineers, full of fight and mean whiskey," which expresses Harris' attitude of long ago toward the civilization-fleeing mountaineers of Ducktown. In revision, Sut sits his horse "among a crowd of mountaineers full of fun, foolery, and mean whiskey." Thus the explicit, surface element of comedy is reinforced—the element of play made clearer in both the vocabulary and the alliteration of the language.

The third paragraph, in dialect like the first, introduces Sut's first speech. It is doubled in length to balance the opening paragraph of banter. Sut's language is as lively and insulting as that of his audience. As the exchange between the mounted Sut and the boisterous crowd of bystanders continues, Sut increasingly dominates by his withering insults and vivid language. The revisions pace the exchange so that the chorus of the crowd grows less in quantity and weaker in power. Two minor characters are added, impressionistically described, to be defeated in their exchanges with Sut. The first, a rat-faced youth whittling on a corn stalk, tries to correct Sut's accuracy. Sarcastically and profanely Sut answers the objection; then he advises the young man to creep back a little into childhood before he gets killed. In the third person Harris adds, "The rat-faced youth shut up his knife and subsided." Thus the symbolism of the knife is made apparent: the youth has threatened Sut's dominance; Sut has accepted the challenge, won, and forced the closing of the knife. The second added character, a red-nosed drunkard in a ragged overcoat, respectfully corrects Sut's counting, calls him "Mister Lovingood," but for his interruption receives a cruel insult and slinks into the doggery, followed by the pitiless laughter of the crowd, which from this point has ears only for Sut.

Such changes show how Harris worked to actualize Sut's

demonically intense personality. Since "Sut Lovegood's Shirt" in 1857, Harris had been developing his concept of the fool from his reading, from his observation, and from his imaginative efforts to express his meanings. The revisions show not only Harris' interest in the traditional archetype of the fool, but also how artfully he worked to create his own version.

At the time of the newspaper piece, Harris had not considered the possibilities of the fool as point of view. In this first version, the word *fool* appears four times, twice in general application, once applied to Sut's brother and once to his father. In the revision the word is often in Sut's mouth; it appears thirteen times in all. In addition to general application—to his audience, and to others—Sut calls his father a fool six times, his brother once, his family as it relates to him once, and—most significantly—he defines himself as a fool twice.

The fourth paragraph of the original had Sut counting his family with laboriously comic inaccuracy, repeating, starting over, puzzled whether or not to include the "prospect" in his mother's belly, and counting himself several times with the self-absorption of the country clown. In revision Harris has changed his intent. He manipulates the action to shift its meaning from a revelation of Sut's incapacity to one of Sut's control of his audience and his prowess as a storyteller. When the ragged drunkard falls into Sut's trap by pointing out that Sut has counted himself five times, Sut replies, "Yas, ole Still-tub, that's jis the perporshun I bears in the famerly fur dam fool, leavin out Dad in course" (21).

In the exchange, Sut not only tells his audience he is "damn fool" in the American vernacular sense, but also his ambiguously prideful explanation reveals to his audience that he is playing the fool. He is an unknown reality behind a mask; his image is enlarged from the stupid fool to the creature whose foolishness is known to himself and is his mask and his armor.

The revisions also sharpen the conflict between Sut and his father and add images of comic impropriety, usually with sexual connotations. When the naked old man runs away, Sut complains there never was a horse fool enough to leap off such a bluff, although a "cussed mule mout a done it, but dad war'nt a acting mule." Then Harris added in revision, "tho' he orter tuck that karacter; hits adzackly sooted tu his dispersition, all but not breedin" (25-26). Thoughts of his father's sexual prowess are never far from Sut's mind. Compared to Johnson Jones Hooper's story of Simon Suggs cheating his father at cards and running away from home, Harris' sketch is far richer. In choosing fantasy over realism in the central fable, Harris moves closer to the symbolizing power of the folk imagination. The ambiguity of triumph and loss, hatred and admiration, sexual jealousy and love, the sense of ugliness and the sense of glory in life float abundantly in the little fable.

Some of the revisions are for the sake of alliteration. Dad's first reaction to the hornets was that he "rared an' kicked once or twice, an' fotched a squeal wus nor ara hoss in the district, an' sot in to runnin' away, jist as natural as ever you seed." Harris rewrote the sentence to add four initial *s*'s: "He rar'd an' fotch a squeal wus nur ara stud hoss in the State, an' sot in tu strait runnin away jis es natral es yu ever seed any uther skeer'd hoss du" (24). There are at least two other examples of alliterating changes in the opening sketch. Such revisions indicate that Harris painstakingly sought his "lyric intensity," to use Brom Weber's phrase, in sound, rhythm, and imagery.

III

Both Harris' revisions and his added sketches express his continuing motive: to evoke laughter. The spirit of his sketches is that of the humorous tale, which asks first how it may tickle the hearer's risibles. Harris' most obvious device to cause laughter is his plots; more than half of the sketches in the *Yarns* are practical jokes. The motive of the prankster Sut is to discomfort his victim, to disrupt social gatherings into wild action. This tradition is of the ancient comic stage: Pheidippides beating his father in Aristophanes' *The Clouds*, or Strepsiades tearing off the tiles from Socrates' house and setting it on fire. It is the tradition that laughs at Don Quixote's beating the mule driver, and later being stoned by the driver's companions.

In the *Yarns*, Sut upsets camp meetings twice, a wedding, a Negro funeral, a quilting, and, indirectly, a dance. Among the individuals he plays violent jokes on are the lawyer Stilyards;

the Yankee lecturer; the lazy son of a country preacher; old farmer Burns; an Irishman at a hunting camp; a stranger suspected of teasing his dog; one local drunkard, Hen Baily; various preachers, sheriffs, school-commissioners; and other characters who are depressing symbols of propriety, power, and authority.

Although the jokes may be monotonous to the sophisticated reader, they evoke the old human pleasure in rhythm of action, in change, alteration, contrast, and climax.[2] In some, one action leads to another, seemingly without plan, until the anecdotes become highly elaborate, fantastic, and impossible in their total consequence. The element of carelessness and spontaneity is notably present.

Harris uses several devices to make the cruelty in some degree acceptable. First, the element of fantasy removes the actions from reality. Their spirit is the spirit of play, violent but free and high-spirited. Next, the objects of the humor within the tales are created to be unworthy creatures: liars, hypocrites, cheats, oppressors of the powerless. They are often officials, always abusers of their authority. Their reduction or dismissal from the world of the *Yarns* is never intended to bring any sense of loss. Instead, the reader's yearning for simple compensation is gratified. Always Harris assumes that vulgarity is not so disagreeable as pretentiousness.

The cruelty is also limited in degree; the consequences of Sut's jokes are not fatal nor permanent. The nearest Harris comes to this margin of comedy is Mrs. Yardley's death. Her sketch opens with Sut's heartless description of the task of burying her, which he first calls helping "tu salt ole Missis Yardley down," and later, "Fixin her fur rotten cumfurtably, kiverin her up wif sile, tu keep the buzzards frum cheatin the wurms" (134). It first seems that Sut's joke has killed the old woman. Later George asks Sut again what killed her, and he replies: "Nuffin, only her heart stop't beatin 'bout losin a nine dimunt quilt. True, she got a skeer'd hoss tu run over her, but she'd a-got over that ef a quilt hadn't been mix'd up in the catastrophy" (137). Not Sut's cruelty, as the reader is first led to suspect, but a broken heart over the loss of a quilt is the point; not violence, but satire on literary sentimentalism is the basis of the comedy.[3] Harris generally observes in his book the comic convention that the outcome of the action should be limited to minor consequences.

Sut's own character is also an element in the meaning of the jokes. Although his victims often deserve their discomfort, Sut is no instrument of a moral universe, and his personality does not magnify the action. His antic character helps define the jokes as play. He is often the victim himself, sometimes of his own foolishness or of another's malicious mischief. Sut is an outsider, one of the insulted and injured; but the reader is not called to pity him. His own disappointments and sufferings provide welcome motive for his exuberant vengefulness. By returning blow for heartless blow, sometimes like the rains of heaven falling on just and unjust alike, he expresses the joy of survival, of triumphant, mindless life which celebrates its inward vitality in outward circumstances of squalor and hopelessness.

IV

Some of the sketches are not practical jokes. "Sut's Sermon" and "Tripetown" use Sut's point of view as a mask to express Harris' own dislike of innkeepers. Both show some lack of control of the material. In such trivial sketches, only Harris' language is worth attention.

Of the other sketches of the *Yarns* which are not practical jokes, "Sut Lovingood's Daddy, Acting Horse," "Rare Ripe Garden-Seed," "Contempt of Court—Almost," and "Dad's Dog School" rank among Harris' most ambitious efforts to create comic fables of poor backwoods mountain life that will express, through the ambiguity of comedy, the yearning for unrestrained existence. In these last stories of the book Harris develops most explicitly the anti-authoritarian impulse that underlies his work —an impulse that reached some peak of intensity in American life during the middle decades of the nineteenth century. Shelley and Byron among the English Romantic poets had developed their distrust of authority to its ultimate conclusion in defiance of a despotic God. Parts of *Don Juan* express the same impulse in comic form. The theme of defiance of authority is as old as the Greek myths to which Shelley turned for his characters and fable. Harris' domestication of the theme utilized a comic folk symbolism that masked the impiety in such a way as to make it a fresh experience of release to his readers.

"Rare Ripe Garden Seed" is a story of comic sexuality and infidelity, and both are in the time-honored tradition of folk humor. A young blacksmith, Wat Mastin, "in struttin an' gobblin time," marries the only daughter of a respectable old widow. The two set up housekeeping and plant a garden of rare ripe seed they have bought from a Yankee peddler. Wat looks forward to an abundant crop and increasing joy of life, but soon he decides to leave home. As Sut says, "He tuck a noshun tu work a spell down tu Ataylanty, in the railroad shop, es he sed he hed a sorter ailin in his back . . ." (232). The new bridgegroom's proverbial exhaustion is a common subject for folk humor.

After four months Wat returns to find his wife has produced a baby. In a scene of comic ignorance, he counts, uncertainly and laboriously, the months of his marriage. His mother-in-law, who had shown great eagerness for the marriage, offers him whiskey and promises to explain. Her explanation, like similar efforts in Chaucer and Boccaccio, depends on the appearance of reasonableness and even more on an ignorant and credulous hearer. With somewhat more subtlety than that of the *fabliaux*, however, Harris develops the almost-conscious element of persistence in Wat's credulity. He needs to be deceived, but he cannot succeed. Mrs. McKildrin's explanation is that the magical effect of the rare ripe garden seed had caused Mary Margaret to produce her baby with unprecedented speed.

During Mrs. McKildrin's explanation, Sheriff Doltin, the real father of Mary Margaret's baby, arrives with gifts for the girl and his new child. Seeing the deceived husband has unexpectedly returned, he composes his face in one of the mask images common in Harris: he "drawed the puckerin-string ove that legil face ove his'n an' fotch hit up tu the 'know'd yu wer at home,' sorter look" (239). The sheriff seconds Mrs. McKildrin's explanation and expresses astonishment at Wat's ignorance concerning the potency of rare ripe seed.

At this point Sut's tale is interrupted by his audience with a reminder that it is bedtime. The ultimate outcome of the plot is delayed through two following episodes until the final exposure of the sheriff as father of the child, and his punishment in an elaborate and humiliating practical joke. Doltin is made the comic victim not because he is guilty of breaking a moral law but because he has shamed Sut's friend, and even more because he is selfish, ugly, oppressive, pretentious authority.

Examples of faithless, lying, deceitful women are common in Harris. Sut's earlier warning to George to beware of "strong minded" women because they can turn a man into a "kidney worm'd hog what cant raise his bristles" in less than a month had explained woman's discontent by observing that she wanted to be a man. Underlying the comic anti-feminism was Harris' very apparent uneasiness about the place of women in Southern society. Since the earlier sketch, it had seemed to Harris that women were trying more openly, like men, to exact satisfaction for grievances done them within the family. Harris' comedy avoids sentimentalizing woman and avoids debate about her condition. His reply to what he thought was her demand for the rights and freedom of a man was to create a gallery of women as faithless and hypocritical as his men—and even more devious in their malice.

Old Sheriff Doltin's alliance with Mrs. McKildrin brings together the institution of the law and middle-class respectability. Harris' attack on female deceit and cunning and on the sheriff's use of his office to keep the surface proprieties is extended to an attack on explanations. As the sheriff and Mrs. McKildrin explain the four-month baby, "they talked so fas', an' so much, that the more Wat listened the less he know'd" (240), says Sut. In Sut's world, explanations are always false. Human reason exists only as an instrument of the self in the struggle with others.

V

Rejection of reason and of order emerges as the major theme in the last story of the collection, which follows the series on Wat's entrapment and cuckolding and Sut's revenge for him on the sheriff. This final tale, "Dad's Dog School," is—like "Sut Lovingood's Daddy, Acting Horse"—a comic fable of the destruction of the father of the Lovingood family. The action belongs to the wild, free folk imagination. It was printed as an anecdote in the comic journal *Yankee Notions* ten years before Harris' elaboration of the central incident.[4] The fable belonged to popular lore and, according to Harris' introduction, to folklore in the sense that it is a traditional oral tale. The yarn, as F. M. Cornford said of the early Greek comedy, is "a scene of Sacrifice and a Feast";[5] it contains the seemingly incompatible elements of cruelty and festival and, like the ancient comedy and many folk tales, is pervaded with a strong erotic element.

Harris' gentleman character, George, appears once again in this last sketch, briefly and ineffectually, to begin the tale; but Sut interrupts with a common folk storyteller's device to announce that he will tell it because the event really happened in his family. He was, he recalls, sixteen at the time. A neighbor gave him a bull pup, "Ugly as a she ho'net an' brave es a trap't rat" (278). His father liked the pup because, as Sut understood it, "thar naters wer sorter like, I reckon. He wer the only critter I ever know'd dad tu be good tu, an' narra pusson yet" (278).

In one of the detailed scenes that Harris constructed with a craftsman's skill, Sut presents a Lovingood Sunday morning service:

> Late one Saturday, we sot in an' kill'd a-tarin big black an' white yearlin bull beastes, an' on Sunday mornin, arter gittin a big bellyfull ove fried liver an' chopp't inyuns, dad sot down ontu the cabin steps, in the sun, a-playin wif "Sugar," that wer the pup's name. I wer mounted ontu the fence a-shaven seed-ticks ofen my laigs wif a barlow knife, an' mam wer in the yard sittin ontu the half-bushel wif three ur four ove the childers' heads in her lap, bizzy rite in the middil ove a big still hunt arter insex (278).

The "famerly devarshin," as Sut calls it, begins when dad decides to teach the pup to bite and hang on, despite mam's protest that he ought to "let that ar blasted roun-headed pup edecate hissef like yer uther childer dus" (280). Dad has his way at first. He sends Sut down to the creek with the dog while he goes into the loom house with his daughter. Here Sal, with pre-Freudian innocence, sews him naked into the bull's raw hide. At the signal, Sut returns to set the pup on the mock bull. On his second try, the dog goes in under the hide and fastens his teeth in the old man's blood besmeared nose and upper lip.

At this point, following one of the traditional folk patterns, the unwelcome outsider arrives in the person of the local deacon, Squire Hanley, on his solemn Sunday horse. The note-shaving old squire is characterized by Sut as "secon enjineer ove a mersheen, made outen a mess ove sturgeon-backed, sandy-heeled ole maids, devarsed wives, ur wimen what orter been wun ur tuther; an' uther thin minded pussons, fur the pupus, es they sed, ove squelchin sin in the neighborhood, amung sich domestic heathins es us, but raley fur the mindin giner'lly ove everybody else's bisness" (287).

Significantly, the squire is the reasonable man, a model of planning, order, and utilitarian regularity:

> He wore a hat ten years, an' wore a nail in the chuch wall bright, a-hangin hit on. He wore a holler spot in the side ove his walkin-stick, wif his finger allers tetchin the same place, an' he wore anuther greasy holler in one ove the groanin bainches, ni ontu the noth corner ove the pulpit, jis' like the sittin hole in a shoemaker's stool. . . . His pea-sticks wer shod wif spikes, his fire wood wer clar ove knots es waggen timber, his hens never laid on a Sunday, an sot when he told em to (286).

The squire's horse, like Don Quixote's, was the image of propriety: "He wer never hearn squeal, belch, ur make eny onsightly soun . . ." (288).

The old deacon hides his impulse to meddle behind the mask of religion. In the voice of the church, he demands to know why the Lovingoods are tormenting the two varmints "on the Lord's Holy Sabbath." The squire's presence causes Sut to see himself, his father, and his mother with the eye of another: "A appertite tu run began tu gnaw my stumick, an' I felt my face a-swellin wif shame" (286). The folk literature of the American backwoods and frontier is filled with expressions of hatred of churches as fierce as Shelley's hatred of orthodoxies. It is customarily cast in the form of scorn of hypocrisy, but it is often grounded on the union of the church with the community caste system and the power that union has to call man to judge his place in it.

Sut's mam, however, helps Sut to see what the old squire

really represents. She tells the deacon to be on his way as the Lovingoods have no girls "ole enuf" to convert. Sut starts the horse by clapping a burr under his tail. Mam's parting advice is not only an expression of scorn for Squire Hanley's hypocrisy; it also expresses the comically ambiguous and ironic attitude of the folk toward faith: She says, "Trus' freely in heving Squire es long es crupper holt lasts" (291). Sut expresses his own release from shame by adding to the mockery of religion. The horse's rearing breaks one of the squire's sentences, and Sut says sarcastically, "Thinks I, *thar* that ar kick wer a interpersision, fur hit kep the Squire frum plain cussin" (291).

After mam and Sut forestall the Squire's attempt to restore order and authority, they turn again to the Dionysian old man bellowing for help from within the bull's hide. The dog's hold on his nose and upper lip so distorts his astonishing obscenities and blasphemies that the family pretend not to understand. After checking to see if the pup's hold is secure, mam seizes a bean pole and beats her husband on the back as dog and man whirl round in frenzied agony. Under the blows and the pain, dad begins to totter. Sister Sal, whom dad has sent for a jug of "Spanish fly whisky, tu make happy cum arter he let out his dorg-school" (297), returns; and Electra like, she is infuriated at her father's suffering. "Yu durn'd yaller son of a b——h," she cries with comic accuracy, "*I'll* break yer holt" (297). This she does with an ax, but in her zeal she chops off the end of Dad's nose and a half-moon of his upper lip, along with part of the dog's snout and lower jaw. Dad fainted, Sut tells his audience; but the dog was ruined forever.

By linking Sut's father and Squire Hanley, the model of regularity, prudence, and religious respectability, the yarn not only expresses scorn of the comic anti-father, but also releases laughter at order, regularity, and reason itself. Within his family as within the world, if the fool Sut has a choice between order and chaos, he prefers chaos. In the opposition of symbolic characters, in the ebullient action of the plots, and in the tension of the style, Harris objectifies to some degree man's inner struggle, where body and mind oppose each other, and reason is the enemy of life.

This aspect of irrationalism, an explicit element in Romantic thought since Blake, has had perhaps its most extreme philosophic statement in Miguel de Unamuno's *The Tragic Sense of Life:*

> For living is one thing and knowing another, and, as we shall see, perhaps there is between them such opposition that we might say that everything vital is not only irrational but anti-rational, and everything rational, anti-vital. . . . Actually, reason is the enemy of life.—Intelligence is a terrible thing. It tends toward death as memory towards stability. What is alive, what is absolutely individual, is, strictly speaking, unintelligible. Logic tends to reduce everything to identities and types, so that each representation may have only a single and identical content in any place, time or relation in which it occurs for us. And there is nothing which is the same during two successive moments of its existence. . . . How, then, can reason be opened to the revelation of life?[6]

The folk feeling that to be thoughtful is to be sad is rooted in some such perception. Harris' final comedy expresses that impulse of life simply to be, and not to know itself. Energy overwhelms order. In this energy, exuberance, revenge, joy, hatred, fear, sexuality swirl together as irreducible facts; and the knowledge that all the impulses of life cannot be enjoyed at once is a knowledge to be fled in comedy.

Once the old squire is seen as a symbol of religion and the orderly life, and once he is linked with the cruel, squalid oppressiveness of dad and with the pretentious social and institutional power of Sheriff Doltin and Judge Smarty of "Contempt of Court," a basic element of Sut's world becomes apparent. The drift toward irrational and absolute freedom is carried in the symbolism to its ultimate conclusion. It is not merely the traditional victim of satiric attack—Yankee, Negro, Preacher, and Woman—that Harris' fables destroy in comic symbol. And it is not merely the escape from institutions that we see in Dickens' *Pickwick* and in Aristophanes' comedies: the fool Sut would escape the outer restraints of others and of institutions and the inner restraints of reason itself. For Sut, every practical joke is a delight because it is a conspiracy against all order.

The final element in Harris' comic symbolism—as the figure of old Deacon Hanley has suggested—is, at its farthest reaches, the transcendent image of God.

In so formally religious a life as Harris', the father figure cannot altogether escape connotations of the heavenly Father. Harris' reduction of the image of the Father is not Romantically heroic as with Shelley and Byron. Nor is it uneasily humorous and speculative as with Melville when he wrote Hawthorne, "The reason the mass of men fear God, and *at bottom dislike* Him, is because they rather distrust His heart, and fancy Him all brain like a watch."[7] For Harris this feeling, although more masked and ambiguous than it was to become in Mark Twain, is like *Letters from the Earth* in its fierce and occasionally ecstatic release of hatred. The reduction of the Transcendent provides a great part of the energy which pervades the comic symbolism of the *Yarns*. As Robert Wiggins in *Mark Twain: Jackleg Novelist* says of Mark Twain's late work, so Harris, too, dimly recognized in his comedy a symbolic mode that enabled him to write more than he knew, and to say the unsayable.

After about 1840, frontier and backwoods American humor abounds in expressions of anti-authoritarian and anti-religious impulses, and Harris' comic expression of the feeling suggests why his work struck so responsive a hidden chord in his readers. Joseph Glover Baldwin's *Flush Times in Alabama and Mississippi* (1853) is mostly satire on the corruption of justice and on general incompetence in his portion of the old Southwestern frontier; but his sketch "Assault and Battery" contains one of the meddling, pretentious religious figures that were shifting from images of ignorance to images of authority in the humor of the middle century. As Burwell Shines passes a doggery, he denounces the loafers standing inside for their Sabbath breaking. They run out to beat Shines, calling, "Kill him! Kill Shadbelly with his praying clothes on!" The passion of the cry has its meaning beyond laughter. Satire on cant is not absolutely separated from scorn of religion in the frontier humorists.

Sometimes these literary creations of the disruption of camp meetings rise to a kind of ecstasy of madness, as in Henry Clay Lewis' story, "The Day of Judgment." In it a group of drunken young men pour turpentine and tar on a mule, set him afire, and drive him into a congregation of Millerites awaiting the last day. This cruel scorn of orgiastic camp meetings is balanced by no praise of religion.

The anti-religious feeling, underlying the more obvious class bias expressed in stories of camp meetings disrupted, suggests community impulses widely shared. John Caldwell (quoted in chapter 3, section I) recorded Ducktown's open scorn for Christianity. The flight from civilization to Ducktown, obviously, was for many an escape from religious ethics; in Europe, the flight was not physical but intellectual: in the Romantic symbolism of Nietzsche, man killed God because he could not bear to have anyone looking at his ugliest side.

Of all the Southwestern humorists, Harris created the most comic assaults on fathers and preachers. Sut defeats them all. The only characters who equal Sut in resilience are creatures of defiant physical strength, like Wirt Staples, the sexually powerful Sicily Burns, and other primitive life-force figures. The constant defeat of the authority of the family, the community, and the church focuses at last on the final, transcendent source of order, law, and authority. Masked in the irony of the fool's point of view, and in the ambiguity of comic fable, Harris provided his readers a source of profound, if unrecognized, release for one of his community's feelings: the unutterable longing for the death of God.

VI

Not only in language and in fable but also through his creation of characters Harris sought to express his sense of the human condition in a way to evoke laughter at it. The *Yarns* present with lavish invention a remarkable collection of backwoods humanity—young and old, ugly and beautiful, strange and familiar—in a variety of occupations and social conditions from the middle ranks of the rural community down. Sut himself, Harris' most careful creation, will be discussed below. Sut's fantastic father, "mean, an' lazy an' ugly, an' savidge, an' durn fool tu kill," and his mother, protective of the children but full of hatred for her husband, have both been mentioned. As memorable as Faulkner's Armstids, they are fuller of the unquenchable vigor of life.

Old Squire Hanley is skillfully developed as both individual and symbol. The beautiful Sicily appears and reappears in images of sensual, sometimes naked beauty, in bloom and decline. Bart Davis, the "no-count, jug-kerryin, slow-thinkin, flea-hurtin, herrin-eatin Noth Calinian"; Wirt Staples, whom F. O. Matthiessen admired as "the central man of the Smoky Mountains to stand beside Emerson's"; the pustle-gutted Sheriff Doltin and Parson Bullen; Mrs. Yardley, that "great noticer ove littil things, that nobody else ever seed"—all these are memorable for the coherence of their being and conduct; for the vivid color of their presentation; and, at their most disguised level, for what they reveal about humanity.

Numerous even more minor characters are presented with swift impressionism: In "The Widow McCloud's Mare" Sut passes "a cabin whar a ole 'oman dress'd in a pipe an' a stripid aprun wer a-standin on the ash-hopper lookin up the road" (46), and these three details are sufficient to fix her in the reader's mind. Some minor characters have little legends of their own. In one of Sut's elaborate similes, retribution is as well deserved as any "since ole Shockly chased Passun Bumpas wif a shot-gun ritribushun, for onsantifyin his wife" (222). When George stops the story to ask if the farmer caught the preacher, Bumpas springs to life in his comic community legacy: "I dunno; he mus' a-run 'im pow'ful clost, fur he fotch back his hoss, hat, an' hyme book, an' bof caps on his gun wer busted, an' nobody name Bumpas hes been seed 'bout thar since, 'ceptin sum littil flax-headed fellers scattered thru the sarkit, wif no daddys, an' not much mammys tu speak ove" (222). What begins as a rambling comparison, ends as a character swiftly and impressionistically summoned into Harris' world to play out the preacher's proverbial devotion to sex and then to disappear with Sut's ironic dismissal.

It is only at the end of the *Yarns* that the reader is aware of the number and variety of characters who have risen in the lavish invention of Sut's language. Neither their ugliness nor their rarer beauty, their occasional honesty nor their more common hypocrisy, nor any detail of their appearance or being strikes the reader as inappropriate. The impression of teeming humanity is both exhilarating and ugly, usually memorable, always rich and full of life.

The effect of Harris' book on its readers has varied widely. Humor is never innocent; it always means something, and in Harris' practice its convention of masking was pervasively called to his reader's attention. Because comedy often communicates the unspeakable, and because it often concerns itself with fundamentals of immediate life, it expresses or collides with our most jealously held feelings. This masking and vivid symbolizing explains why F. O. Matthiessen could say that Harris' language possesses something on the comic level that Melville's has on the tragic; and why Edmund Wilson could say that *Sut Lovingood's Yarns* is the most repellent book of any literary merit in American literature.[8] Although Mr. Wilson's assessment is subjective, the two comments are not incompatible. In the *Yarns* there are elements of triumphant life, exuberance, and joy; there are elements of hatred, disorder, and terrible human ugliness. The power of its evocations is tribute to Harris' extensive reading, long apprenticeship, and painstaking craftsmanship—all issuing in a work which is one of the minor masterpieces of American humor and the best book of its kind before *Huckleberry Finn*.

CHAPTER 6

'Well! Dad's Dead'

FROM THE APPEARANCE of his *Yarns* until his death two and one half years later, Harris published eleven known sketches in Chattanooga and Knoxville newspapers. These established no new lines of development, but many of them are significant efforts. In general, they show an increase of unusual fantasy, a greater amount of sexual reference and symbolism, and more use of folklore.

"Saul Spradlin's Ghost" describes a folk method of exorcising a spirit, but the second installment of the story is still unlocated. The awkwardly titled "Sut Lovengood Reports What Bob Dawson Said after Marrying a Substitute" has as its motif the disappointed bridegroom. When George asks Sut why he has never married, Sut responds with the story of Bob Dawson. On a horse-trading trip to Tennessee, Dawson meets a girl he likes, woos her, and suddenly finds himself married. During the wedding party, the new bride whispers to him to slip off to bed and she will follow shortly. Amidst the coarse jokes of the crowd, Dawson races upstairs.

The second installment describes Dawson's anticipation until the bride enters, begins drawing out her hair pins and throwing them right and left. Astonished, Dawson asks if she would not prefer to blow out the light. She replies coolly, "You will see me strip, sooner or later, and I might as well begin tonight." Rapidly emerging from her Victorian mass of clothing, she divests herself one by one of a series of false and cosmetic devices: false calves, false breasts, false teeth, false eye, and false hair. The first two revelations are comic; the last three culminate in a disgusting act: "She, with her fore finger bounced out one of her eyes, and put it in her mouth, while she lifted her whole head of hair, leavin' her skull white and glossy as a billiard ball." As she looks in one-eyed speculation at her new bride-groom and then at the candle, the false series explodes into Dawson's comically obscene fantasy: "I busy all the while recapitulatin' 'False calves, false breasts, false teeth, false eye, false hair' what next? The most horrible idear that ever burnt an' blazed in the brain of man, was now fast resolving itself into its dreadful shape in mine. . . ." When the bride says significantly she is *almost through*, Dawson can look no more; fearing the ultimate imitation, he runs downstairs in his shirt tail, out of town and out of the state.

The sketch ends with Sut saying that the fashion for false breasts—which he calls "palpititytators," with a characteristic in-fixed pun—has caused even his sister Sal to make herself some: "She saw'd a round dry gourd in two, a gourd as big as my head, an' then made a hole in the middil ove each half, an' stuff'd in white oak acorns, butt first, an' dad shave me if she dident hist the whole contrapshun intu her buzzum. I wish I may be dam if you cudent see the bulge ove the acorns across a field."

The humor of discovering male or female beauty as falsely created by mechanical devices is old: Poe's "The Man that Was Used Up" and Hawthorne's "Mrs. Bullfrog" are painful ex-amples. Harris' sketch is more complex than either of these in the emotions it expresses, and considerably franker physically. The undressing scene parallels the first half of Swift's "A Beautiful Young Nymph Going to Bed," and the whole sketch, beyond its comedy of duplicity discovered, expresses both desire for and loathing of the female. Phallic symbolism of great variety abounds in the piece during Dawson's anticipatory wait-ing; the actual undressing, however, is not an erotic but a dis-gusting act. The traditional sexual elements of primitive comedy and folk humor are pervasive and are presented with increas-ingly less disguise in Harris' work.

Bob Dawson's story has a comic echo of a line from Pope's "Essay on Criticism"—"as soon as the doleful half hour devoted to delicacy should drag its slow sled away"—and Harris' next sketch, "Sut Lovengood's Big Music Box Story," opens with a slightly misquoted line from Congreve's *The Mourning Bride*: "Music hath charms to soothe the savage breast." Other references indicate that Harris was a particularly careful reader of Pope and Congreve. It would appear he long studied eighteenth-century drama and poetry for the techniques to create Sut's backwoods imagery.

In the spring of 1868, Harris wrote two rambling installments for a project titled "Sut Lovengood, A Chapter from His Autobiography." The first includes a fight between mam and Sall Simmons over dad. From a dogwood tree Sut watches the women pull hair in a stream. He cheers impartially for both,[1] pleased to see the women almost naked, their clothes wet. The plot of the two sketches is loose; the language is colorful, but not carefully wrought in either dialect or imagery.

Later in the spring Harris wrote a parody of Jesse Grant's campaign biography of his famous son, General U. S. Grant, then a candidate for President.[2] The fiction is that old Hoss Lovingood is writing the life of his son, Sut. Harris failed to work out any central metaphor for his series; his comedy is merely reductive satire, and his judgment of the Civil War is not original: it was fought for profit; Lincoln was a coward; and Grant was an inept, obstinate, destructive winner. J. J. Hooper's *Simon Suggs* had been structured as a campaign biography burlesquing John Henry Eaton's *Memoirs of Andrew Jackson,* and the form gave Harris opportunity, as it had Hooper, to practice literary satire as well as to attack a political enemy—to express artistic as well as political interests.

"Bill Ainsworth's Quarter Race," which follows, is a nostalgic return to the East Tennessee of 1833. The sketch is leisurely in its movement, full of detail lovingly presented. The tone is elegiac; the descriptions of people—Negroes, old women, officials even—are pleasant and affectionate. The attempt to re-create the fun of the old days is much less compressed and violent than in "The Knob Dance," and does not imply, like the earlier sketch, that the American Eden is to be found in the mountains of East Tennessee. The sketch concludes with two footnotes to country customs which show the careful attention Harris was still giving to the popular beliefs and traditions which were so important in his art.

George's voice, which opens "Sut Lovengood's Allegory," is heavy and weary; but Sut's portion, only slightly infected by George's mood, grows increasingly coarse and vigorous. The world, Sut says uncharacteristically, is going backward: "No, boys, we aint as *good* as we wer forty years ago. We am too dam artifishul, interprizin, and *sharp*—we know too much." At George's resigned invitation, Sut tells how Brakebill served his "meterfistickal, free will billygoat . . . , showin' many marks ove progress, an' higher law." The goat's sign of progress is that it begins to breed with all the animals on the farm, and old Brakebill's solution is to castrate the creature.

In the fall of 1868, the Knoxville *Press and Messenger* printed one of Harris' strangest stories, "Well! Dad's Dead," an account of the death and funeral of old Hoss Lovingood. Donald Day takes its publication date, after Grant's election, as significant; he reads the sketch as a political satire, dad symbolizing the Old South and mam the surviving New.[3] The sketch, however, shows no very convincing evidence of political intention or meaning. It seems best read as a grotesque comedy of death that is to some degree comparable to Faulkner's *As I Lay Dying*, as M. Thomas Inge has pointed out.[4]

The sketch opens with the comic impropriety of Sut's opinion of his father's death: "Thar never wer a man yet, so mean, but what some time, or other, done at least one good thing. Now, my Dad, put off doin his good thing, for an awful long time, but at last he did hit, like a white man. He died, by golly." Mam's inverted praise for the old man is equally incongruous: "Mam declar'd that Gineril Washington never did a better thing in his whole life." Her only regret is that he did not get the idea twenty years earlier. To spite her, he had hung on until she had broken her last tooth.

The largest portion of the tale details the funeral procession. Dad is sewn up in an old bed cover, placed on a borrowed shingle sled, and dragged by two borrowed steers to his grave. Sut, mam, and Sister Sal—all mindful of the proprieties of grief—are filled with solemn satisfaction. As the eldest son, Sut drives: "I sot in front an' was driver, an' a feelin' come over me, like I think a darn'd, starvin' one-hoss lawyer mus' a had, when he fust foun' hissef Captain ove Company A, at the beginin' ove the war. I'd a cuss'd a man in a minit, but fortinatly for any man, he warnt about jist then." The pride of the occasion issues in a fantasy of clownish insolence, not characteristic of the Sut of the *Yarns*.

Frightened by the smell of the corpse, the steers run away. As the body lunges about the flying sled, it knocks all the family off; and mam wonders "when the devil *will* go out of *him*." When the sled crosses the grave, Sut kicks his father's body out, and it falls neatly into the earth. For a moment Sut is worried because the old man's back is to the east, and he will be slow to rise on Judgment Day. But his second thought is that his father will rise with his "back to the danger," and can all the better run.

The improperly placed corpse is an ancient element in folk literature. At Till Eulenspiegel's funeral, the coffin falls so that Eulenspiegel stands upright in his grave. The people say, "Leave him as he is, he was strange in his life, he wants to be so after his death."[5]

The surface element of the comedy lies in the Lovingoods' inability to conduct even a funeral with propriety and in their lack of decent feeling, like the coarseness of the gravediggers in *Hamlet*. Like the Bundrens in Faulkner's *As I Lay Dying*, the Lovingoods are not only creatures of poverty and inflexible ignorance, but also half-proud victims of an antically perverse fate. The comedy goes beyond an expression of amusement at the coarseness of the low-born, however, to a more universal celebration of satisfaction and even triumph at the death of another.

Seen in relationship to the earlier stories of old Hoss Lovingood, this final tale reinforces the reader's perception of his special significance. He is the necessary figure of power and authority. However, he serves not to protect and assist, but to spoil and destroy the lives in his keeping. His death, like that of the divine fertility kings of ancient comic ritual, is occasion for disorderly festival. Harris achieves the minor but significant tone of solemn elevation through the ceremonial elements of the wild funeral ride and through his avoidance of condescension. Sut's voice is calm in his new apotheosis: "Well! well! charm's broke at last." Unlike "Dad's Dog School," the sketch develops no satire against the church. The tone is comic resignation to the human lot.

What were to be Harris' last two sketches are both minor efforts. The rich texture of his style seems to have been achieved by careful working and revision, but Sut's language in these final sketches is thin by comparison. "On Old Gals and Young Ones" contains an imaginative reconstruction of a woman's sexual fantasies, but is otherwise insignificant. "Sut Lovengood Sets up with a Gal—One Pop Baily" is intended as a comic account of Sut's wooing, but it does not rise above the level of ordinary journalistic humor. Harris' other writing for 1869 may have been for the last manuscript he completed, *High Times and Hard Times,* a work that remains undiscovered. By the end of 1869 Harris was dead.

CHAPTER 7

The Fool as Point of View

I

WHEN WILLIAM FAULKNER, in the *Paris Review* interviews, was asked for his favorite fictional characters, he offered Dickens' Mrs. Gamp, Falstaff and Prince Hal, Don Quixote and Sancho, Huck and Jim, and a few others; he devoted his longest discussion to the least-known character in his list: "And then I like Sut Lovingood from a book written by George Harris about 1840 or '50 in the Tennessee mountains. He had no illusions about himself, did the best he could; at certain times he was a coward and knew it and wasn't ashamed; he never blamed his misfortunes on anyone and never cursed God for them."[1] The august company seems surprising, and Faulkner's point that Sut is an admirable literary creation invites examination.

The framework device of the earlier Southwestern humorists—A. B. Longstreet, T. B. Thorpe, and Johnson J. Hooper—always gave the gentleman observer superior comprehension and a moral system competent to understand and judge the native backwoodsmen whose oral stories he reproduced. Harris, by the time he prepared the *Yarns* for publication, had abandoned this framework except as the briefest convention and had endowed Sut with a vividness of language, expansiveness of spirit, and even a perceptive intelligence superior in vitality to those of gentleman George. Sut is a highly sophisticated point of view in the technical literary sense, a personality rich enough to evoke interest for itself and to perceive and refract the world. With careful craftsmanship, Harris exploits Sut's point of view to destroy in his reader old habits of perception and to introduce a fresh and original vision of the world.[2]

In time and place Sut is to some degree a local type. He shares a language, a social condition, a set of traditions that define the outward form of his existence. From the first, however, he is detached both in life and in spirit from his community. Outwardly, he seems often to be one of the insulted and the injured—to have reason, as Faulkner felt, to curse God; but he is not one of Dostoievski's introspective underground men, or one of Dickens' victimized and terrified poor. Although mean-souled and often cruel, Sut is at the same time large-spirited, triumphant, and free. To achieve Sut's triumph over life, Harris has chosen one of man's ancient modes of existence within society; Harris defines his broadest intention for Sut in his subtitle by terming Sut a "nat'ral born durn'd fool."

The reader is early aware that Harris is not using the term in any loose, careless, or general way. Instead, Sut is created in the literary tradition of the fool, a type which has since Classical antiquity been constantly reinvigorated by a parallel folk tradition.

Sut is always conscious of his mode of existence. In this sense, despite his constant disclaimers, his life is a free choice he has made for himself; his existence is the product of his own will. His choice frees him from the necessity of deceiving himself and thus provides him an authentic mode of being. His existence is not, like that of the average man, dead in the world of tradition, habit, and illusion.

In his preface, Sut calls himself an eternal fool. Writing prefaces, he tells George, "Smells tu me sorter like a durned humbug, the hole ove hit—a littil like cuttin ove the Ten Cummandmints intu the rine ove a warter-million; hits jist slashed open an' the inside et outen hit, the rine an' the cummandmints broke all tu pieces an' flung tu the hogs, an' never tho't ove onst—them, nur the 'tarnil fool what cut em thar" (ix). Harris' conception of his fool, then, is not the antic simpleton but the wise fool; Sut is the ironic hero who perceives the human condition and knows he himself is a fool to communicate his perceptions, to cut his ten commandments in the rind of a watermelon.

In "Sut Lovingood's Daddy, Acting Horse," Harris provides

one of the rare objective descriptions of Sut: a "queer looking, long legged, short bodied, small headed" creature. He is five times the fool any other member of the family could claim to be, excepting his dad, of course. Sut's dad is called a damned fool and he calls his son a damned fool; and variously throughout the sketch the Lovingoods, father and son, are cursed as eternal fools. At the opening of the book, Harris defines Sut primarily in action. He is a demonically ebullient creature, commanding and free.

For the following sketch, Harris chose "Sut's New-Fangled Shirt," which is something of a falling-off from the opening; but Sut as fool is further developed by his telling a tale of his own ignorance. In Sut's authentic existence as fool, he always knows his own weakness and stupidity; and his expressions of comic despair are both recognition and acceptance of his life.

During 1858 Harris had begun considering more carefully how he might utilize the mode of Sut's existence to present a version of life. References in his sketches show that at the time he was reading Pope, Burns, Byron, and particularly Dickens and Shakespeare; from these sources he drew techniques and concepts to help him shape Sut's being. At the end of "Sicily Burns's Wedding" one of Sut's definitions introduces the element of irony possible to the point of view:

> Hit am an orful thing, George, tu be a natral born durn'd fool. Yu'se never 'sperienced hit pussonally, hev yu? Hits made pow'fully agin our famerly, an all owin tu dad. I orter bust my head open agin a bluff ove rocks, an' jis' wud du hit, ef I warnt a cussed coward. All my yearthly 'pendence is in these yere laigs—d'ye see 'em? Ef they don't fail, I may turn human, sum day, that is sorter human, enuf tu be a Squire ur school cummisiner (97).

To become "sorter human" is not plaintive longing, but the ironic man's disdainful scorn for unrealized and, to Sut, unrealizable humanity. Sut has chosen not to try to become human.

After rejecting the human condition, Sut also rejects the religious life. In "Old Burns's Bull Ride" Sut repeats his comic fear, but what he fears is pain of the body. He has no fear of the hereafter, for he has no soul:

I'se a goner I 'speck, an' I jis don't keer a durn. I'm no count, no how. Jis' look at me! Did yu ever see sich a sampil ove a human afore? I feels like I'd be glad *tu be* dead, only I'se feard ove the dyin. I don't keer fur herearter, fur hits onpossibil fur me tu hev ara soul. Who ever seed a soul in jis' sich a rack heap ove bones an' rags es this? I's nuffin but sum new-fangil'd sort ove beas', a sorter cross atween a crazy ole monkey an' a durn'd wore-out hominy-mill. I is one ove dad's explites at makin cussed fool invenshuns an' cum afore my time. I blames him fur all ove hit, allers a-tryin tu be king fool (107).

Within the *Yarns* the image of mam as a worn-out kitchen machine and of dad as a lascivious beast is appropriate; behind the tale the mechanical inventiveness of Harris himself and of his foster father Samuel Bell provides possible psychological applications. But most important for the point of view he is constructing, Harris has freed him from any transcendental significance in making Sut soulless.

As has been argued in the discussion of "Rare Ripe Garden Seed" and "Dad's Dog School," Harris' work embodies expression of anti-authoritarian and anti-rational feelings. Sut as fool personifies this concept in another of his characteristics, his mindlessness. Sut says he talks, acts, and "thinks at random" because he has no "steering oar" to his brain. He then develops a comic biology to explain the imperfection of his mind:

Well, I thinks peopil's brains what hev souls, am like ontu a chain made outen gristil, forkid at one aind; wun fork goes tu the eyes, an' tuther tu the years, an' tuther aind am welded tu the marrer in the backbone. . . . Idears start along the chain, an' every link is smarter nur the wun ahine hit, an' dergests em sorter like a paunch dus co'n, ur mash'd feed. . . . Now, in my case, thar's a hook in the chain, an' hits mos' ove the time onhook'd an' then my idears stop thar half made. Rite thar's whar dad failed in his 'speriment; puttin in that durn'd fool hook's what made me a natral born fool (210-11).

Planning and thinking, says Sut, are "ginerly no count" (67). One's fate is determined by how one conducts himself at the moment of action. Harris, like W. G. Simms, feared that thought and contemplation enfeebled life; both expressed a yearning to solve the problem of the conduct of life in moments of dramatic action.[3] Sut's conduct is uninfected by reason.

The elements of Sut's nature and his experience of life issue in a formulated philosophy. One of the primary elements of Sut's character is his search for joy. Such passages as "kissin an' fitin am the pepper an' salt ove all soshul getherins" (139) image his world and express his reason for being. His philosophy insists on the joy of sex: "Yere's my sentimints ontu folks: Men wer made a-purpus jis' tu eat, drink, an' fur stayin awake in the yearly part ove the nites: an' wimen wer made tu cook the vittils, mix the sperits, an' help the men du the stayin awake" (88). Sometimes the conflict between pleasure and the de- mands of social morality and religion are openly acknowledged, as in Sut's evaluation of Sicily Burns's function in the world:

> George, this worl am all 'rong enyhow, more temtashun than perventitive; ef hit wer ekal, I'd stand hit. What kin the ole prechurs an' the ugly wimen 'spect ove us, 'sposed es we ar to sich invenshuns es she am? Oh, hits jis' no use in thar talkin, an' groanin, an' sweatin tharsefs about hit; they mus' jis' upset nater ontu her head, an' keep her thar, ur shet up (77).

Expressions of the joys, frustrations, and occasional horrors of sexual activity are possible to Sut because of his comic freedom as fool. The formal public man, George Washington Harris, abhorred, on a rational level, what he took to be Brigham Young's sexual license; and in his political satires he ridiculed the free-love utopias of nineteenth-century America. Harris found only the comic mode satisfactory to contain what he both abhorred and, at a deeper level, desired.

While Sut seeks joy, he also sees the harsh, bitter competition for existence. Harris' emphasis on the poverty and cruelty of the American backwoods implies a profound disappointment with life in the New World that was envisioned in his early Mr. Free essays. In "Rare Ripe Garden-Seed," which came late in Harris' career, Sut speculates on the social cannibalism of village America:

> Well, es I wer sayin, mam wer feedin us brats ontu mush an' milk, wifout the milk, an' es I wer the baby then, she hilt me so es tu see that I got my sheer. Whar thar ain't enuf feed, big

childer roots littil childer outen the troff, an' gobbils up thar part. Jis' so the yearth over: bishops eats elders, elders eats common peopil; they eats sich cattil es me, I eats possums, possums eats chickins, chickins swallers wums, an' wums am content tu eat dus, an' the dus am the aind of hit all. Hit am all es regilur es the souns from the tribil down tu the bull base ove a fiddil in good tchune, an' I speck hit am right, ur hit wudn't be 'lowed (228).

Harris' familiarity with Pope's *Essay on Man* assures his acquaintance with the "Vast chain of being! which from God began," vibrating in perfect, holy harmony. Sut's concluding ironic submission to a guiding divinity and his mock-faith that "whatever is, is right" reinforce the satiric tone of his version of the heavenly order of the universe.

It is a mistake to see in the vision of human wickedness the grasp of original sin. There can be no knowledge of original sin without knowledge of the will of God and without sacrifice to make that will be done on earth. For Christianity, the will of God is expressed centrally in the Sermon on the Mount. The *Yarns* are not concerned with the knowledge of God or with the will of God; on the contrary, they are a symbolic escape from the discipline of love, as well as the discipline of authority. Sut exists outside Christianity.

Some of Sut's vitality lies in his being conscious of the discipline of love but his choosing to be free of it, and thus he is free to express the reality of his primitive hatreds. His explanation of his hatred of an encyclopedia salesman who expressed boredom at one of his tales goes beyond revenge to embody the human impulse to inflict and to contemplate pain:

I hates ole Onsightly Peter, jis' caze he didn't seem tu like tu hear me narrate las' night; that's human nater the yearth over, an' yere's more univarsal onregenerit human nater: ef ever yu dus enything tu enybody wifout cause, yu hates em allers arterwards, an' sorter wants tu hurt em agin. An' yere's anuther human nater: ef enything happens [to] sum feller, I don't keer . . . how sorry yu is fur him, thar's a streak ove satisfackshun 'bout like a sowin thread a-runnin all thru yer sorrer. . . . An' yere's a littil more; no odds how good yu is tu yung things, ur how kine yu is in treatin em, when yu sees a littil long laiged

lamb a-shakin hits tail, an' a-dancin staggerinly onder hits mam
a-huntin fur the tit, ontu hits knees, yer fingers *will* itch tu
sieze that ar tail, an' fling the littil ankshus son ove a mutton
over the fence amung the blackberry briars. . . . Ur a baby even,
rubbin hits heels apas' each uther, a-rootin an' a-snifflin arter
the breas', an' the mam duin her bes' tu git hit out, over the hem
ove her clothes, don't yu feel hungry tu gin hits jis' one 'cussion
cap slap, rite ontu the place what sum day'll fit a saddil, ur a
sowin cheer, tu show hit what's atwixt hit an' the grave; that
hit stans a pow'ful chance not tu be fed every time hits hungry,
ur in a hurry? (245-46).

In spite of the rationalizations, the piece expresses primarily the
impulse to give pain. Beneath is a strong sense that life is
struggle and disappointment; man's natural response to the
cruel urgency of the infant is not always kindness but often an
equally selfish cruelty.

This passage not only expresses Sut's vision of life but also
reveals his power to observe and to verbalize as a commanding
storyteller. He is no simple poor white, and he goes considerably
beyond Davy Crockett and the Big Bear of Arkansas in his
grasp of his world. The movement of Harris' imagination toward
myth is revealed in these presentations of Sut's vision of existence
and in his numerous passages of advice to George about how to
live. The impulse to give Sut supernatural characteristics is
shown in the bird imagery associated with him. The farthest
movement toward mythic birth does not appear in the *Yarns*,
but in "Sut Lovengood Lands Ole Abe Safe at Last," where Sut
tells a newspaper reporter: "We kep a sand-hill crane, and Mam
and him had a difficulty, and he chased her under the bed"
(Weber, 232).[4] Our source of delight in the "mythy" Sut is not
far to seek.

At his farthest symbolic meaning Sut escapes the Christian
conception of man fulfilling himself by abandoning himself to
Divine truth and goodness. Instead, he finds the significance of
his existence within himself. He is the creator of his own being.
His project is to identify himself and define himself to himself.
Once he discovers his authentic desires, he wants to realize them
in some condition of purity and permanence. By making Sut a
self-conscious symbol of the essential poverty and mortality of

human life, by restricting the meaning of his existence to the flesh's reality, by making comedy of the idea of resurrection (in "Well! Dad's Dead"), but by keeping undiminished in him the will of life to survive and enjoy itself, the fool Sut becomes the irrational comic figure who realizes the ancient yearning to escape death and to become God himself.[5]

II

By having Sut present his version of the world and the nature of his own being through self-analysis, Harris defines Sut's point of view as that of the fool as seer. He is outside the law, outside social morality, outside religion, even outside rational life. As fool, he can express the logically incompatible elements of comedy: cruelty and joy, logic and license, the knowledge of mortality and the insistence on permanence.[6] The summary reveals the parallels and affinities Sut has with the Fool of tradition.

Enid Welsford's *The Fool*, a study of the "historical origin and role of the Fool as comic entertainer," defines the fool's esthetic significance as he appears in the folk tradition, in society, and in the literary tradition. The fool, according to Welsford's definition, is the one who gets slapped, the ancient scapegoat of mankind; but also he is emotionally and spiritually tough, none the worse for his slapping:

> For the genius of the fool is manifested by his power of deluding us into the belief that he can draw the sting of pain; by his power of surrounding us with an atmosphere of make-believe, in which nothing is serious, nothing is solid, nothing has abiding consequences. Under the dissolvent influence of his personality the iron network of physical, social, and moral law, which enmeshes us from the cradle to the grave, seems—for the moment—negligible as a web of gossamer.[7]

The fool, Miss Welsford argues, does not lead to revolt against the law; on the contrary, he acts as preserver of social life by exposing pretension, by providing a safety-valve for our own unruliness, and by nourishing the sense in us "of secret spiritual independence of that which would otherwise be the intolerable tyranny of circumstance."[8]

The illusion of freedom must be created by relief from pressures. In Sut's experience, his defiance of order and propriety, and his urge to revenge himself on Sicily are all outward symbols of inner pressures. His desires are real and at the same time impossible. It is less the pressure from without than the pressure from within that Sut symbolizes. As fool, he is creator not of order, not of beauty, but of freedom.[9] He is free to create his being and to be that self.

III

Harris' work and his literary associations contain many hints about possible sources for the fool Sut. The American folk tradition is rich in terms for fools and in anecdotes about simpletons, antic clowns, and clever rogues. Many of these tales found their way into the *Spirit of the Times* and *Yankee Notions* during the years Harris contributed to those periodicals. In 1845 and 1846—when "The Knob Dance" was printed in the *Spirit* and reprinted in Porter's anthology, *A Quarter Race in Kentucky*— Johnson J. Hooper's crafty rogue Simon Suggs was also appearing in the same journal and volume. The young Suggs cheats his father at cards and runs away from home, the grown Suggs swindles a camp meeting, the middle-aged Suggs deceives his neighbors into electing him to a military office. Harris never makes Sut a sharper, but he may have found in Suggs's freedom from morality and social ties hints for a type freer even than the rogue.

Harris was fond of Alexander Pope; he paraphrased for comedy a line from the *Essay on Criticism*[10] and quoted from the *Essay on Man*, which is full of references to fools. According to Pope, man cannot escape being a fool; he can only learn and then mourn his condition. From Robert Burns, whom Harris also read and quoted (*Yarns*, 158), he could have found, had he needed, precedent for Sut's caustic satire on social pretentions and religious hypocrisy. Somewhat more remotely, "Sut Lovengood's Adventures in New York" echoes lines from Byron's *Don Juan*, Stanzas 128, and 132:

> This is the patent age of new inventions
>   For killing bodies and for saving souls,
> All propagated with the best intentions.

A greater amount of evidence exists for the influence of Charles Dickens. Sut's victim in "Old Skissim's Middle Boy" is modeled, Harris writes, on "Charley Dickins's son, the fat boy" (67), from *Pickwick Papers*. In a headnote to "Hen Baily's Reformation" Harris calls his mock temperance tract to the attention of Dickens' Reverend Mr. Stiggins, leader of the Grand Junction Ebenezer Temperance Association (198). Some of Dickens' most ebullient satire on religious cant and affectation is focused on the Reverend Mr. Stiggins. More significant for the creation of Sut's view of life may have been Harris' reading of *Hard Times* (1854). He intended to title his last manuscript *High Times and Hard Times,* which seems in the nature of a special tribute. Dickens' work may have been useful to Harris both in content and in the technique it manifested. Dr. F. R. Leavis has pointed out that the appropriateness of the vocabulary, rhythm, and imagery to the burden of meaning in *Hard Times* places Dickens among the greatest masters of the English language.[11] These three elements are strong qualities in Harris' work.

Hard Times is Dickens' most comprehensive version of the inhumanities of Victorian civilization, particularly in the way its harsh philosophy fostered and sanctioned "the aggressive formulation of an inhumane spirit."[12] These inhumanities reduce workers to "hands" in Bounderby's factory; children to numbers in Gradgrind's school, where only "facts" are allowed; and life itself to the measure of the "deadly statistical clock very hollow." Sut's objection to the excessive order of Squire Hanley's life, his complaint that "we know too much," his dissertation against planning might all have been reinforced by the reading of Dickens.

One of the ways in which Harris transmuted material from Dickens is indicated in what is at first glance one of Sut's more original flights of fancy. Discussing circuit riders in "Sicily Burns's Wedding," first published in 1858, Sut tells George: "Suckit-riders am surgestif things tu me. They preaches agin me, an' I has no chance tu preach back at them. Ef I cud I'd make the institushun behave hitsef better nur it dus. They hes sum wunderful pints, George. Thar am two things nobody never seed: wun am a dead muel, an' tuther is a suckit-rider's grave" (89). In *Pickwick Papers* the ingenious comic servant Sam Weller theorizes that postboys are immortal. He asks the medical student, Bob Sawyer:

> "Never . . . see a dead postboy did you?" inquired Sam, pursuing his catechism.
> "No," rejoined Bob, "I never did."
> "No," rejoined Sam, triumphantly, "Nor never vill; and there's another thing that no man never see, and that's a dead donkey. . . ."[13]

In conceptualizing objections to the utilitarian society, in the techniques of rhythm, dialect, and imagery, even in items of comic fantasy, Harris is indebted to Dickens.

When Sut is considered in his generalized form, however, he seems to have most affinities with the Renaissance Fool of court and stage: he is a lean, ugly creature; he leaps and runs; he has a rapid, commanding flow of talk; he is cruel or witty in repartee; he is sometimes privileged truthteller; he is sometimes the antic, diverting jester; he is sometimes the scapegoat; he is often the bitter seer. Harris could have learned most of this tradition of the fool from Shakespeare. *The Merchant of Venice*, from which Harris borrows twice in one sketch (67, 69), has a good traditional fool in Launcelot Gobbo. Launcelot tricks his father, can be both kind and cruel, and is the witty jester and privileged truthteller. Falstaff, Touchstone of *As You Like It*, and Feste of *Twelfth Night*—all represent the fool's flight from civilization, the freedom from law and order that many an American frontiersman yearned for.

The influence of one artist on another is never a simple matter, but Harris' utilization of material from other writers forms a significant pattern. His quotation from Pope reveals his interest in poetic techniques to control sound and speed of language. His utilization of material from Shakespeare and Dickens concentrates on the comic figures of Gobbo and Sam Weller, revealing his fascination with the clever, witty, free ironic

character, and the capacity of such a point of view to refract a
vision of life and evaluate a society. Byron and particularly
Burns provide satiric elements. As one result, Sut becomes the
most technically sophisticated point of view in Southwestern
humor—one capable of exploring a variety of qualities of American and Southern life that lie obscurely along the fringes of
perception.

CHAPTER *8*

The Texture of a Language

I

SINCE the mid-1930's critics have recognized Harris' language as his finest artistic achievement. His revisions for the *Yarns* show he etched Sut's language with painstaking care. Several times Harris presents Sut as speculating about the limitations of words. Of breaking up the Negro camp meeting, Sut says, "Well, when I larns tu spell an' pernounce the flavor ove a ded hoss, play the shape ove a yeathen war-jug [earthenware jug] ontu a fiddil, ur paint the swifness ove these yere laigs ontu a clapboard, then I'll 'scribe the nise ove that meetin . . ." (158). The analogies with music and painting reveal in what artistic terms Harris was considering his problem. Other instances occur in the *Yarns* where Harris, from behind the mask of comedy, calls his language to the attention of his audience. Two aspects of Harris' language present the most problems to the reader: his dialect and his imagery.

The dialect is the first quality of language to strike the reader—and often also the last; for many readers give up trying to penetrate the maze of rustic idiom complicated by phonetic spelling of dialectal pronunciations and by "comical" misspellings of no linguistic significance.

Like the other Southwestern humorists, Harris intended his dialect partly to be realistic and partly to be humorous. These humorists were attempting to re-create an oral tradition in writing; and storytellers like Jim Doggett, Simon Suggs, and Sut had to be presented as speaking a believable vernacular. The original function of the frame stories, as they appeared in Porter's *Spirit of the Times,* was to distinguish the folk tellers from the gentleman listeners by their speech habits.

Longstreet, Thorpe, and Hooper used the framework to imply the superior education and social status of the gentleman. Harris expanded the technique to reveal contrasts in character and even, tentatively, in moral vision. George speaks standard English of a stilted, traditional, and formal variety; Sut speaks a lively, vigorous vernacular. The dialect accentuates a basic irony: the illiterate yokel is revealed by his speech as considerably more speculative and articulate than his educated friend, who has achieved stability and accuracy in his language at the expense of its vitality. Pascal Covici has noted that Harris anticipated Twain in turning the ridicule implied in dialect outward against the sophisticated audience rather than against the backwoodsmen.[1] From the Mr. Free epistles and "The Knob Dance" of the 1840's to the Lovingood tales of the 1850's Harris' interest shifted from focus on customs and speech as picturesque curiosities for an assumedly superior audience to an interest in dialect for its own qualities and for its possibilities for humor and meaning.

To the formally educated reader there is something incongruous and therefore often comic about dialect. The term itself implies deviation from some norm of propriety. The incongruity and therefore the comedy are intensified when dialect speech is put into writing—when an attempt is made to write what is not a written language. Talk like Sut's, readers feel, should be heard, not seen; and to recognize its form is to feel superior in one's own form. Natives of Tennessee who heard such a dialect all their lives could, and obviously did, find it comical when used as a literary vehicle.

The same dialect could operate successfully as a medium for serious material, as is evidenced by Mary Noailles Murfree's later use of it in such works as *In the Tennessee Mountains* (1884) and *The Prophet of the Great Smoky Mountains* (1885). Mary Murfree, who wrote under the name Charles Egbert Craddock, creates a quite different tone from Harris'; but her dialect is very similar linguistically to his. Her work is cited by both Krapp and Mencken, neither of whom seems to have read Harris.

Sut speaks that dialect of American English which linguists call Southern Highland or Appalachian. Mencken said of it:

It is interesting because the people speaking it have been isolated for many years, and have thus preserved speech forms that have become archaic elsewhere. They are also, in the main, of low economic status, and it is among the poor that ancient forms are least affected by pedagogy and fashion. The dialect of Appalachia is based primarily upon the Southern English of the late Seventeenth Century, but it has been considerably modified by the Northern English brought in by the Scotch-Irish. . . . The dialect was put to extensive literary use before it got much attention from philologians, but since an account of it by Dr. Josiah Combs appeared in 1916, it has been investigated at some length.[2]

Mark Twain, in his brief review of the *Yarns* for the *Alta California* (July 14, 1867), showed his persistent interest in accuracy of dialect writing when he remarked, "The book abounds in humor, and is said to represent the Tennessee dialect correctly." Contemporary Tennessee newspaper accounts agree that Harris had a keen ear and captured the qualities of the dialect well. Close analysis of a portion of the *Yarns* will provide the materials for some generalizations about his method. The following random sample is from "Mrs. Yardley's Quilting":

"But then, George, gals an' ole maids haint the things tu fool time away on. Hits widders, by golly, what am the rale sensibil, steady-goin, never-skeerin, never-kickin, willin, sperrited, smoof pacers. They cum clost up tu the hoss-block, standin still wif thar purty silky years playin, an' the naik-veins a-throbbin, an' waits fur the word, which ove course yu gives, arter yu finds yer feet well in the stirrup, an' away they moves like a cradil on cushioned rockers, ur a spring buggy runnin in damp san'. A tetch ove the bridil, an' they knows yu wants em tu turn, an' they dus hit es willin es ef the idear wer thar own" (141).

It is obvious that by no means all of the passage varies from normal usage. Of the 118 words (counting compounds as two), fifty are perfectly standard English, including four complete phrases in which no ecentric form appears: "But then, George," "fool time away on," "feet well in the stirrups," and "on cushioned rockers." The last two of these have even a slightly literary flavor.

There are eight instances of misspellings without phonetic significance: *tu* for *to, cum* for *come, ove* for *of, dus* for *does,* and *wer* for *were.* Since educated George is supposed to be writing the book for Sut, the misspellings are not in character as are those in *Huckleberry Finn* and other illiterate autobiographies. They represent rather Harris' use of a traditional comic device. Such spellings were considered intrinsically funny, according to the same feeling which makes our writers of comic strips and comic books write *wuz* for *was* and *duz* for *does.*

Analysis of the remainder of the passage presents some uncertainties. English does not have a phonetic alphabet; and, since there is a wide geographical variation in American pronunciation, it is often hard to ascertain exactly what a dialect writer means to indicate by his attempts at phonetic spelling. (The classic example of this dilemma is the case of *marster* for *master* in the dialect writing of many Southern authors. They intended the intrusive *r* to indicate a long broad *a,* as in *father,* but readers who are not themselves speakers of a Southern dialect are likely to think an *r* sound is intended). We can safely say, however, that the remaining portion is a mixture of general colloquial, low colloquial, and local dialect forms.[3]

General colloquial means typical of the casual or rapid speech of even educated persons. It includes expressions such as *yer* for *your, es* for *as, ef* for *if, an'* for *and, ole* for *old, fur* for *for, yu* for *you, ur* for *or, em* for *them, san'* for *sand,* and *goin', kickin', willin', standin', playin',* and *runnin'* for *going, kicking, willing, standing, playing,* and *running.* Harris apparently means to indicate the dead vowel ə by the *u* in *fur, yu,* and *ur,* and the *e* in *es* and *ef.* Since he spoke a Southern dialect, he probably intended the final syllable in each of the last six words listed to be pronounced *in* rather than as syllabic *n* or ən.

Low colloquial means belonging to the speech of careless or uneducated speakers anywhere. It includes many archaic forms not found in standard speech. Into this category fall the pronunciations *haint* for *aint* (itself a low colloquial form), *hit* for *it, widders,* for *widows, gals* for *girls, skeerin* for *scaring, clost* for *close, hoss* for *horse, purty* for *pretty, idear* for *idea, tetch* for *touch;* the archaic *a-throbbin* for *throbbing;* and constructions such as *yu gives, yu finds, they moves, they knows, yu wants,* and *they dus.* These low colloquial forms are no respecters of geography. They occur in New England, in the Lowland South, and in the West as well as in the Appalachians. In some of these areas certain of the pronunciations (such as *idear* in New England) may occur in educated speech.

A few expressions remain which might be classified as local dialect, though some of them occur in other areas of the South also. For example, *thar,* for *there, years,* for *ears,* and *arter* for *after,* are used by Joel Chandler Harris in his Georgia stories.[4] Other dialect forms with a local flavor are *naik* for *neck, rale* for *real, wif* for *with, smoof* for *smooth,* and *sperrited* for *spirited.* Among the most puzzling forms are *sensibil, cradil,* and *bridil,* in which Harris may be trying to suggest the peculiar quality of Southern light *l* by his spelling. If so, this is a triumph of aural perception and of an esthetic delight in subtility beyond distinctions any audience could make.

Harris wrote Sut's dialect with remarkable consistency. There is seldom a word, a grammatical form, or a pronunciation which does not ring true; and some of the apparent inconsistencies may well be typographical errors—Harris' spelling is admittedly a typesetter's nightmare. Most of the unorthodox spellings are not used in the spirit of the literary comedians, but indicate characteristic details of pronunciation which make an important and cumulative difference in the total effect. There is, for example, a real difference between a Northern *chicken* and a Southern *chickin* to the sensitive ear.

Harris wrote his dialect with increasing respect; and, by the time he finished the *Yarns,* he was using it without condescension and with a "true ear," as Robert Penn Warren has noted.[5] Eventually the vernacular became an object of esthetic delight for him. Henry Nash Smith found in Edward Eggleston a similar interest in folk speech for itself, and not as a simple inch-rule to measure status or refinement. Professor Smith's analogy with the Dutch genre painters is instructive.[6] Harris came to concern himself with the items of dialect as objects of esthetic contemplation and pleasure for their own sake.

The young Mark Twain's interest in Harris' dialect, as well as his re-reading of the *Yarns* during the composition of *Huckleberry Finn*, implies a significant evaluation of Harris. No other American artist could have suggested so much to Mark Twain about the creation of an American literary prose based on the vernacular.

II

As carefully worked out as the dialect, and of even greater power to create meaning and tone, is Harris' imagery.[7] By artful selection from the vernacular, by original invention, by mining earlier sketches, and by painstaking revision Harris created an imagery through which he projects indirectly Sut's vision of the American backwoods—the people, animals, cabins, doggeries, and clearings of Frog Mountain, Rattlesnake Spring, and Lost Creek. A subtly perceptive, often dark vision is projected through a varied, complex, and tonally consistent body of images. This body is capable, like Harris' few best fables, of bearing the double occasions of laughter; and it shows an even greater capacity to carry incompatible emotions. In his imagery Harris' art is shown at its best, masterful and ingenious in evoking the dark atmosphere of life, somberly fleshly at times, graphic and gestural, to use Erich Auerbach's phrase.[8]

The numerous imagery studies of modern critics have demonstrated that symbolism is not simply a phase of rhetoric. Imagery at its best is not only technique, but also revelation of the author's conscious and less conscious intentions and preoccupations. Harris' imagery embodies his philosophy, his humor, his assessment of reality—in short, his moral vision. His work provides an opportunity to observe the function imagery serves in providing a counterpoint to surface meanings. Notably in the *Yarns*, what his images communicate is not always the same thing that his plots and characters communicate. The coarse and impish, sometimes cruel surface of the tales celebrates the joy of physical movement; delight in food, drink, sexual experience; the excitement of wild confusion; and freedom from all restraint. The tone of the imagery is equally turbulent but darker, more pervasively magical and sensory in its elements of the ugly, the broken, the erotic.

From the first Harris warns his readers that the vision of the world he communicates will not "sit purfeckly quiet ontu the stumicks ove sum pussons" (x). The sense of the difficulty of writing and of its absurdity, of the yearning for some permanent esthetic achievement, the sense of a burden of message is heavy in Harris' Preface to the *Yarns*. It is the language, and primarily the imagery, that carries the greatest weight of the vision Harris would communicate.

Most apparent in Harris' images is the frequency with which he uses epithets and complexly developed metaphors and similes. The similes are often extended by elaborate addition and qualification of detail. Almost every line of the *Yarns* contains some kind of imagery. The detail used is concrete, closely packed, and graphic.

The first effect of this frequency is speed and intensity. The reader is whirled into the illusion of ebullient delight in motion and wild action. Racy colloquialisms, nonce words, corruptions of names and of bookish terms, compression of detail, astonishing expansion of connotation, and controlled changes in the tensions of the action and of the language, shifting from litotes to the wildest hyperbole, create an illusion of speed, movement, freedom. Images are expanded by piling detail upon detail until the reader is bewildered in a complexity of emotions and ideas.

The subject matter of the imagery reveals that Harris' world of reference was limited, doubtless with the conscious intent to achieve a close and intense focus. From this world the great body of his metaphors and similes can be classified into a few broad categories that all point to the sharp center of the focus.

The largest group, constituting well over one-third of all images employed, is made up of animal images—mammals, birds, fish, and insects. Usually these are comic and, abstracted from the text, unpleasant, whatever the animal. Harris uses horses, mules, and asses most frequently: a woman may be as "ugly es a skin'd hoss" (36), Sut's starched shirt stands like "a dry hoss hide" (32), words fall from one's lips "sorter like a ole heart-broken hoss slobbers" (61), an attractive woman does more devilment than "a loose stud hoss et a muster groun'" (77), and a deceitful woman can look as "solemn es a jasack in a snow storm, when the fodder gin out" (80).

The next largest group within the animal category consists of comparisons to bulls and cows. Sut's starched shirt sat as close to his skin "es a poor cow dus tu her hide in March" (33); a Negro, smelling Sut's stink bomb, "histed the pint ove his snout up atween his eyes, turn'd his upper lip inside out, throw'd his head back, an' scented slowly all roun'" (162); and, of the naked Parson Bullen, "his belly wer 'bout the size an' color ove a beef paunch" (57).

The third sub-group is made up of insects, usually poisonous or verminous ones—mosquitoes, hornets, ants, bees, locusts, bed bugs, weevils, cockroaches, fleas, and others. After insects come comparisons to dogs and cats followed and approximately equaled by those to hogs and sows. For example, the victim of one of Sut's jokes lies as "quiet as a sick sow in a snowstorm" (44). A strong-minded woman may browbeat her man until she changes him into "a kidney worm'd hog what cant raise bristles in less nor a month."[9] Many of the comparisons to domestic beasts are to diseased animals, to skinned carcasses, or to the bloody parts of butchered creatures. Whiskey goes down a circuit-rider's throat "like a snake travelin thru a wet sassidge gut" (185). One man has a mouth "es red es a split beef" (199); another goes home "es nakid es a well-scraped hog" (121).

Miscellaneous animals, not all appropriate to Sut's natural environment, make up the rest of the sample: alligators, elephants, lizards, snakes, worms, eels, rats, fish, ganders, sheep, squirrels, panthers, wolves, buzzards, ferrets, and weasels. The fish image quoted above (Chapter 4, Section II) of the hanged and shot radical Republicans strung on a chain driven through their mouths and out their rectums with a harpoon and hung over the side of the devil's ship to writhe and leap in the brimstone will illustrate one of Harris' most cruel and hallucinatory conceits.

At times the image refers to no specific animal but merely to general animal characteristics. In a sexual image, a joker watches for opportunities "jist es clost es a ole 'oman what wer wunst onsanctified hersef, watches her darters when a suckus ur a camp meetin am in heat" (61). Sut says of a Yankee whom he hates: "He wer hatched in a crack" (37). And Sut's starched shirt, with bits of his skin clinging to it, "looked adzactly like the skin ove sum wile beas' tore off alive" (35).

The total effect of Harris' animal imagery is disturbing. It implies speed, wild action, grotesque appearance, suffering, decay and death. Bloody flesh, meat, skin, and bones are everywhere in a welter of disorder.

Next to animals, the second largest category, accounting for one-fifth of Harris' similes and metaphors, is that of machinery and implements: steam engines, locomotives (a pair of angry bulls clash "like two drunk locomotives" [99]), threshing machines, pumps, steamboats, sawmills, grist mills, cotton gins, whiskey stills, corn shellers, welding torches, knives, axes, and the like. The feelings they generate are reactions to sharpness, hardness, threat, motion—frequently of powerful, fearsome, and mindless action.

The third most frequent group of images has to do with the human being in his actions, trades, and professions. An action may be "quick es an 'oman kin hide a strange hat" (239), or one may be "pow'ful b'lever, not a sarcumsised b'lever, but a lie b'lever" (198), or mam, to insult the neighbor woman with whom she is pulling hair over dad, calls her a "merlatter lookin strumpit."[10] Animal characteristics and human trades may be combined: Sut says he may "turn buzzard, an' eat ded hosses fur a livin" (171). Sut once says of George that "eaves-drappin am a durn'd mean sorter way tu make a livin" (116). Of a dog fight, Sut says, "When the ballunce ove the dorgs cum up, (human like,) they all pitched into the poor helpless devil" (106). Thus Harris' characters are compared to types or to typical actions of churchgoers, circuit riders, congressmen, soldiers, rough-and-tumble fighters, drunks, auctioneers, farmers, butchers, tailors, coffinmakers, and other classes, trades, racial groups of the backcountry.

The category next in size is household goods and utensils. A fat man is "a tub ove soap-greas" (51) or pot-bellied (51); women are quilts (usually old quilts); an unconscious man may be "es cold es krout" (73); while another has a head "as big es a wash pot" (28) or "as black as a pot" (155).

Various smaller categories can be formed for images referring to the appearance and power of whiskey, called skin-gut, fester gut, rot-gut, popskull, churn brain, limberleg, tangle-leg, tangle-foot, kill-devil, bald face, etc. (31, 85, 113, 173, 199, 58); of the imagined actions and appearance of the devil and of hell; of vegetables and plants; of gunpowder, poisons, drugs, and diseases.

Many incongruous or incommensurate comparisons, common in American humor, appear in Harris' descriptions. One may be "a bigger fool nor ole Squire Mackmullen, an' he tried tu shoot hisself wif a onloaded hoe-handle" (58). Retribution comes "es big es a car shed" (179). A Negro camp meeting, disrupted by Sut, "looked like forty-eight cords of black cats a-fitin" (167). Sheriff Doltin pursed his mouth to blow "a whistil seven foot long" (240), and Sut, singing

> Daddy kill'd the blind bull,
>   Human nater, human nater!
> Mammy fried a pan full,
>   Sop an' tater, sop an' tater,

claims that the song is prettier than Longfellow's "Exelcider" "by a gallun an' a 'alf" (123).

III

Several generalizations are possible after Harris' imagery is abstracted from the total work and examined as a separate element. First, it rarely suggests beauty or any of the softer emotions. It reinforces the impression Sut creates that the benevolent or good-natured man does not exist. The effect of images of flayed and butchered animals, of diseases and verminous insects, of fatness and thinness, of occasionally seductive women fills the *Yarns* with a sense of the ever-present flesh. The dark chaos of flesh emphasizes Sut's solitary isolation. There is no meaning to discover or to recover in this dark atmosphere but the feeling of the flesh. At the broadest, the human condition is isolated, ugly, dying, without transcendental meaning.

However, it is equally apparent that the effect is not merely ugly. Harris' imagery is formally varied and complex. Usually it is concrete and graphic, but at times it conveys no picture at all. It becomes cryptic and intellectual, communicates ideas and judgments. One example of such sunken imagery is mam's invitation to ole Squire Hanley to leave her home: "We's got no notes tu shave nur gals ole enuf tu convart" (289). Harris' image implies that the squire is interested in cheating and in girls, and that the interest in girls is sexual rather than spiritual. The image comprehends too much for simple visualization. It approaches abstraction. Specifically, it compares the present child with the nubile adolescent to be, and then, shifting the object of the comparison, suggests that a deacon can have no concern for little children. Such sunken imagery exists for its content of ideas. Its generalization is expansive. Recurring images of circuit riders fathering illegitimate children, seducing young girls, fleeing irate husbands, continue an ancient folk tradition of humor and communicate an impression of the hill-country preacher as ignorant, immoral, and as baldly hypocritical as Chaucer's Pardoner or Boccaccio's Friar Onion. Behind the comic fantasy of Harris' practical jokes plays the counterpoint of the imagery, sounding the deeper discords of the American Eden.

Next, the imagery reveals that Harris' imagination ranged from the keen and incisive to the expansive, myth-making visions, and functioned with natural ease and telling effect in symbols and allegories. For example, the imagery associated with Sut's birth moves him in the direction of the heroes of legend. "No," Sut once answers a reporter, "But we kep a sand-hill crane, and Mam and him had a difficulty, and he chased her under the bod" (Weber, 232). The excesses of the imagery, wild, vigorous, and compelling, match the vaultings of a large and strange imagination—an imagination at times irrational and compulsive but bodying forth from a microcosm of homely images a macrocosm of emotions and ideas.

Finally, the imagery is one of the most enduring elements of comedy in Harris. The most common humorous tendency of the language is to expose foolish or knavish characters to ridicule. The satiric and reductive elements in the imagery are balanced by its frequency and vividness to communicate a sense of the vigor and joy of life. A clerk-like newspaper reporter is "a little, mild, husband-lookin feller in gold specks and a pencil" (Weber,

231). Among the many tendencies of the satire here, one of them is something near to affection for human variety.

Much of Harris' imagery is witty in the vernacular tradition. One of his techniques is to begin with a common English expression which he then qualifies in some way to cancel its cliché meaning and thus surprise the reader. Two bloody-headed men are dismissed with "Jis' a fis' fight, with sticks: that's all."[11] Recalling an early episode of his poverty-stricken life, Sut remembers mam feeding the "brats ontu mush an' milk, wifout the milk" (228). Sometimes Sut plays on dead images: "wimen went head-fust intu the houses, doors slam'd, sash[es] fell, cats' tails swell'd es they treed onder stabils" (223).

Another kind of verbal humor turns not on imagery but on logic. This type is best exemplified by Rabelais' report of Pope Alexander, who took "the advice of a Jew, his physician, and . . . lived till his dying day in despite of his enemies," or by Mark Twain's telegram which complained that the report of his death was greatly exaggerated. Parson Bullen, excusing his nakedness after Sut loosed lizards up his trousers, took as his text the following Sunday: "Nakid I cum intu the world, an' nakid I'm a gwine outen hit, ef I'm spard ontil then" (59). When Sut expresses sympathy, it is often in an ambiguous form, as when he tells George of a poor, "misfortinit devil [who] happen'd tu steal a hoss by accidint" (38).

Harris is fond of vernacular images which both break categories and offer satiric comment, as when old Simon Jerrold chases his wife "wif a drawn corn hoe."[12] A man trying to kill his wife is scandalous enough, but the image of the drawn sword applied to the hoe calls attention to the indignity and impropriety of both the act and the method. The class bias is clear here; Harris' assumption is that the more cultured elements of the community would never use hoes.

The element of fantasy in Harris' imagery is at its best both comic and functional, unlike that of the literary comedians; and it may be conceit-like in the logic of its applications. In "Sut Lovengood in New York," an angry woman is described as "a standin' with all her laigs so clost together that a buckit hoop w'u'd a went roun' all ove em." The comic impropriety of the "all" disappears, almost, as Harris presents the image of a cat in the next line.

As the reader examines the imagery associated with Sicily Burns or her father, with Sut, with Sut's father, and with other characters, it becomes apparent that it is coherent, that it expands their meanings, and that it objectifies the ancient comic ambivalence of hatred and joy. Sicily is all flesh, power, beauty —as tempting as naked Eve; and the smell of the devil is about her. Old man Lovingood is ugly and cruel authority, and floats before the mind's eye in the harness of a horse, or naked, or dressed in the skin of a bull and lying, at the end of the *Yarns,* bloody-faced on the ground, a poleaxed sacrifice. Connotations of powerful sexuality and of Sut's jealousy cling to the old man. The fool Sut is imaged in his long legs, in his heroic, mythic birth, sired like a Greek hero by a wild bird on a wild hill-country woman. He follows in the succession of his father: dark, fierce, inhuman, squalid, but magical and commanding, ritualistically driving out scapegoats. His life is hatred and revel, attack and flight;[13] and the imagery associated with him is that of isolation, of escape, and of freedom.

Our argument has been that Harris' imagery will bear close scrutiny; it is art of no mean order. It is art as a means to rigorous and austere pursuit of reality. Sut appears to seek sheer fun, but the imagery associated with him, like the fables at their best, enlarges his stature to a figure ambiguously comic and mythy, perceiving an awful reality, and desiring and ritualistically asserting an impossible freedom.[14] He pursues intensity of experience in the flesh, and an abandonment to the obsessive and the irrational. Beneath the plain practical jokes swirl the dark currents of the imagery which bodies Sut's world as occasionally satisfying, but more often ugly, harsh, deceitful, transitory, and meaningless. In it Sut lives detached in the comic triumph of the fool.

CHAPTER 9

The Bull among the Butchers

I

NOT UNTIL the 1930's did Harris begin to receive serious critical analysis, but the author of only one published book is not without an audience when he can number among his admirers Mark Twain, William Faulkner, and Robert Penn Warren—and such critics as F. O. Matthiessen and, with qualifications, Edmund Wilson. Harris himself looked forward to his reception by the critics—"book-butchers," Sut calls them, "orful on killin an' cuttin up, but cud no more perjuce a book, than a bull-butcher cud perjuce a bull" (x)—with a comic warning not to tear and eat his flesh. As Harris foresaw, the thick flesh-and-blood texture of his style and his symbolically ambiguous representation of life and of social, political, and religious institutions have been a source of uneasiness to many readers from his time to our own.

William T. Porter cheerfully assumed that his contributors to the *Spirit of the Times* were benevolent collectors of American scenes and characters. The early Harris fit easily in the *Spirit*, and Porter's comments on his work were the most general praise, except for his refusal of one sketch in 1848 as "too highly seasoned." The anthologies in which Harris was reprinted before the Civil War—Porter's own *A Quarter Race in Kentucky* (1847), Thomas Chandler Haliburton's *The American's at Home* (London, 1854), and S. P. Avery's *The Harp of a Thousand Strings* (1858)—all praised him, first, as a comic writer and, second, as an accurate portrayer of provincial scenes and characters. Elbridge Gerry Eastman, in the *Union & American*, presented him as the "best delineator of a peculiar class of southwestern characters," and assured his readers they might without reproach read of Sicily's adultery with Doc Fabin because Sut was "a great favorite in the refined and educated circles of the Southern and Eastern Cities." Neither Porter nor Eastman was squeamish; both found Harris strong meat. Only his comedy and his low characters made him acceptable.

With the publication of the *Yarns,* Harris gained, unknown to himself, his greatest reader. In 1867 Mark Twain reviewed the book briefly for the San Francisco *Alta California.*[1] Mark Twain's notice shows his familiarity with Harris' newspaper work; he remembered "Sut Lovingood's Daddy, Acting Horse," "Parson Bullin's Lizards," and others. "The book abounds in humor," young Mark Twain wrote appreciatively, and added carefully, "it is said to represent the Tennessee dialect correctly." He perceived that genteel readers would be shocked at Harris' humor: the book would sell in the West, he predicted, but "the Eastern people will call it coarse and possibly taboo it." Mark Twain's casual judgment was correct. The book invokes its reader's system of taboo.

Later in his life Mark Twain read Harris again. In the 1880's, when he began compiling his anthology, *Mark Twain's Library of Humor* (1888), he included "Old Burns's Bull Ride"—and wrote two more versions of the already traditional tale himself. As Walter Blair's research into the making of *Huckleberry Finn* has shown, in 1879-80 Mark Twain began jotting in his notebooks the names of the humorists who might provide material for the anthology. His working notes include the names of Augustus Baldwin Longstreet, Joseph Glover Baldwin, Johnson Jones Hooper, William Tappan Thompson, and George W. Harris. From examination of the notebooks, it is Blair's opinion that Mark Twain's concept of the ante-bellum South was to some extent re-formed by his reading of Harris and the other humorists.[2] Stuck in the composition of *Huckleberry Finn* at the time, and perhaps reading Harris after his disillusioning revisit to the Mississippi River and after his liberating talks with George W. Cable, Mark Twain could have found Harris' masterfully complex texture and his harsh version of the rural church, officialdom, and oppressively conforming community life both liberating and exhilarating. The extreme implications of Harris' anti-religious symbolism would not have been lost on Mark Twain.

II

For sixty years after Harris' death, the critics gave his work little attention. His name appeared in a few reference works and his tales in a few regional anthologies. Henry Watterson's *Oddities of Southern Life* (1882) includes three sketches. In this era of local color, Watterson tried to provide a category for Sut by saying he was representative of a class; but, unable to characterize this supposed class or to identify its geography, he added it was "little known even in the South." Observing that the stories did not state their meanings abstractly nor through any form he could praise, Watterson wrote that Harris made "little attempt at technical literary finish . . . the author seeming to aim merely at his point and, this reached, to be satisfied to leave it to work out its own moral effect." Watterson perceived the objectivity of Harris' presentation and his intention to create a "moral effect"; but he failed, in spite of the rich texture of Harris' style, to perceive the meanings or the degree of control and technical finish it displayed.

The many-volumed *Library of Southern Literature* (1907-1923), reflecting like Watterson the time's interest in local customs, reprinted "Bart Davis's Dance," with four pages of biographical and critical information by J. Thompson Brown. To Brown, also bewildered by Harris' emotional complexity, the stories were "unsavory." Explaining his own theory of humor, he argued "it must laugh *with* and not *at;* past bounds of friendly give-and-take it breaks into horse-play or takes on the acerbity of wit." The theory that humor had to be amiable, a civilizing agency exciting to sympathy and benevolence, had undergone a long development by English critics following the Restoration.[3] By the mid-nineteenth century academic critics and genteel readers believed humor had become benevolent and compassionate. What was not compassionate, they felt, was not the best humor. Wit was held in low esteem. Some parts of Harris' work seemed to Brown "unfit for either humorous or intellectual diet"; the stories were repellent because of their "most minute and disgusting details." In practice this theory could not translate Aristophanes; it corrected Chaucer, bowdlerized Shakespeare, and found Donne incomprehensible or repulsive. But in perceiving the "minute and disgusting details" of Harris' style, Brown did glimpse uneasily one of the basic qualities of Harris' tone.

The first extensive effort to assess Harris' work, to present it to a national audience, and to recover the facts of his life began in the 1920's and 1930's, briefly with Napier Wilt and Jennette Tandy, and more fully with the work of Walter Blair, Bernard DeVoto, and Franklin Meine, in each of the latter three related to the knowledge these scholars had of Mark Twain's ideas and artistic techniques. For his pioneering anthology, *Tall Tales of the Southwest* (1930), Meine used not only the *Yarns* but turned also to the files of the forgotten *Spirit of the Times* for the "Snake-Bit Irishman" and "The Knob Dance." Intending to illustrate the tradition out of which Twain developed, Meine sampled generously from a variety of writers, particularly Harris and Hooper. The introduction is largely an appreciation but does distinguish the character of Sut from that of the rogue and sharper of frontier literature. Later Edmund Wilson was to object to Meine's observation that Sut had a "keen delight for Hallowe'en *fun*," apparently taking Hallowe'en fun to mean the innocent trick-or-treat ritual of modern suburban children and not the destructive and vengeful pranks of the older folk tradition. Meine also assembled the first extensive collection of biographical material on Harris, comprising information from nineteenth-century Tennessee newspapers, county court records, local traditions, and the like. From this material he prepared the Harris entry for the *Dictionary of American Biography*.

Neither Constance Rourke's *American Humor* (1931), nor Bernard DeVoto's *Mark Twain's America* (1932) offers any extended analysis of Harris' art, but both include significant comment on him. Miss Rourke's compressed and elliptical study of the esthetic and psychological meanings of American humor remains the best broad survey of the topic. She places Sut among the rootless drift of the backwoods, those who "pursued uncharted ways, breaking from traditions, bent on triumph."[4] These were the characters who expressed the mood of disseverance in the American experience, the revolt against all fixed or traditional heritage.[5] Her demonstration of how American humor could relieve fear, transcend reality, express the forbidden, contain irreconcilables, and rise into ecstatic, wild emotion reminds the tame reader of literature's ancient magic power. Her two quotations from Harris are both examples of his aggressive, satiric humor.

DeVoto's polemical defense of the richness of American frontier humor and its profound importance for Mark Twain also subsumes Harris into a tradition and makes no extended effort to define the original quality of his art. His brief references call attention to Harris' delight in sexual beauty by quoting Sut's description of Sicily Burns, and he notes correctly the element of literary satire on the popular ballad formula of the snow-white breast. DeVoto's effect is to emphasize the realistic frankness, the color, the element of joy in Harris' work. Without mentioning Harris specifically, but certainly including him, DeVoto wrote that the fiction of these humorists was "the conscientious work of writers, frequently intelligent and sometimes very talented, who knew quite well what they were doing."[6]

Walter Blair's *Native American Humor* (1937) contains a careful introduction to the "Humor of the Old Southwest" which represents the fullest attempt to its time to identify the writers, to study the conditions out of which they grew, and to define briefly their content and techniques. Blair ends his chapter with a six-page analysis of Harris' work which remains the most comprehensive definition of his achievement. Harris' artistry—still insufficiently appreciated, Blair observes—is revealed in the three principal elements of the *Yarns*: the character of Sut, the language, and finally, the comic world created in Sut's flow of talk.[7]

Sut's character—revealed directly in George's rare comments and indirectly in the reactions of others—expresses delight in fun; in passion for sex, food and drink; and in venting hatred for Yankees, sheriffs, and others. His harrowing pranks, Blair believes, could not be funny if they were not removed several steps from reality. Although Blair does not press his definition of play, it may be observed that Sut plays in a world which Harris does not envision with the order and equanimity of

Cervantes, whose mad Don Quixote also moves in a world of play.[8]

Blair characterizes Harris' language as "poetic in an almost Elizabethan fashion." Its qualities are a seemingly fresh creation, satiric and comic antithesis, contrast, and conceit-like figures of speech that startle with their ingenuity. The dialect Blair does not evaluate but characterizes, after Watterson, as a "wild jargon."

Sut's world of comic fantasy, Blair says, is pervaded with an interest in backwoods religion which is grotesquely warped. Everywhere the sense of coarse, crowded, earthy life is vivid in "scent, sound, form, color, and motion," Blair observes, "coarser and earthier perhaps, than any other in our literature during the nineteenth century."

Of his group, Blair concludes, Harris made the most of oral humor, of the framework technique, of colloquial richness and vivid detail: "If his writings were better than the rest, they were better because he had more sense of incongruities, more exuberance, more imagination, and because he had greater genius than his contemporaries for transferring the unique artistry of the oral narrative to the printed page."[9] Although highly compressed and allusive, and although limited primarily to Harris' more rational and pleasant meanings, Blair's analysis still remains the most comprehensive and the most sensible reading of Harris.

Edd Winfield Parks's *Segments of Southern Thought* (1938), and his *Sut Lovengood Travels with Old Abe Lincoln* (1937) contain biographical material on Harris, and the latter volume republished for the first time in book form Harris' three satires on Lincoln.

For his study of America's first artistic and cultural maturity, *American Renaissance* (1941), F. O. Matthiessen chose Harris to represent the comic response to the national myth of the common man. Because Sut admires Wirt Staples, Matthiessen takes Wirt as Harris' ideal common man within the comic myth. Wirt, however, is a highly derivative figure, a half-horse, half-alligator frontiersman roaring his contempt for the "watch-tinker" (one of Harris' trades) and the Negro, as well as his defiance of the sheriff and the judge. He is too simple a creation of beautiful strength, existing in an Edenic home with an Eve-like wife, to represent Harris' vision of the American experience. Wirt occupies only a small place in the *Yarns,* and his nature and experience are not representative of the book's most comprehensive meaning.

Matthiessen's definition of Sut's hard and knowing character generally follows Blair and Rourke, except where, noting Sut's admiration of Wirt, he sees Sut as creating a "hymn to fertility." Matthiessen's analysis of Harris' style is his most original criticism. He notes Harris' significant animal imagery, Sut's technique of deprecating his speech while at the same time demonstrating astonishing inventiveness of expression, and Harris' use of expanded similes to compress scenes or character sketches within his main narrative. These vignettes are not irrelevant to Harris' narrative, however, as Matthiessen maintains; instead they establish its contrapuntal tone, like the digressions of Congreve and Byron, whom Harris studied during the mid-1850's. Matthiessen summarizes his evaluation of Harris' prose by comparing its rich complexity to Melville's: "Harris possesses on the comic level something of what Melville does on the tragic, the rare kind of dramatic imagination that can get movement directly into words."[10]

Mathiessen closes, as he had opened, with the observation that Harris "brings us closer than any other writer to the indigenous and undiluted resources of the American language, to the tastes of the common man himself." By placing Harris briefly in the company of Whitman, Thoreau, and Melville, the brilliant Matthiessen gave courage to those critics under the ferule of fashion and academic gentility to look at what they had heretofore dismissed as quaint and crude without benefit of careful reading.

III

In 1942 Donald Day completed a doctoral dissertation under the direction of Walter Blair, and out of this research Day published three essays: one on Harris' humor, another on his political satires, and one on his life.[11] The critical generalizations are of indifferent quality, but the carefully documented biographical essay—for which Franklin Meine made his research available— remains the starting point for any study of Harris' life. To go much beyond Day's and Meine's work in locating biographical information will be a difficult task, but students of American culture and literature would find a full life of great interest.

Until the 1950's Harris was known only to the scholar, the antiquarian, and the special taste, partly because of his dialect and comic misspellings. In brief quotations, DeVoto, Blair, and Matthiessen had all changed Sut's language to make it more understandable to their readers. In the mid-1950's Brom Weber undertook the formidable task of regularizing on sensible principles essentially all of the *Yarns* and the three Lincoln satires and of providing a historical and critical introduction to make Harris available to the general reader. Grove Press issued the volume in 1954, an event significant both for Weber's critical introduction and for the readers the edition gained.

Writing after the great upsurge of interest in myth and symbol in literature, and with knowledge of the Lincoln sketches, Weber was able to see farther reaches of Harris' comic mythology than even Matthiessen could have been aware of. By calling attention to Sut as offspring of the sandhill crane who chased Betts Lovingood under the bed, Weber invited renewed exploration of Sut's symbolic meaning.

Weber's discussion of Harris' language, after his own intimate reworking of it, offers the most precise definition yet of the qualities of the style:

> The smaller compass of Harris, however, fostered a lyric intensity which reflects itself in his prodigious outpouring of poetic similes and metaphors. Characters and situations may at times be repetitive in outline, but they are vivified and transcended by imagery which practically never repeats itself. Details flash by at breathless speed; their insight into motive, their re-creation of the sensuous texture of life plunge the reader deep into the heart of Sut's strange world. Working intensively within a limited scope, Harris veritably embraced almost every aspect of his chosen reality and . . . seems to have gone beyond it too. There is not elsewhere in American literature, certainly not in the Nineteenth Century and not even in Twain's masterpiece, *Huckleberry Finn,* a similar portrait of primitive, insular man in all his bestiality, glory, and humor. Nor, for that matter, has anyone equalled the concentrated richness of his style.[12]

Out of the brilliant style and the chaos of Sut's adventures, Weber notes, a structure of ideas arises revealing that the whole is informed with a moral vision. By calling some of Harris' values "traditional" and "wholesome," Weber offended genteel critics and those disturbed by the demonic in Sut.

Newspaper critics who commented on Weber's edition generally enjoyed Harris' comedy. The reviewer for the Cincinnati *Enquirer* wrote that it was "the funniest damn book" he had even seen; and it was variously characterized as broad, extravagant, bawdy, ribald, raw, tart, and gusty. Some reviewers commended Harris' satire of gentility and pretention and his deflation of fraud, vanity, and phony humility. Several complained of the cruelty. The novelist Stephen Longstreet, reviewing it for the Los Angeles *Daily News* (September 13, 1954), delighted in the characteristically American qualities and evaluated Harris as "one of the greatest writers of native dialogue we've ever had," a version of the praise Robert Penn Warren was to offer independently a few years later. A number of writers may have discovered Harris first in Weber's edition: Longstreet probably, Warren possibly, Flannery O'Connor certainly.[13]

Faulkner's admiration of Harris was old. His father had owned a copy of the 1867 edition. In 1932 William Faulkner inscribed his own name, the date, and the name of his home, Rowanoak, in the volume; such inscriptions were the only mark of esteem he left in his books, according to Joseph Blotner in *William Faulkner's Library*. At Weber's request, the publisher sent Faulkner a copy of the new edition; Faulkner placed it in the bookcase beside his bed, where he kept books he was reading, and here it remained at his death.

A third significant result of Weber's edition was a long review in the *New Yorker* by America's most eminent man of letters, Edmund Wilson, an essay reprinted with few changes in the fascinating but erratic *Patriotic Gore*.[14] As a critical analysis, the essay is disappointing because Wilson clearly perceived the oppressively dark atmosphere of life Harris created but turned his attention away from defining the meaning of the darkness, and toward a denunciation of Weber's project and of Harris' and of Sut's immorality.

From some knowledge of Harris' life, Wilson concludes that Sut's "ferocious fantasies" express Harris' feelings and, too simply, that Harris' feelings arose from a sense of frustration with an economically trapped life. The instrument of Harris' expression, Sut, has not the excuse of a frontiersman enduring a cruel ordeal; he is simply a sordid, malevolent poor-white type, a "peasant squatting in his own filth."[15] The criticism is largely denunciatory, and the word "peasant" is to be understood in the provincial, American sense. It could be argued that, if Sut is a malevolent Southern type, it is because the type's ancestors had lost the old, formal peasant culture, had found nothing to replace it, and had sunk out of culture into effortless barbarism. Wilson's criticism is disappointing because it veers away from examination of the fullness of Harris' meanings and into simplified psychological and sociological assessments.

Although the quality of Harris' art has escaped Mr. Wilson, and although he has no taste for and little interest in understanding its complex humor, his essay does open to discussion the elements of sadism and hatred in Harris' comedy. Unfortunately, Wilson explains this passionate malignity too simply as hatred of gentility (which Harris practiced) or idealism or education (which Harris sought). As has been argued, Harris' malevolence does not end with fantasies of destruction of enemies, which is simple enough; it extends to reason itself, to the ground conditions of social life and eventually of human life, which Sut presents as both joyful and disgusting, without any transcendental meanings. He presents the human creature as a strange, impenetrable animal. What Wilson calls Sut's sadism and hatred are universal, and they demand what they have not yet received: a reading in the light of European Existential comedy; and finally they call for some Ortegan critic's utmost moral and intellectual attention.

Kenneth Lynn's *Mark Twain and Southwestern Humor* (1959) gives a usefully extended though narrow treatment to this whole group of humorists. It is primarily an analysis of their social and political milieu, with some interpretations of their strategies and meanings. Lynn documents extensively Blair's earlier insight into the function of the framework in defining the gentleman's intellectual and moral superiority to the common folk he reports.

Marred by numerous errors of fact and interpretation, this study contains, however, some perceptive work, such as the analysis of J. G. Baldwin's style, and of the allegorical elements (which are unfortunately dropped short of completion) in Hooper's *Simon Suggs*.[16]

Lynn sees Sut as one of a growing number of instances of a new strategy on the part of secessionist writers: a strategy of abandoning the self-controlled gentleman type in favor of a figure more suitable to express the South's hatred and fanaticism born of guilt, fear, and a growing sense of isolation.[17] The study overemphasizes the Southerner's sense of guilt. If anything, the South, like most of America, was well along toward becoming a shame culture (if such a generalization can be applied at all), by the mid-nineteenth century. However, Lynn rightly adds that Harris' best stories are not his political satires but those which arise from the deeper levels of the imagination.

Lynn's short analysis of Sut's character is the silliest misreading of Harris to be found among twentieth-century critics. He sees Sut as a teen-age boy; but this sufficiently indefinite term, taken, perhaps, from Jennette Tandy, becomes "child"; then "the child becomes the author's persona," and, finally, "not until Huckleberry Finn would an American book sustain a child's point of view more faithfully than the Sut Lovingood stories." This supposed child becomes, by sentimental progression, a neglected child, lonely, afraid, and, regrettably, "often half-drunk," for "the boy has a whisky jug for his closest friend."[18] Instead of seeing Sut as a creature seeking to pierce the masking, lying, and hypocrisy of all human existence, and trying to live free of it, Lynn sees him as merely innocent of pretensions. Quoting Matthiessen's reading of the Wirt Staples passage as a hymn to fertility, Professor Lynn continues, "a hymn, it must be added, with an ache in its music, for Sut affirms a life which is beyond his youthful grasp. At the very heart of his vernacular style is the wistfulness, and the awed attention to details, of a lost and lonely boy." Even though in quoting Lynn a sentence at a time, the trite sentimentality of the passage is emphasized, still it is hard to imagine anything farther from Sut's effect on the reader or from Harris' intention.

This genteel, sentimental version of Sut's character as a psychologically and sociologically deprived child is not only an impossible simplification of Sut's meaning, it is itself cast in the form of a literary mode which Harris believed was false to human experience. Ironically for Lynn's reading, Harris had once tried a sentimental description of Sut in "Sut Lovengood Blown Up," but later, as he rejected the mode as false, he cut the whole passage out in preparing the story for republication. In fairness to Lynn's book, this example of poor scholarship and shallow, imperceptive reading is not characteristic of the work as a whole.[19]

In summary then, as a minor artist in his own right, as a part of the terrible Civil War experience, as an influence on other writers, and as a version of American common life, Harris has since the 1930's been receiving a slowly broadening recognition. The *Cambridge History of American Literature* merely listed him among Southern humorists, but now he has a paragraph of analysis in the *Literary History of the United States*. Among the standard encyclopedias, *Americana* still omits him, but *Britannica* includes a fairly full article by Donald Day. Harris' work is included in numerous anthologies of American humor, and in an increasing number of college anthologies of American literature —sometimes in Weber's version rather than the original without the editor's knowing the difference. M. Thomas Inge has published several essays on Harris and is preparing an edition of the newspaper sketches. Under the editorship of Ben Harris McClary, founder of The Sut Society, one volume of a journal called *The Lovingood Papers* appeared in 1962, reprinting three sketches from newspapers and including essays about Harris and a brief working bibliography. The 1963 issue, published by the University of Tennessee Press, republished seven more sketches. The editor plans annual volumes.

Discussion of Harris' critical reputation would be incomplete without recalling the varied reactions of creative writers to Harris. Mark Twain, William Faulkner, Robert Penn Warren, and Stephen Longstreet have all rendered him high praise. Flannery O'Connor numbers Sut among American grotesques. Stark Young long ago had one of his old women in *So Red the*

Rose recall with gusto the story of Sut and the starched shirt. Hamlin Garland once praised Harris to Whitman, who objected that he failed to show the typical in human experience and the decorum of American common life.[20] For artist and critic alike, Harris calls to judgment their image of man and of art: he fascinates the explorers of the twilight fringes of human existence; he repells those who fear the vision of the irrational and the destructive in human experience.

Notes and References

Notes and References

Chapter One

1. Letter from J. Cleveland Harris to Franklin J. Meine, July 12, 1930, reporting his interview with Harris' daughter, Amanda Pillow Harris Raymond.

2. Letter from Mrs. W. L. Stoner to John J. Heflin, in "George Washington Harris" (unpublished master's thesis, Vanderbilt University, 1934), pp. 2-8.

3. Donald Day, "The Life of George Washington Harris," *Tennessee Historical Quarterly*, VI (March, 1947), 3. Hereafter cited as Day.

4. Day, p. 3.

5. Day, p. 5; Elizabeth Bell's name and birthplace from U. S. Census of 1850, Knox County.

6. Quoted from Day, p. 4.

7. U. S. Census of 1850, Knox County.

8. Knoxville *Register*, December 20, 1843.

9. "In Memory of George W. Harris," Knoxville *Press & Herald*, December 14, 1869.

10. Donald Davidson, *The Tennessee* (New York, 1946), I, 245-48.

11. "In Memory of George W. Harris," Knoxville *Press & Herald*, December 14, 1869.

12. Quoted from Grant Foreman, *Indian Removal* (Norman, Oklahoma, 1953), p. 255.

13. "Another Head Off," Knoxville *Register*, October 18, 1855; Knoxville *Argus*, February 16, 1841. Day believes Peter Nance was Mary's father; but Harris' daughter, Mrs. Raymond, told J. Cleveland Harris it was Pryor. See n. 1.

14. Day, p. 13.

15. George F. Mellen, "George W. Harris," Knoxville *Sentinel*, February 13, 1909.

16. U. S. Census of 1850, Knox County; Knox County Records, Deed Book "Z," I, 482.

17. Blount County Records, Book "O," p. 207.

18. Jesse C. Burt, "Elbridge Gerry Eastman," *The Lovingood Papers* (1962), p. 14.

19. *Ibid.*, pp. 13-14.

20. Day, p. 9.

21. George W. Harris, *Sut Lovingood. Yarns Spun by a "Nat'ral Born Durn'd Fool* (New York, 1867), xiii. Hereafter cited as *Yarns*. Page references to this work will be included in the text.

22. Blount County Records, Book "Q," p. 144. The inventory is printed in Day, pp. 9-10.

23. Blount County Records, Book "Q," pp. 173, 174.

24. Day, p. 11. The advertisement is found in at least three Knoxville newspapers and runs for several years.

25. "The Mechanics of East Tennessee," Knoxville *Register,* July 5, 1843.

26. Knoxville *Register,* June 19, 1844.

27. Day, pp. 15-16.

28. Norris W. Yates, *William T. Porter and the Spirit of the Times* (Baton Rouge, 1957), p. 28.

29. The "Mr. Free" letters are not absolutely identified as Harris', but Franklin J. Meine makes a convincing case, summarized as Appendix A in Donald Day, "The Life and Works of George Washington Harris" (unpublished Ph.D. dissertation, University of Chicago, 1942), pp. 102-3.

30. Day, p. 22, from the New York *Spirit of the Times,* December 23, 1848.

31. Letter from Mrs. W. L. Stoner to Franklin J. Meine, July 7, 1930. Mrs. Stoner was Harris' granddaughter.

32. Mellen, *op. cit.*

33. Day, p. 21, quoted from the *Spirit of the Times,* June 24, 1848.

34. Letter from J. Cleveland Harris to Franklin J. Meine, July 12, 1930.

35. Day, pp. 23, 26. Day believes Harris surveyed the Ducktown Copper Mines early in 1857, but this is too late for Harris' first contact with the region. "Sut Lovengood's Daddy, 'Acting Horse,' " *Spirit of the Times,* October 21, 1854, is set in the copper basin. For the death of the real Pat Nash, mentioned in the tale, see Ben Harris McClary, "George and Sut: A Working Bibliography," *The Lovingood Papers* (1962), 8-9, item 31.

36. Ben Harris McClary, "The Real Sut," *American Literature,* XXVII (March, 1955), 105-6.

37. McClary, "George and Sut: A Working Bibliography," *The Lovingood Papers* (1962), item 31.

38. For this insight, see Walter Blair, *Native American Humor* (San Francisco, 1960), p. 101.

39. Walter Blair, *Horse Sense in American Humor* (Chicago, 1942), pp. x-xi, 154-55, *passim.*

40. Day, p. 24.

41. Edd Winfield Parks, ed., *Sut Lovingood Travels with Old Abe Lincoln* (Chicago, 1937), p. 17.

42. Knoxville *Register,* September 17, 1857.

43. Donald Day, "The Political Satires of George W. Harris," *Tennessee Historical Quarterly,* IV (March-December, 1945), 326-28.

44. Day, p. 30.

45. Mary R. Campbell, *Attitudes of Tennesseans Toward the Union* (New York, 1961), p. 208.

46. Pryor Nance Harris, "Interesting Reply to a Question," *Confederate Veteran,* June, 1897, p. 296.

47. George W. Harris [Harris' second son], "Dead Angle—Georgia Campaign," *Confederate Veteran,* December, 1903, p. 560.

48. Day, p. 31.

49. Gilbert Govan, "William Crutchfield," *The Lovingood Papers* (1962), p. 16.

50. *Ibid.*

51. "American Humor and American Culture," *American Quarterly,* XIV (Fall, 1962), 505.

52. *Patriotic Gore* (New York, 1962), p. 509.

53. "Letter from 'Mark Twain,'" July 14, 1867.

54. Letter from Edna Cahill to Milton Rickels, April 23, 1962.

55. Quoted from Day, p. 35.

56. Day, "Political Satires," p. 332.

57. Letter from Virginia Pride Binger to Franklin J. Meine, May 23, 1929.

58. Letter from Ross Smith, Conductor, E. T. & Va. R.R., to the Editors, published Knoxville *Press & Herald,* December 15, 1869.

59. "George W. Harris (Sut Lovengood)," Knoxville *Press & Herald,* December 14, 1869. See also Knoxville *Press & Messenger,* December 15, 1869.

60. *Ibid.*

61. *Ibid.*

62. For careful reading of the two contemporary accounts of Harris' illness and death (notes 58, 59 above) and for their medical opinion, I am indebted to Charles Marston McClure, M.D., Lindsay, California, and Charles Chester Martin, M.D., Lafayette, Louisiana.

63. Letter from Mrs. F. R. Sykes, another of Harris' granddaughters, to J. Cleveland Harris, September 10, 1928.

Chapter Two

1. Quotations from Harris' newspaper writings may be examined by locating the title in the bibliography.
2. Thomas Bangs Thorpe, "The Big Bear of Arkansas," reprinted in *The Hive of "The Bee-Hunter"* (New York, 1854), p. 90.
3. *Virgin Land* (Cambridge, 1950), pp. 123-24.
4. Quoted from Norris W. Yates, *William T. Porter and the Spirit of the Times* (Baton Rouge, 1957), p. 135.
5. Johan Huizinga, *Homo Ludens* (Boston, 1955), pp. 5-6, 52.

Chapter Three

1. R. E. Barclay, *Ducktown back in Raht's Time* (Chapel Hill, 1946), p. 46. *Ducktown* is a translation of the Indian place name.
2. *Ibid.*, p. 47.
3. See Chapter 1, n. 35, for McClary's reference to Pat Nash, who is also mentioned in Barclay.
4. William R. Taylor, *Cavalier and Yankee* (New York, 1961), p. 310.
5. Walter Blair, *Mark Twain & Huck Finn* (Berkeley, 1962), pp. 242-43.
6. See Taylor, pp. 162-76.
7. Jean-Paul Sartre, *Being and Nothingness*, trans. Hazel E. Barnes (New York, 1956), p. 364, argues that the basic relation between people is conflict.
8. Carl Sandburg, *Abraham Lincoln: The War Years* (New York, 1939), I, 81.
9. José Ortega y Gasset, *Meditations on Quixote*, trans. Evelyn Rugg and Diego Marín (New York, 1961), p. 158.
10. Northrop Frye, *Anatomy of Criticism* (Princeton, 1957), p. 224.

Chapter Four

1. Day, p. 31.
2. Reprinted from the October 13, 1844, *Spirit of the Times* in Franklin J. Meine, ed., *Tall Tales of the Southwest* (New York, 1930), pp. 385-88.
3. See G. Legman, "Toward a Motif-Index of Erotic Humor," *JAF*, LXXV (1962), 227.
4. *Anatomy of Criticism*, p. 45.
5. Taylor, pp. 337-39.

Chapter Five

1. *The American Adam* (Chicago, 1955), p. 86.
2. Huizinga, p. 75.
3. Brom Weber, "A Note on Edmund Wilson and George Washington Harris," *The Lovingood Papers* (1962), p. 49.
4. The anecdote appeared on the page where "Sut Lovegood's [*sic*] Shirt" ended, *Yankee Notions*, VI (October, 1857), 291. The story was still alive in the oral tradition in the 1870's. See Frank Harris, *My Life and Loves* (New York, 1963), p. 187.
5. *The Origins of Attic Comedy* (Cambridge, 1914), p. 3.
6. The standard English version is that translated by J. E. Crawford Flitch, London, 1931, where see p. 90; but the present quotation, closer to the original Spanish edition of 1912, is from Rugg and Marín, translators, Ortega y Gasset, *Meditations on Quixote*, n. 15, p. 179.
7. Merrell R. Davis and William H. Gilman, eds., *The Letters of Herman Melville* (New Haven, 1960), p. 129.
8. See Chapter 9 below.

Chapter Six

1. See Richard Dorson, *American Folklore* (Chicago, 1959), p. 71, for the impartial spectator; Dorson's book is indispensable background for reading Harris.
2. Donald Day, "The Political Satires of George W. Harris," *Tennessee Historical Quarterly*, IV (December, 1945), 332-35.
3. *Ibid.*, p. 336.
4. "William Faulkner and George Washington Harris: In the Tradition of Southwestern Humor," *Tennessee Studies in Literature* (1962), 54-57.
5. Quoted from Blair, *Native American Humor*, p. 101, n. 1.

Chapter Seven

1. Republished in Malcolm Cowley, ed., *Writers at Work* (New York, 1958), p. 137.
2. For a useful definition of comic points of view see John Gerber, "Mark Twain's Use of the Comic Pose," *PMLA*, LVII (June, 1962).
3. Taylor, pp. 294-96.

4. Quotations from Weber's edition will be included in the text, with the editor's name within the parentheses.

5. For a psychological study of this impulse, see Sartre, p. 566.

6. Wylie Sypher, "The Meanings of Comedy," in Sypher, ed., *Comedy* (Garden City, New York, 1956), p. 218.

7. Welsford, p. 321.

8. *Ibid.*

9. *Ibid.*, p. 326.

10. In "Sut Lovengood Reports What Bob Dawson Said after Marrying a Substitute." See also letter to Eastman, Nashville *Union & American*, June 16, 1858.

11. *The Great Tradition* (Garden City, New York, 1954), p. 297.

12. *Ibid.*, p. 274.

13. Editions of Dickens' *Posthumous Papers of the Pickwick Club* exist in great variety. The quotation is from Chapter 51.

Chapter Eight

1. *Mark Twain's Humor* (Dallas, 1962), p. 73.

2. Henry L. Mencken, *The American Language,* 4th ed. (New York, 1936), p. 358. Mencken summarizes pioneer linguistic scholarship in this dialect, pp. 350-62. For more recent studies, consult the bibliographies in *American Speech* and the Publications of the American Dialect Society.

3. George Philip Krapp, *The English Language in America* (New York, 1925), pp. 225-75.

4. See Sumner Ives, *The Phonology of the Uncle Remus Stories,* Publications of the American Dialect Society, Number 22 (Gainesville, Florida, 1954).

5. "Elizabeth Madox Roberts: Life is from Within," *Saturday Review,* March 2, 1962, pp. 21, 38.

6. *Virgin Land,* p. 240.

7. The editors of *American Literature* kindly gave permission to use large portions of my essay, "The Imagery of George Washington Harris," XXXI (May, 1959), 173-87.

8. *Mimesis,* trans. Willard R. Trask (Princeton, 1953), p. 54.

9. "Sut Lovengood's Chest Story."

10. "Sut Lovengood, A Chapter from His Autobiography."

11. "Bill Ainsworth's Quarter Race."

12. "Sut Lovengood's Big Dinner Story."

13. See Sypher, p. 242.

14. Freud argues the *liberating* element is basic in humor: "Ob-

viously, what is fine about it is the triumph of narcissism, the ego's victorious assertion of its own invulnerability. It refuses to be hurt by the arrows of reality. . . ." Sigmund Freud, *Collected Papers,* ed. James Strachey (London, 1950), V, 217.

Chapter Nine

1. July 14, 1867.
2. *Mark Twain & Huck Finn,* pp. 242-46.
3. Stuart M. Tave, *The Amiable Humorist* (Chicago, 1960), *passim.*
4. P. 63.
5. *Ibid.,* 86.
6. P. 243.
7. Pp. 96-99.
8. Auerbach, p. 357.
9. P. 101.
10. P. 644.
11. Listed in the Bibliography.
12. P. xiii.
13. Verified in conversation.
14. New York, 1960. My references will be to *Patriotic Gore,* which Alfred Kazin calls "the greatest single work of Wilson's unique career," in *The Reporter,* XXVI (May 24, 1962), 44.
15. Wilson, p. 510.
16. See Robert Hopkins, "Simon Suggs: A Burlesque Campaign Biography," *American Quarterly,* XV (Fall, 1963) 459-63. See above, Chap. Six.
17. Lynn, pp. 129-31.
18. *Ibid.,* p. 135.
19. Lynn's factual mistakes are numerous. A listing would grow tedious, but the reader should use the book with caution. Some mistakes invalidates his conclusions, as his incorrect date for Henry Clay Lewis' book, p. 104. See John Q. Anderson, *Louisiana Swamp Doctor* (Baton Rouge, 1962), p. 53. Anderson's volume includes a life of Lewis and reprints most of his work.
20. Matthiessen, p. 603.

Selected Bibliography

Selected Bibliography

PRIMARY SOURCES

Recovery of Harris' newspaper work began with the searches of Franklin Meine, J. Cleveland Harris, and John J. Heflin through the files of the *Spirit* and through New York and Tennessee journals. Donald Day enlarged their list and noted republication of each sketch as he could discover it for his doctoral dissertation, University of Chicago, 1942. Day made his compilation available to M. Thomas Inge, who emended and added items for his master's thesis, Vanderbilt University, 1960. Inge kindly gave permission to base the following list on his. Of his fifty-one items, this omits three letters as insignificant (Inge's items 20, 21, and 22) and three sketches as probably not Harris' (Inge's items 9, 17, and 50). One date is corrected. The following list, as the first published bibliography, attempts to include the first appearance of all Harris' fiction now known.

1. *Works*

"Sporting Epistle from East Tennessee," *Spirit of the Times*, February 11, 1843.

"Quarter Racing in Tennessee," *Spirit of the Times*, April 15, 1843.

"Sporting Epistle from East Tennessee," *Spirit of the Times*, June 17, 1843.

"Sporting Epistle from East Tennessee," *Spirit of the Times*, September 2, 1843.

"The Knob Dance, A Tennessee Frolic," *Spirit of the Times*, August 2, 1845.

"A Snake-Bit Irishman," *Spirit of the Times*, January 17, 1846.

"A Sleep Walking Incident," *Spirit of the Times*, September 12, 1846.

"There's Danger in Old Chairs," *Weekly Nashville Union*, October 6, 1847.

"How to Marry," *Spirit of the Times*, October, 21, 1854.

"Sut Lovengood's Daddy 'Acting Horse,'" *Spirit of the Times*, November 4, 1854.

"Playing Old Sledge for the Presidency," Nashville *Union & American*, October 18, 1856.

"Sut Lovengood Blown Up," Savannah *Morning News*, date unknown; reprinted Nashville *Daily Gazette*, July 21, 1857.

"Sut Lovegood's [sic] Shirt," *Yankee Notions,* October, 1857.

"Sut Lovengood's Lizzards," Nashville *Union & American,* November 15, 1857.

"Sut Lovengood's Dog," Nashville *Union & American,* January 8, 1858.

"Sut Lovingood at Sicily Burns's Wedding," Nashville *Union & American,* April 15, 1858.

"Old Burns's Bull Ride," Nashville *Union & American,* April 22, 1858.

"Sut Lovengood's Chest Story," Nashville *Union & American,* June 30, 1858.

"A Shell Bark Lawyer," Nashville *Union & American,* July 7, 1858.

"The Doctor's Bill," Nashville *Union & American,* July 10, 1858.

"Sut Lovengood in New York" (Second Installment), New York *Atlas,* date unknown; reprinted Nashville *Union & American,* August 15, 1858.

"Sut Lovengood at Bull's Gap," New York *Atlas,* date unknown; reprinted, Nashville *Union & American,* December 5, 1858.

"Sut and the Locomotive," New York *Picayune,* April 16, 1859.

"Sut Lovingood's Love-feast of Varmints" (Four Installments), Nashville *Union & American,* April 19, 21, 30, and May 3, 1859.

"Sut Lovengood Travels with Old Abe as His Confidential Friend and Adviser," Nashville *Union & American,* February 28, 1861.

"Sut Lovengood with Old Abe on His Journey," Nashville *Union & American,* March 2, 1861.

"Sut Lovengood Lands Old Abe Safe at Last," Nashville *Union & American,* March 5, 1861.

"Sut's Hog Ride," Nashville *Press and Times,* September 14, 1865.

"Sut Lovingood Come to Life," Nashville *Union & American,* May 3, 1866.

"The Coat of Faded Grey" (poem), Nashville *Union & American,* July 1, 1866.

"Sut Lovengood's Big Dinner Story," Nashville *Union & American,* August 10, 1866.

"Sut Lovingood, on the Puritan Yankee," Nashville *Union & American,* October 16, 1866.

"Sut Lovingood's Dream," Lynchburg *Daily Virginian,* January 23, 1867.

Sut Lovingood. Yarns Spun by a "Nat'ral Born Durn'd Fool["]. *Warped and Wove for Public Wear.* By George W. Harris. New York: Dick & Fitzgerald, 1867.

"Saul Spradlin's Ghost" (First Installment), Chattanooga *Daily American Union,* October 31, 1867.

"Sut Lovengood Reports What Bob Dawson Said after Marrying a

Substitute" (Two Installments), Chattanooga *Daily American Union*, November 27 and 28, 1867.

"Sut Lovengood's Big Music Box Story" (Two Installments), Chattanooga *Daily American Union*, December 11 and 12, 1867.

"Sut Lovengood's 'Hark from the Tomb' Story," Chattanooga *Daily American Union*, March 17, 1868.

"Sut Lovengood, A Chapter from His Autobiography" (Two Installments), Chattanooga *Daily American Union*, March 31 and April 2, 1868.

"Sut Lovengood, The Early Life of Sut Lovengood, Written by His Dad" (Four Installments), Knoxville *Press & Messenger*, April 30 and May 7, 14, and 21, 1868.

"Bill Ainsworth's Quarter Race," Knoxville *Press & Messenger*, June 4, 1868.

"Sut Lovengood's Allegory," Knoxville *Press & Messenger*, September 17, 1868.

"Well! Dad's Dead," Knoxville *Press & Herald*, November 19, 1868.

"On Young Gals and Old Ones," Knoxville *Press & Herald*, May 13, 1869.

"Sut Sets Up with a Gal—One Pop Baily," Knoxville *Press & Herald*, date unknown; reprinted in Knoxville *Press & Messenger*, September 29, 1869.

2. Modern Editions

Sut Lovingood Travels with Old Abe Lincoln, by George Washington Harris. Introduction by Edd Winfield Parks. Chicago: The Black Cat Press, 1937. Includes useful biographical information and reprints the three Lincoln satires. Only 150 copies were printed.

Sut Lovingood. By George Washington Harris. Edited with an Introduction by Brom Weber. New York: Grove Press, 1954. This edition regularizes the language and reprints eighteen of the twenty-four sketches in the *Yarns.* It includes the three Lincoln satires.

SECONDARY SOURCES

1. *Bibliography*

BLANCK, JACOB, comp. *Bibliography of American Literature.* III. New Haven: Yale University Press, 1959. Bibliographical information on Harris appears pp. 384-86.

McCLARY, BEN HARRIS, "George and Sut: A Working Bibliography," *The Lovingood Papers* (1962), pp. 5-9. An arbitrary, but highly useful list of 35 secondary items, arranged chronologically.

2. Biography

DAY, DONALD. "The Life of George Washington Harris," *Tennessee Historical Quarterly*, VI (1947), 3-38. Still the most extended record of Harris' life. Although it makes little attempt to interpret, it remains invaluable for its factual material and careful documentation.

3. General Criticism

BLAIR, WALTER. *Horse Sense in American Humor*. Chicago: University of Chicago Press, 1942. The work traces the American tradition of homely wisdom. It defines Harris' intention in writing of Sut's imaginary trip with Lincoln.

————. *Native American Humor*. San Francisco: Chandler Publishing Co., 1960. The work originally appeared in 1937. The new edition includes a chapter on twentieth-century humorists, and an indispensable bibliography. The discussion of Harris, pp. 96-101, remains one of the most complete general introductions to his art.

————. "Sut Lovingood," *Saturday Review of Literature*, XV (1936), 3-4, 16. A popular introduction to Harris.

BROWN, J. THOMPSON, JR. "George W. Harris," *Library of Southern Literature*, eds. E. D. Alderman and J. C. Harris. V. Atlanta: Martin and Holt Co., 1907. Brown records turn-of-the-century reactions to and traditions about Harris. He perceives with genteel horror the texture of Harris' style.

BUDD, LOUIS J. "Gentlemanly Humorists of the Old South," *Southern Folklore Quarterly*, XVII (1953), 232-40. Dealing with the pre-Civil War humorists, Budd warns against the facile labeling of these writers.

COHEN, HENNIG. "Mark Twain's Sut Lovingood," *The Lovingood Papers* (1962), p. 19-24. Reprints in its entirety Twain's short review of the *Yarns* and discusses briefly most of the points Twain raises. It calls attention to Walter Blair's most recent discussion of the Twain-Harris relationship in *Mark Twain & Huck Finn*.

DAY, DONALD. "The Humorous Works of George Washington Harris," *American Literature*, XIV (1943), 391-406. A general survey of the humor rather than an analysis in depth, which makes extensive use of the unpublished stories from Tennessee newspapers.

————. "The Political Satires of George W. Harris," *Tennessee Historical Quarterly*, IV (1945), 320-38. Day's is the only comprehensive discussion of the subject; carefully documented.

Selected Bibliography

DEVOTO, BERNARD. *Mark Twain's America.* Boston: Little, Brown and Co., 1932. A polemical reply to Van Wyck Brooks's *The Ordeal of Mark Twain,* this work defines the tradition out of which Twain grew. It emphasizes the element of joy Harris expresses, calls attention to his literary satire and the conscious artistry of all these humorists.

DORSON, RICHARD M. *American Folklore.* Chicago: University of Chicago Press, 1959. Dorson mentions Harris only briefly, but the book is invaluable for its careful definition and illustrations of folklore.

————. "The Identification of Folklore in American Literature," *Journal of American Folklore,* LXX (1957), 1-8. Observes that although the work of Harris and others is striated with folk material it is nonetheless a sophisticated literary product; urges that the "dark and somber" themes merit as much attention as humorous exaggeration. Excellent.

INGE, M. THOMAS. "Sut Lovingood: An Examination of the Nature of a 'Nat'ral Born Durn'd Fool,'" *Tennessee Historical Quarterly,* XIX (1960), 231-51. This chapter from an M.A. thesis, Vanderbilt University, is a sympathetic appreciation.

————. "William Faulkner and George Washington Harris: In the Tradition of Southwestern Humor," *Tennessee Studies in Literature,* VII (1962), 47-59. This carefully documented study restricts itself to a few parallels between the two writers.

LONG, E. HUDSON. "Sut Lovingood and Mark Twain's *Joan of Arc,*" *Modern Language Notes,* LXIV (1949), 37-39. Compares Harris' and Twain's accounts of bull rides.

LYNN, KENNETH S. *Mark Twain and Southwestern Humor.* Boston: Little, Brown and Co., 1959. A lively but ill-informed book. Praises Harris' artistry, but misunderstands it almost completely.

McCLARY, BEN HARRIS. "The Real Sut," *American Literature,* XXVII (1955), 105-6. The essay reports an 1858 obituary which wrote that a Polk County, Tennessee, farmer, "Sut" Miller, was Harris' pattern for Sut Lovingood.

————. "Sut Lovingood's Country," *Southern Observer,* III (1955), 5-7. Locates settings of the *Yarns.*

McKEITHAN, D. M. "Mark Twain's Story of the Bull and the Bees," *Tennessee Historical Quarterly,* XI (1952), 246-53. Notes that Twain probably borrowed Harris' bull ride not only for *Joan of Arc* but also for a proposed chapter for *The Prince and the Pauper,* printed separately in the Hartford, Connecticut, *Bazaar Budget,* June 4, 1880.

————. "Bull Rides Described By 'Scroggins,' G. W. Harris, and

Mark Twain," *Southern Folklore Quarterly*, XVII (1953), 241-43, continues the collection of bull rides.

MATTHIESSEN, FRANCIS OTTO. *American Renaissance*. New York: Oxford University Press, 1941. The first extensive esthetic criticism of Harris' work. This perceptive reading compares the power of Harris' language to Melville's and praises the evocations of joy in the life of the flesh. The main discussion of Harris occurs near the end of the book, but the reader should check index and notes for valuable comments and information.

MEINE, FRANKLIN J. *Tall Tales of the Southwest*. New York: Alfred A. Knopf, 1930. Meine's pioneering anthology selects richly from Harris; includes sketches from the *Spirit* as well as the *Yarns*. The enthusiastic introduction discusses the lighter elements of Harris' humor. Meine prepared the Harris article for the *DAB*.

MELLEN, GEORGE F. "*Sut Lovingood's Yarns*," "George W. Harris," and "Lovingood's Settings," Knoxville *Sentinel*, February 11, 13, 1909, and March 7, 1911. These popular newspaper essays deal with Harris' lighter surfaces. Mellen was a University of Tennessee professor who collected a number of local recollections of Harris.

PARKS, EDD WINFIELD. *Segments of Southern Thought*. Athens, Ga.: The University of Georgia Press, 1938. Contains useful biographical information, as does Parks's introduction to his edition of the Lincoln tales.

PENROD, JAMES H. "Characteristic Endings of Southwestern Yarns," *Mississippi Quarterly*, XV (Winter, 1961-62), 27-35. A brief, general structural study.

————. "The Folk Hero as Prankster in the Old Southwestern Yarns," *Kentucky Folklore Record*, II (1956), 5-12.

————. "Folk Humor in *Sut Lovingood's Yarns*," *Tennessee Folklore Society Bulletin*, XVI (1950), 76-84. Enumerates some of the better known folk customs to be found in the *Yarns*.

RICKELS, MILTON. "The Imagery of George Washington Harris," *American Literature*, XXXI (1959), 173-87. An imagery count and classification study which argues that the imagery is darker in tone than the elements of plot or character, and handled with skillfull artistry.

ROURKE, CONSTANCE. *American Humor, A Study of the National Character*. New York: Harcourt, Brace and Co., 1931. This penetrating study of the uses of humor and of the traditional comic character types discusses Harris briefly. Indispensable.

STEWART, RANDALL. "Tidewater and Frontier," *Georgia Review*,

XIII (1959), 296-307. Commends Harris' style and compares both language and tales glancingly to Chaucer's.

TANDY, JENNETTE R. *Crackerbox Philosophers in American Humor and Satire*. New York: Columbia University Press, 1925. An early, carefully documented study, not reliable in its insights. Sut is seen as the first well developed "bad boy."

THORP, WILLARD. "Suggs and Sut in Modern Dress: The Latest Chapter in Southern Humor," *Mississippi Quarterly*, XIII (1960), 169-75. Relates the early humorists to Erskine Caldwell, Flannery O'Connor, Carson McCullers, and others.

TURNER, ARLIN. "Realism and Fantasy in Southern Humor," *Georgia Review*, XII (1958), 451-57.

————. "Seeds of Literary Revolt in the Humor of the Old Southwest," *Louisiana Historical Quarterly*, XXXIX (1957), 143-51. Argues that Harris clearly "intended to defy the rules of polite letters," and represented a challenge to the rules and prohibitions of genteel literature.

WATTERSON, HENRY. ed. *Oddities in Southern Life and Character*. Boston: Houghton, Mifflin and Co., 1883. The brief introduction to the three Harris selections classifies him as a kind of local colorist.

WEBER, BROM. "A Note on Edmund Wilson and George Washington Harris," *The Lovingood Papers* (1962), 47-53. Responds strongly to Wilson's review of Weber's edition of Harris by demonstrations of the weakness of certain portions of Wilson's argument. Weber's introduction to his edition of Harris is perceptive criticism, as are his comments on Harris in his recent *Anthology of American Humor*, which reprints two uncommon Harris selections.

WILSON, EDMUND. "Poisoned!" *New Yorker*, XXXI (1955), 150-54+. This review pays negative tribute to the power of the writing and deplores Harris' cruelty, Sut's squalidity, and Weber's editing. It does open to discussion the demonic and sadistic elements of the work.

————. *Patriotic Gore: Studies in the Literature of the American Civil War*. New York: Oxford University Press, 1962. As part of Chapter 12, the preceding item is reprinted almost without changes.

YATES, NORRIS W. *William T. Porter and the Spirit of the Times*. Baton Rouge: Louisiana State University Press, 1957. This lively work defines Porter's tastes and the nature of his journal. It contains much material on Harris. The standard study of its topic.

Index

Index

Abolitionists, 56

Anti-feminism, 54, 80, 90

Aristophanes, 76, 123

Auerbach, Erich, 112

Avery, S. P., *The Harp of a Thousand Strings*, 120

Baldwin, Joseph Glover, 121; *Flush Times in Alabama and Mississippi*, 85

Beckett, Samuel, *l'Innommable*, 46

Bell, Elizabeth, 20, 26

Bell, Samuel, Jr. (foster father), 19, 20, 28, 30, 98

Bell, Samuel, Sr., 19

Blair, Walter, 70, 123, 126; *Native American Humor*, 124-25, 129

Blake, William, 84

Blotner, Joseph, *William Faulkner's Library*, 128

Blount County, Tennessee, 22, 23

Boccaccio, Giovanni, 79, 117

Brooks, Preston, 68

Brown, John, 59-60

Brown, J. Thompson, in *Library of Southern Literature*, 122-23

Buchanan, James, 48, 49

Burns, Robert, 23, 39, 97, 103, 106

Butler, Benjamin F., 67, 68

Byron, George Gordon, Lord, 23, 85, 97, 106, 126; *Don Juan*, 78, 103

Cable, George W., 121

Caldwell, John, 44, 52, 86

Cash, Wilbur, 41

Chaucer, Geoffrey, 79, 117, 123

Christianity, 51, 86, 100

Civil War, 32, 63, 91, 131

Clemens, Samuel L., *see* Mark Twain

Comedy, ambivalence of, 119; anti-authoritarian elements in, 47, 52, 78, 81-86, 93, 98; anti-religious and impious elements in, 51, 85-86, 100, 102; anti-feminism in, 54, 80, 90; asserts power, 58; celebrates joy of life, 52, 88, 99, 112, 117; communicates unspeakable, 88; destructive element of, 62; as escape or flight, 53, 62, 84; evokes ecstasy, 41; freedom in, 40, 96, 103, 113, 119; Greek, 76, 81, 84; hatred in, 57, 66, 69, 88, 100-1; irrationalism of, 84, 98, 102; laughter as aim, 76-77; mask of, 51, 88, 107; obscenity in, 64; political, 48, 58-62; ritual and ceremony in, 47, 93; satire, 57-58, 65-66, 118, literary, 47-48, 77-78; scapegoating of, 48, 50; selection for, 62; symbolic revenge in, 66, 69; symbolism in, 85; variety in, 77, 86; Victorian attitude toward, 122

Congreve, William, 23, 126; *The Mourning Bride*, 90-91

Cornford, Francis Macdonald, 81

Covici, Pascal, 108

Craddock, Charles Egbert, *see* Murfree, Mary Naoilles

Crockett, Davy, 37, 55, 101

Crutchfield, William, 32

Davis, Jefferson, 32

Day, Donald, 24, 25, 36, 59, 92, 126-27, 131

DeVoto, Bernard, 72, 123, 124; *Mark Twain's America*, 123, 124

Dialect used by Harris, 107-12

Dickens, Charles, 23, 34, 51, 95, 96, 97; *Hard Times*, 34, 104; *Pickwick Papers*, 104, 105

Index